THE END OF THE 'ASIAN MODEL'?

Advances in Organization Studies

Advances in Organization Studies includes cutting-edge work in comparative management and intercultural comparison, studies of organizational culture, communication, and aesthetics, as well as in the area of interorganizational collaboration — strategic alliances, joint ventures, networks and collaborations of all kinds, where comparative, intercultural, and communicative issues have an especial salience. Purely theoretical as well as empirically studies are included.

General Editors

Stewart Clegg
School of Management
University of Technology Sydney
Quay Street, Haymarket
P.O.Box 123
Broadway, NSW 2007
Australia
s.clegg@uts.edu.au

Alfred Kieser
University of Mannheim
D 68 131 Mannheim
Germany
kieser@bwl.uni-mannheim.de

Volume 2

Holger Henke and Ian Boxill (eds)

The End of the 'Asian Model'?

The End of
the 'Asian Model'?

Edited by

HOLGER HENKE
Iona College, New Rochelle, NY

IAN BOXILL
University of the West Indies, Jamaica

JOHN BENJAMINS PUBLISHING COMPANY
AMSTERDAM/PHILADELPHIA

TM The paper used in this publication meets the minimum requirements of American National Standard for Information Sciences — Permanence of Paper for Printed Library Materials, ANSI Z39.48–1984.

Library of Congress Cataloging-in-Publication Data

The end of the 'Asian model'? / edited by Holger Henke, Ian Boxill.
    p.   cm. -- (Advances in organization studies, ISSN 1566-1075 ; 2)
    Includes bibliographical references and indexes.
    1. Industrialization--East Asia. 2. Finance--East Asia. 3. East Asia--Economic policy. 4. East Asia--Economic conditions. I. Henke, Holger. II. Boxill, Ian. III. Series.
HC460.5.E53   1999b
322'.095--dc21   99-046719
ISBN 90 272 3299 7 (Eur.) / 1 55619 745 4 (US) (Pb: alk. paper)   CIP

John Benjamins Publishing Co. · P.O.Box 75577 · 1070 AN Amsterdam · The Netherlands
John Benjamins North America · P.O.Box 27519 · Philadelphia PA 19118-0519 · USA

Table of Contents

Introduction

Holger Henke and Ian Boxill

For years the rapid growth of several East Asian economies has recommended what has often been called the "Asian Model" as one to be emulated by developing countries worldwide. However, the long term viability of this model is now being seriously challenged by economic analysts and development specialists following (and even prior to) the severe economic crisis which has hit this region in the second half of 1997. A number of East Asian countries, including South Korea, Thailand, Indonesia and even Japan are currently facing serious economic challenges brought on by plunging currencies and the concomitant spiraling inflation as well as growing unemployment. More than ever before the provocative question implied in the title of this book appears to be justified, "Is this the end of the Asian model of development?" While it will take some time to unravel the causes of the current debacle, it has been argued that factors such as "falling exports, rising labor costs, white-elephant construction projects, a bribe-based business ethic and way too much capacity in too many industries" (*Businessweek*, January 26, 1998, 1) are to be blamed for the current crisis. So severe is the crisis that Western nations, including the U.S., have agreed to bail out these countries by providing loans of unprecedented values through the IMF and other multilateral lending agencies. According to one report "[b]ailing out East Asian banks, it must be made clear, will neither be easy nor cheap ... the non-performing loans of the south-Asian banks alone will peak at $73 billion" (*Economist*, November 15, 1997).

Although the scope of this book was conceived before the recent financial crisis hit, we seek to establish two basic points. Contrary to the predominant perceptions in the West of Asia as a homogenous high-growth area, the region has always been and remains to be highly diversified. In the view of the editors, as well as most of the contributors, this perception has not yet attained sufficient recognition, and in fact, in many small developing countries the view of Asia as the cradle of a new industrial revolution has reached almost mythological levels. Secondly, it is the intention of this volume to increase the readers' awareness of the dangers of attempting to transplant development experiences from one region/country to another. As the chapters in this book remind us, as far as the construction of a valid development theory is involved, to extract an abstract "model" from such a diverse region involves a "leap of faith". Readers ought to be reminded that almost all chapters in this book were completed before either the financial crisis of 1997/98 transpired or the Indonesian regime under Suharto crumbled and most authors were only able to make preliminary observations regarding the effects of the crisis.

By the way of an introductory overview, Henk Houweling delineates the trajectories of industrialization in East Asia since World War II. His findings show in which way historically different patterns of variables account for the high growth achieved by Japan, the Northeast Asian NICs, and the Southeast Asian economies. With regard to the latter, Houweling states the challenging proposition that "these countries may be considered to be a manufacturing equivalent of raw material suppliers from an earlier epoch in their history." While underlining the importance of "who comes first to a market", the author based on his analysis also makes some observations which are critical of the neoliberal model pursued in many developing countries.

In the following chapters, two distinguished Singapore-experts, W.G. Huff and Philippe Régnier, offer their interpretation of the development in this city-state. In line with the above made observation about the urban bias in East Asian development, Régnier's chapter places Singapore into a longer historical tradition of flourishing commercial emporia in Southeast Asia. While confirming several of the observations in the preceding chapter, he places particular significance on the role of external security and Singapore's perceived need to have a strong economy in order to guarantee national independence. Régnier's observations of multiracialism in the context of a meritocratic economy with sufficient opportunities in education are presumably of great importance to policy-makers in regions such as the Caribbean or the Pacific. Huff's detailed report about various macroeconomic factors and different aspects of capital accumulation comes to the conclusion that in Singapore's case the distinction between "the market versus the Plan offers too crude a dichotomy."

The following two chapters provide further evidence of the diverse developmental experiences in the East Asian region. First, Remenyi supplies a rather sobering account of the scope and depth of poverty experienced in Mongolia. He concludes that although this country is rich in natural resources and can boast one of the highest literacy rates in the Third World, the abrupt transition from socialism to market economics has made it one of the most aid-dependent economies in the world. Mendis' paper complements Remenyi's perspective with an analysis of income distribution and economic growth in Sri Lanka. Although his research shows that — in the short run — "direct public policy intervention can abruptly change the direction of income inequality",

Mendis recommends that in the long run and without losing sight of the human dimension of development "the best way to achieve a higher human development is ... by promoting economic growth."

Jayasuriya's juxtaposition of competing models for the explanation of the 1997–98 financial crisis in Southeast Asia provides readers with a useful heuristic analysis of each model's analytical biases and epistemological traps. Exposing the shortcomings of the neo-classical, institutional and globalization approaches to the crisis, this author concludes that "a fuller understanding of the crisis needs a dynamic analysis which locates the economy in the context of broader political structures." At first sight Jayasuriya's conclusion appears to imply an indictment of IMF analysis and prescriptions.

Following this theoretical perspective, Bustelo discusses some empirical evidence of the crisis by taking a closer look at South Korea's economic situation. Interestingly, this author argues that the recent Korean crisis "has been a *crisis of underregulation*." His observation that Western creditors not only decreased their lending, but actually withdrew money from the region at a time when sustenance of lending would have appeared to be beneficial, sounds very similiar to the scenarios in many Caribbean and Latin American countries during the 1980s. Bustelo concludes that Korea might have to abandon its original development model, not least because of the unreasonable conditions imposed by the IMF.

Following this perspective, Michael Goldsmith's analysis suggests that "the basis for Asian-style development does not exist in most Pacific states and territories." In addition, he finds several instances in which Asian interests have developed a "predatory nature" in their overseas operations in Pacific territories such as Papua New Guinea and Vanuatu. He therefore concludes that neither economic, nor political conditions in the Pacific islands would seem to allow the sustenance of development à la East Asia.

The concluding chapter by the editors introduces the reader to some of the conceptual problems associated with drawing inferences from the experiences of countries which have achieved or are in the process of achieving economic development and making prescriptions for those countries which have not developed economically. We argue that globalization has produced an uneven playing field and the context of economic development is different for all countries. Therefore, the use of abstract economic models is fraught with many dangers. We are not against drawing lessons or proposing alternative paths based on these lessons; rather we favor an analysis which recognizes the limits of abstraction and the appropriateness of these lessons.

In sum, the articles gathered in this book compare aspects of industrialization and development in a variety of Asian countries. Because the authors' analyses focus on different variables, use various indicators and employ different approaches, the reader is enabled to arrive at a more comprehensive and objective perspective about the prospects of these countries than is usually produced in the mass media and by economistic accounts of Asia's development, in general, and the new "Tigers", in particular. It is the hope of the editors and the authors gathered here that the results of their analyses may contribute to a steadily evolving body of literature about the relevance of the Asian development experience. At the same time, the editors expect that rather than providing a definitive judgment about this subject matter, this book may initiate more and systematic comparative research into the trajectories and results of industrial policy in the late and so-called late late developers in both Asia and the rest of the developing world. Too often economists tend to forget or deliberately exclude from their analyses the fact that both economic growth and social development are depending on the multihued, composite and heterogeneous influences of different social actors and that — paraphrasing Karl Popper's warning against the pitfalls of historicism in the social sciences — societal processes are most times too complex for our inferences to enjoy privileged status.

At this point in an introduction editors customarily thank the institutions, organizations, or individuals which enabled them to assemble the fruits of their research and efforts of bringing together a number of contributors. However, while the chapters of individual contributors here may have been supported institutionally, materially and/or by the personal assistance of numerous individuals, the editing and publication of this book was largely achieved without any of these admittedly convenient facilitating factors. The editors, therefore, would like to think that this book is also a testimony to the commitment, personal resourcefulness and creativity of all the contributors and individuals who worked to make it a reality. However, we wish to express our gratitude to Ralf Kneer for his valuable help in redesigning some of the graphics included in this book. In particular, however, the editors would like to take the opportunity to thank all contributing authors for their patient collaboration and instant willingness to make the results of their work available for this collection of essays in comparative development. Above all, their example demonstrates that established and well-known intellectual resources can be profitably invested in an "investment location" which at first glance may appear to many as a less than safe environment. While the general thrust of the research presented in this book may cause some observers to become more skeptical about future prospects of growth and development in East Asia and other small "underdeveloped" economies, it would appear that it also provides room for the hope that — despite the velocities of international capital — some investors will in due time recognize that maximizing their profits may sometimes require a willingness to take detours.

August 1998

CHAPTER 1

Industrialization in East Asia
A Developmental Approach

Henk Houweling

The problem that is usually being (investigated by economists) is how capitalism administers existing structures, whereas the relevant problem is how it creates and destroys them. As long as this is not recognized, the investigator does a meaningless job. — Joseph Schumpeter

1. Introduction: Approach to the Topic and Organization of this Chapter

As suggested by Schumpeter's critical comment on the task of the analyst stated above, I study in this chapter the spread of industrial capitalism into East Asia as a process of institutional and behavioral transformation. That transformation began in earnest in the decade of the 1970s. In the 1960s, inward-oriented Latin America and autarchic Soviet economies had been (with the exception of Japan) the most important centers of growth of manufacturing. In the 1976–80 half-decade, export-oriented East Asia (excluding Japan) took over that role. In the 1980s, a reforming China began to integrate into the world economy. At present, China is the second largest destination in the world (after the United States) of inflowing foreign capital.[1] It is estimated that about 145,000 foreign-funded firms employ over 17 million people. The country has a large surplus in the balance of trade with both the European Union and the United States.

Economies in Southeast Asia have also attracted investment capital, from Japan, the United States, South Korea, and Taiwan. As I will further discuss in Section IV, Southeast Asian economies are integrating into the industrial division of labor at the bottom of the value-added chain. These countries are not repeating the catch-up experience of Japan and the Northern newly industrializing countries (NICs). Northeast Asian economies caught up by breaking into markets of established producers and achieved full control over the value-added chain of branded manufactured products in export markets. In Southeast Asia and China, globally competing enterprises from developed countries outsource production *processes* in which these low-wage economies have a cost advantage. Southeast Asian economies therefore do not have complete import substitution. They produce with imported capital goods, which are partly owned by foreign firms, have little or no capacity to add new knowledge to production at the beginning of the product cycle, and do not have control over the transoceanic part of trade channels of their external trade. China and Southeast Asian economies also find in their domestic markets foreign companies at the sales and servicing end of locally manufactured and imported consumer products.

The importance of the decade of the 1970s as a turning point in global economic relations is revealed by the relation between trade expansion, economic growth, and foreign investment. In the 1960s and 1970s the expansion of foreign direct investment closely followed the growth of international trade and of world output. Between 1985 and 1995, direct investment flows increased annually by about 16 percent, whereas world output increased by only 2 percent and world trade by 7 percent. In the years 1992–94, developing countries purchased about 25 percent of industrial country exports and received about 40 percent of global inflow of foreign direct investment, leading to cross-border restructuring of corporate activity.

Governments in developed countries are participants, and may be willing partners, in the cross-border activities of enterprises. Governments prepare the national location for business practices. Labor markets, subsidization, deregulation of public monopolies, infrastructure, and tax legislation on capital and labor incomes are fields in which enterprises require state activity. For example, between 1989 and 1993, OECD governments increased subsidization by 27 percent. From the early 1980s the tax rate on income from capital began to decrease. Tax rates on income from labor increased as before, as governments shifted the cost of social protection of labor from capital to labor.

In North-South relations, the decade of the 1970s was equally a turning point. Southern demands raised in the 1970s for a redistributive new international economic order in which political decision-makers would intervene for the benefit of poor countries have instead been succeeded in Latin America, the Middle East and sub-Saharan Africa by economic restructuring, by massive expansion of World Bank lending, and by promoting market-oriented policy reform, though without boosting economic growth.[2] The result is the appearance of a "Fourth World."

The chapter is organized as follows. Drawing upon Schumpeter, I introduce in Section II the notion of catch-up industrialization as a process of "creative destruction" on a grand scale. I introduce in Section III a set of definitions of concepts concerning the transformative impact of the spread of capitalist industrialization on East Asian societies. In Section IV, I discuss catching-up by Japan,

South Korea, and Taiwan. Section V focuses is on Southeast Asia. In Section VI, I discuss the present financial crisis in East Asia. Section VII contains conclusions.

2. Catch-up Industrialization as a Process of Creative Destruction on a Grand Scale

Schumpeter's expression "creative destruction" is a useful tool to comprehend the effects of the spread of capitalist industrialization: it is a corrective to both the optimism of Enlightenment theorists of the eighteenth century as well as to the developmental pessimism of dependency scholars.

Students of social change in eighteenth-century Europe like Godwin and Condorcet assumed that the expansion of knowledge would result in increasing control over the natural and social worlds, thereby leading to an improvement in the human condition. Their optimism, however, was countered by the developmental pessimism of Malthus and most classical economists of his time.

Indeed, in the last five centuries humanity has proved able to transform both the social and natural surfaces of the planet to an unprecedented degree. Out of a collection of (unconnected) localized societies, one world society has been created. In developed parts of the world, society is no longer exposed to untamed nature. Industrialization has instead created a man-made shelter within the system of nature. The cost of that transformation, however, has been horrendous, without any assurance that the shelter will hold or can be extended to the entire world's population.

To comprehend this cost, one should realize that anthropological evidence suggests that the number of ways in which human groups have been able to survive by adapting to nature is very large.[3] The number of ways of becoming "human" within the system of nature is at least as large as the number of cultures localized groups of people have brought to life. East Asia used to offer an impressive collection of human possibilities, but the transition to industrial capitalism uprooted these localized communities. In the mercantile era, businessmen did not need to control local populations. The expatriate trader living on the margins of the host society is the best reminder of that fact. Industrial capitalism, on the other hand, operates high-cost factories, and depends on commodified labor and on markets for land, capital, and natural resources. The social transformation implied by these things cannot occur without the exercise of state power on a vast scale and over large populations.

Where does the destructive impact of capitalist industrialization come from? Under industrial capitalism, a decreasing proportion of population has direct access to means of subsistence. The implication of the international spread of capitalism into East Asia therefore is that inhabitants of formerly localized societies are to be "separated" from their lands and other natural resources they may occupy. The proclamation of state sovereignty over natural resources is the first step of a removal process, to be followed by their lease or sale to private domestic entrepreneurs and foreign investors. Since decolonization, newly independent governments have taken over the task of commodifying land, natural resources, and labor. Since the departure of Western colonial governments, scholars in the West have developed statistics of peoples under threat [cf. Gurr (1993: Table 3A) for peoples under threat in East Asia].

At the world level, the novelty of the development process is revealed by the fact that for about 0.2 percent of the time humanity is estimated to have been around on the planet, it lived in a state in which all the resources required for survival could be obtained by hand tools at best. During that long period of social stasis, the world population grew imperceptibly. Nor did the tools of war and of production move beyond the stage of hand-operated implements.

The suggestion is that social transformation on the scale required for industrialization is imposed by superior power. Or, in other words, development spreads via the capacity of actors coming from the first developed groups to overcome resistance met on their path of expansion. That suggestion is compatible with the following evidence:

2.1 The Worldwide Expansion of Peoples Coming from Western Europe during the Mercantile Era

Mercantile capitalism is the first stage of what has become the hype of "globalization." But it has only been in the last 250 years that the rising Atlantic economy of Western Europe and North America overtook China. In 1820, on the eve of the spread of industrialization from areas in England to parts of Northwestern Europe, Asia as a whole is estimated to have accounted for about 58 percent of world production; by 1940 its share had fallen to 19 percent although it held 60 percent of the world's population.

2.2 Worldwide Colonial Expansion of Countries That Industrialized First and the Imposition of Markets for Land and Labor in the Host Society

In the second or colonial phase of globalization, between the 1870s and 1914, state officials from Western countries and traders set foot on land overseas. They began to organize primary commodity production using commodified labor — which was partially brought in from outside — for industrial processing at home. In precolonial Southeast Asia, for example, the number of people originating in China was very small. Colonial authorities, in need of workers for plantations and mines, organized the "piggy-trade" in which people from China were brought in. When the Qing Empire began to collapse at the end of the nineteenth century, the exodus reached its peak, to be followed by another exodus in the 1930s and 1940s. After decolonization, these people would become very successful in establishing themselves in retail, mining and plantations, transportation, manufacturing, and finance. Colonial governments used these people as middlemen between indigenous primary commodity producers and port traders. However, colonial governments appropriated — for entrepreneurs from their home countries — the transoceanic part of the value-added chain of goods produced. Uprooting local communities by road building, followed by the formation of a market for land, leading to a labor market, set the stage for capitalist development of production.[4] (In independent Thailand, the monarchy, under British and French pressure, began in the era of colonialism to function as a colonial government itself.)

2.3 *External Compulsion on Independent Governments to Catch Up*

In the third stage of globalization, independent governments and enterprises from developed countries, instead of colonial governments, are the driving force in the imposition of capitalist transformation on late-developing societies. However, they face the choice either to catch up with developed countries or to be overrun, if not destroyed, by them. At that stage, international production, international trade, and the servicing of the local consumer market define the globalization process.

After decolonization, independent governments in Southeast Asia tried on their own initiative to implant into their societies the power-wealth generating machinery of industrial capitalism. However, the effort to catch up by state-administered, low-wage, labor-intensive production for domestic markets began to falter in the mid-1980s and 1990s. In these decades enterprises from developed economies, driven by a decline in labor costs of finished consumer products relative to the cost of capital and servicing, built production and sourcing networks in the low-wage economies of China and Southeast Asia. Instead of labor-intensive *sectors,* labor-intensive *production processes* moved to these developing economies. These companies also sell and service on the spot locally produced and imported manufactured products.

2.4 *The Importation from Abroad of Legal Systems*

Capitalist development brings within-group ethics, originally based on the notion of common survival of a subsistence community dominated by nature, now set on a commercial (individualist) basis within a man-made world. When industrial capitalism spreads and deepens, "outsider ethics" (raiding, conquest, cheating, loans at exorbitant interests for foreigners) has to be brought into the domain of commercial exchange. "Insider ethics," relating to family, locality, religion, or race, is to be bracketed and to be brought up to the national, and subsequently to the international level. International trade and investment law link national legal systems with host societies. However, during the transition, the commercialization of insider and outsider ethics is in multisociety states the principal cause of ethnic conflict, and even of state collapse (Newman 1991). The commercialization of "insider ethics" and "outsider ethics," leading to a supraethnic business community and an impersonal labor market, together with the violence that its formation generates, dramatically decreases variability in ways of life. The social homogenization (Inglehart and Carballo 1997; Latouche 1996) under way in East Asian societies testifies to the direction of the process of sequential development.[5]

It should be noted, however, that the development process still operates in East Asia within very different societies. Japan, South Korea, and Taiwan have rather homogeneous nation-states and a long state tradition. Due to these characteristics, political elites have been able to construct a national consensus about the priority of catching up as the preeminent survival strategy for the nation, to impose that consensus on society, and to implement it.

The People's Republic of China, on the other hand, originates in a traditional agrarian-aristocratic empire that over time expanded in the north, the south, and the west of the three river valleys in which the Chinese as a people originated. Agrarian aristocratic empires as a species of political organization (Kautsky 1982) are much more difficult to reform; if they do, they tend to fall apart into warlordism or to fragment further into groups of roving bandits.[6] Chinese history between 1840 and Mao's victory in 1949 testifies to these events in modern times. Therefore, to keep a weak and fragmented state structure together during the onslaught of the development process will be the priority task of the Chinese government, which strongly shapes its developmental objective of catching up with the West.

States in Southeast Asia began their developmental careers after having achieved independence. States in this part of Asia originated in the ambitions and policies of rival colonial powers. Colonial governments put economies in this region in a primary commodity–exporting niche (Dixon 1991:Chapters 3 and 4), and brought in ethnically different laborers from China and India to work on plantations and to serve as middlemen between the colonial administration and the raw material producers in indigenous society. Colonial governments in this region resorted to ethnic politics, biased military recruitment, and clientelist economics as a strategy to control indigenous society. Postindependent development policy in this part of Asia therefore faces the challenges of keeping the country together first,[7] to ward off foreign intervention and to create a national bourgeoisie.[8] In Northeast Asian societies, state intervention in the economy operates through a national entrepreneurial class and is geared to productivity. As I will further discuss in Section III, government intervention in Southeast Asia is primarily aimed at countering the ethnic-biased distribution of economic assets in favor of Chinese entrepreneurs, which originates in colonial times. In these states, the entrepreneurial class has to grow up within the state apparatus itself. Consequently, economic policy in Southeast Asia bears a strong imprint of ethnic claims balancing or redressing.

East Asia's incorporation into the world economy is rather different from what happened elsewhere. In the Western Hemisphere, indigenous societies between the sixteenth and nineteenth centuries were thoroughly destroyed by Europeans after their Atlantic expansion. In this part of the world "initial differences" between precolonial societies are no longer relevant. (Destruction of host societies that came into contact with countries that were developing first is not limited to the Western Hemisphere. In sixteenth- and seventeenth-century England, British lords transformed Ireland into a beef-producing supply zone for wool-producing England. Assisted by the plague, they began under Cromwell to depopulate the island by slaughter, by compulsory emigration of the Irish as slaves to sugar- and tobacco-producing Caribbean islands, and by the imposition of famine.)

Sequential development implies differential reproduction. Between the mid-seventeenth century and the 1930–50 decades, differential reproduction favored European populations. Since the 1950s, due to the spread of preventive medicine outside its home region and food exports (due to the industrialization of agriculture and of cattle ranging in developed countries) it favors poor populations.

In Spanish America, the Spanish conquest between 1519 and 1540 created virtually empty land (Diamond 1997: 359ff.). Many studies of central Mexico estimate the size of the preconquest population in 1519 at around 25 million; for 1523 the estimated figure is 16.8 million; for 1580 it is 1.9 million and for 1605 it is one million, a decline of 95 percent. Data on Peru also show continuous and stark decline, from 1.3. million to less than 600,000 in 1620. However great the uncertainty of these figures may be, there is no doubt that a demographic calamity beyond comprehension occurred.[9] In the nineteenth century, between about 5 and 10 million North American Indians were "separated" from their land by an elected government that supported "privatizing" farmers whose work of "removing" the Indians was funded by majority voting in the U. S. Congress. In Australia, the work of pushing aside aboriginal society continued under democratic governments until the late 1970s.[10] This is destruction due to capitalist development on a vast scale.

What happened in Latin America on a continentwide scale, did occur on the local level in Southeast Asia. For example, in 1623 Coen, handling the spice trade on behalf of the Dutch East Company, overran the Banda Islands, whose inhabitants refused to give up their trade in spices. Separating native peoples from the land was achieved by killing off inhabitants and banishing survivors. This prepared the way for capitalist production when workers from Sri Lanka were brought in to labor on what had become company land (Drooglever 1978: 123ff.).

However, during the mercantile era, populations in East Asia were too numerous and their rulers often too strong to prevent mercantile capitalism from developing into production capitalism. In the mercantile era in this part of the world, people could not be separated from the land on which they subsisted.

Compared with events in the Western Hemisphere, societies in Northeast Asia and in China were hardly affected by mercantile capitalism. During the colonial era these countries did not experience a transition to primary commodity production.[11] Yet they responded in very different ways to invasions from the West. Initial differences go far to explain the different development performance of Japan and South Korea on the one hand, and of China on the other hand. Or, in other words, responses to the development process are not determined by that process itself, but by its interaction with local conditions at the time of incorporation. Therefore, to better understand differences in development performance between East Asian countries, due attention should be given to initial differences on the eve of their incorporation into the world economy.

In Southeast Asia it is more difficult to link "initial differences" to differences in postindependence performance. States and economies as we now know them originated in the mercantile and colonial periods. For these societies, being integrated into the international industrial division of labor was the third stage of their encounter with the West, after the mercantile and colonial eras had come to an end.

3.   Concepts and Approaches in the Study of the Spread of Capitalist Industrialization

3.1   *Industrial Capitalism*

In the spirit of Schumpeter (Heertje 1981), Max Weber (Collins 1986: Part I), and inspired by Burnham (1941: Chapters 6,–8),[12] industrial capitalism is defined in this chapter as the provision of everyday human needs by professionally managed enterprises that *operate on markets* for the sake of profit by producing and selling to anonymous customers at home and abroad, who supply these firms with labor, part of their capital, and land, though without getting control over business operations.

Societies in transition to industrial capitalism are said to be entrapped in the "process of sequential development," which will be defined below. At the core of that process is a transition in the method of mobilizing the capacity of humans for work and for violence or, in other words, their historically evolved strategies of survival. During the course of the development process, strategies of survival become detached from hunting/gathering ways of life, or alternatively, from subsistence farming under feudal or imperial control systems. In the transition process, these strategies get attached to the emerging "state," which interacts with the rising "enterprise" and the penetrating "market." In the course of the development process, these institutions increasingly take over as regulators of interaction in the spheres of production, distribution, use of violence, and reproduction. The transition to production capitalism begins to emerge when agricultural land is commodified and thus when a labor market is formed as subsistence peasants are getting expelled from the land by "privatizing" owners and produce gets commodified. In the relevant literature, there is not a unified theory of how industrial capitalism, as defined above, really works. However, two distinct subbranches may be distinguished.

3.2 Exchange-Oriented and Production-Oriented Views on Industrial Capitalism

3.2.1 The Exchange or Barter Theory of Industrial Capitalism
In this conception, enterprises are linked to each other and to their customers by prices set on perfect markets. Producers maximize profit within the constraint of known and market-determined prices in their buyer and seller markets, or go bankrupt. Accordingly, the market system of exchange between anonymous buyers and sellers determines the behavior of profit-seeking firms and welfare-minded consumers.

In this theory, producers are assumed to produce at increasing cost, to have cost-free access to complete price information, to confront externally created consumer demand, and to innovate by applying new knowledge to production, which originates in inventions and discoveries from outside the economy.

In this approach, economic growth is achieved by increasing the capital to labor ratio, leading to decreasing marginal productivity and by population growth. Except for inventions made outside the economy, long-term growth in productivity tapers off. Countries with the same propensity to save converge toward the same level of productivity and income.

In this conception of how market economies work, firms are encouraged to expand production until marginal cost on buyer markets equals marginal revenue on seller markets. Consequently, profits dwindle to zero in the long term. As gains in total factor productivity translate into lower prices for consumers at home and abroad, producers have no incentive to innovate.

Accordingly, in the barter conception of industrial capitalism, economies grow by (1) increasing the quantity of factors of production, that is, by population growth and increased use of machinery and raw material inputs, (2) by exogenously determined technological progress, (3) by giving free range to market forces at home, and (4) by "opening up" for free trade closed areas beyond borders, which improves welfare for all, thus irrespective of the sorts of goods traded. In classical and neoclassical free trade theory, it does not matter which goods are produced and internationally traded. Potato chips or coffee beans are just as good for an economy to specialize in as computer chips or airbuses.

In the 1980s, several neoclassical economists, responding to the export success of Northeast Asian producers, began to propagate the view that Northeast Asia industrialized by means of essentially free trade. These authors also had in mind the collapse in the 1980s of protected import-substitution industrialization in Latin America. Accordingly, governments are believed to be unable to improve upon market-produced outcomes.

Probably the most extensive empirical critique on the body of work that conceives industrialization in East Asia as governed by the market is offered by Wade (1990). Empirical studies of world income distribution demonstrate that at least since the 1850s, levels of per capita income in the world as a whole diverge, instead of converge, from the mean per capita income.

3.2.2 The Production, Capital Accumulation, and Innovation-Oriented Conception of an Industrial Market Economy

During Western Europe's preindustrial transition to capitalism, Enlightenment and mercantilist authors (Reinert 1996, 1997, 1998) began to create a production, capital accumulation, and innovation-oriented theory of progress.[13] These authors focused on the enterprise and its decision-makers. They also speculated on how wealth and power could be best created in a society in which merchants and their trade were becoming a source of power for rulers (Hirschman 1962, 1978: 90–107; Lane 1966). In the nineteenth and twentieth centuries, the intellectual heritage of Enlightenment authors commenting upon how entrepreneurs create wealth was picked up by, among others, Marx, Marshall, Schumpeter, and Weber.[14] After World War II, the theory of production-oriented economics was continued by development economists and others, and still later by "endogenous growth theorists" and by "new trade theorists."

The essence of production-innovation-oriented capitalism is probably best summarized by Schumpeter:

> The introduction of new methods of production and new commodities is hardly conceivable with perfect — and perfectly prompt — competition from the start. And this means that the bulk of what we call economic progress is incompatible with it. What we have to accept is that [the large unit of control] has become the most powerful engine of that progress and in particular of the long run expansion of total output. (1976: 105–6)

In the production, capital accumulation, and innovation-oriented approach, following Weber, the focus is on the *creation, use, closure, or abolition of markets* by agents, such as enterprises interacting with governments of states. Accordingly, enterprises, interacting with states, *use* markets in the creation of production power. Banks play a vital role in that process by financing expansion on the basis of a very long time horizon. Banks are therefore doing more than merely selling financial services for profit. In late-industrializing countries, such as Germany, banks are investment banks. In Japan and South Korea, the functional equivalent of the investment bank is the business group. The members of such a group, though active in different markets, have a common, nonmarket system of entrepreneurial and financial control. As cross-stockholders, participating enterprises have a long-term interest in each other's well-being.[15] Compared with Western practices, in which banks were traditionally not allowed to hold the stock of clients, banks in East Asia are accepting a higher level of risk in financing industrial expansion. [As will be further discussed in Section V, financing a long-term investment strategy pays off as long as (1) it is geared to productivity, which is tested in export markets, and (2) the capital market in the capital account of the balance of payments is closed to short-term dealers in stocks and currencies.]

Enterprises from countries that do catch up in production power *operate* on markets, however, without becoming their captives, as they are supposed to do in the exchange theory of industrial capitalism. "Catching up" implies realizing the potential for production power within the technological frontier. Innovating enterprises at the beginning of the product cycle cross the technological frontier by investing in research and development, by creating human capital, by shaping demand for new products on world markets, and by selling these under financial conditions that make production and further innovation possible.

New products have high investment costs, but as production expands, unit costs fall and thus create a temporary barrier to entry for those who try to follow from behind. By integrating, enterprises may abolish markets altogether; by differentiating they may create new markets. It all depends upon cost/benefit calculations in capital accounting. In the production-oriented version of capitalism, it does matter for growth which goods are produced and internationally traded. It matters even more who sells these products first.

Insights that are brought together in this section under the heading of production- or firm-oriented capitalism are thus not new, nor have they been completely forgotten. In 1923, Graham pitted a country that exported watches, in which it had a comparative advantage and produced at decreasing unit cost, against a country exporting wheat, in which it had a comparative advantage, but produced at increasing cost per bushel. He concluded that under these conditions free trade induced the wheat-producing country to specialize in a dead-end street (as quoted in von Haberler 1954: 198ff.).

Innovating enterprises create for themselves legally protected first-comer advantages, which translate into higher wages and higher profits, part of which will be used for new expenditures on research and development.[16] Information relevant to production is thus created within enterprises and is not freely available to others. Investments in innovation are highly interdependent. Consequently, the advantages of innovation accumulate over time. They spread out in society as higher-factor incomes in cartelized factor and product markets. Factor incomes rising with productivity on cartelized labor and capital markets translate into higher prices for buyers of output. Primary commodities, on the other hand, are produced by dispersed producers at increasing cost. In market exchange, producers of the latter therefore see terms of trade turn against them. This is the fate of countries that have a large external sector but that lag behind others in the expansion of their production power.

3.3 Production Power

The production power of enterprises in a society is defined as their ability to design,[17] produce, shape demand for, and retail on national and international markets sophisticated manufactured goods and services consumers and enterprises are willing to buy at prices they can afford.[18] For an economy to catch up in production power means its ability to break into markets occupied by enterprises in economies that industrialized first.

The potential for catching up comes from the fact that economies that industrialized first are producing at the frontier of technological knowledge. That frontier will change over time, though rather slowly. The result is a rather slow increase in labor productivity in mature economies.

For a late-industrializing economy to catch up in production power means its ability to install state-of-the-art technology more rapidly than first-industrializing economies are able to shift the technological frontier outward. In this situation, labor productivity in the late-industrializing country grows faster than in the leader country. The result is a convergence between both in levels of productivity and income (Abramowitz 1994).

As I will further discuss below, there can no longer be any doubt that Northeast Asia, by its transition to production-oriented capitalism, realized the potential for catching up. Japan is also capable of shifting the technological frontier. Industrial capitalism invented in this part of the world is "plan-rational" (Johnson 1995: Chapter 2; Amsden 1989: 55ff.; Lazonick 1991), as compared with presumably the "market-rational" capitalism of the West. In plan-rational capitalism, managers extend the scope of planning of the industrial division of labor on the work floor across the boundaries of legally independent enterprises in interaction with state bureaucracies whose political bosses ratify and legitimize this activity. Plan-rational capitalism provides the organizational means to realize the potential for catching-up.

During World War II, America's wartime mobilization created a surge in labor productivity. With about 8 million young men located in battlefields across the globe, the United States supplied its own armed forces. Trading casualties against the fruits of its production power, U. S. enterprises also supplied the armed forces of its allies with huge quantities of heavy equipment and food.[19] American wartime production offered a rich field of study for economists discovering sources of growth internalized into the act of production itself. After World War II and supported by the United States, Western Europe and Japan did succeed in catching up with American production power by their higher levels of growth in labor productivity.

3.4 Development, Sequential Development

Building on the historical experience of the first-industrializing region of Western Europe, "development" may be defined as the social process that generates simultaneously:

1. a long-term rise in per capita income, or intensive economic growth; as discussed above, long-term intensive economic growth is a feature of production-oriented industrial capitalism;
2. a process of political change, correlated with the transition to industrial capitalism, defined as a sequence of (absolute) state-formation in a multistate system, (ethnic-group-destroying) nation-building and thus societal homogenization, to be followed by democratization.[20]

Accordingly, the political side of the development process may be summarized as the *subjection* of the members of a group to the apparatus of the state, to be followed by their *identification* with and *participation* in the procedures for selecting political leadership on the basis of universal suffrage and the rights of citizens and be elected to office. Democratization is the stage of political development in which an *impersonal, bureaucratic-legal* nation-state evolves. Unlike their absolute predecessors, democratic states have an unprecedented capacity to penetrate society by administrative means and thus to ensnare homogenized society in administrative regulations. "Development" as used in this text is thus conceived institutionally and behaviorally.[21]

The concept of development, as defined above, intends to bring together the social forces of relations of production, or history from below, with nation-state formation, or history at the societal level, with territorial expansion of the development process at the international level.

In East Asia the relationship between the level of per capita wealth, degree of state stability, achieved level of nation-building, and democratization is very tight. Only the richest country, Japan, has a representative government that derives from multiparty elections in which all citizens have the right to vote and to be voted into office, leading to a transfer of power between elected governments. However, whether or not elected governments really govern — the alternative being governments simply legitimizing what has been decided upon in business/

bureaucracy interaction — is contested. The notion of Japan Inc. expresses concern about the undue influence of money and business in politics, despite the transfer of power by elections.[22] However, democracy in Japan has been consolidated in the sense that military rule or dictatorship is out of the question. Taiwan and South Korea, both with a history of authoritarian rule, have in the 1990s joined the ranks of democracies. Middle-income Thailand has a democracy on trial, whereas Malaysia has a rather authoritarian government. In Indonesia, a lower-middle-income country, the "Pancasila democracy" of the "new order" since the end of the 1980s has been challenged from within (Suryadinata 1997).[23] In least-developed Myanmar, the military government is involved in a protracted battle with hill people. In Cambodia the war between brothers, instead of the financial crisis, makes headlines.

To my knowledge, there is no example of late industrialization under the aegis of a democratic political system. Likewise, there is no example of a country at the top level of the per capita income hierarchy that does not have a democratic polity as defined above. Accordingly, one might expect that democratization that precedes substantial economic development will be reversed.

The concept of development as defined above is a simplifying lens, its focus on the making of a particular social order. That order results unintended from a welter of relations between individuals, families, enterprises, and entire communities whose reasons for action are unrelated to the emerging social order. Second, the concept conceives this order as an expansive force, causing the overturning of societies that come into contact with it. How human societies and individuals respond to that force is not determined by that force alone. Prior history, initial position, timing, and a host of other factors are involved in that response. To use a metaphor, the concept of development refers to a direction on a map, but it should not be confused with the winding paths in the underlying terrain.

In order to refer to the directional thrust in international social change, development is defined as a process of social change. That process advances through a series of events, which have been produced by many independently operating causes, but which cluster in the distinct patterns singled out in the definition given above. To be more precise, and introducing the modifier "sequential," the expression "sequential development" refers to the operation over time across a plurality of localized human societies of an anonymous process of social change in the ways and rules (in the sense of a regularity that has obtained normative force) concerning the life of work (production, distribution), reproduction, and the exercise of power and influence in that society.

The modifier "sequential" refers to two basic facts of history: (1) not all regions and countries of the world experience the process of development simultaneously, (2) nor do they make the transition toward that system in the same way. The diachronic nature of the process of development has created in the twentieth century wealth-power gaps between human societies that are without precedent in the preindustrial age. Until the industrial transformation of agrarian society began in mid-eighteenth century England, the differences in living conditions *within* states and other political units were vastly larger than differences *between* countries and regions of the world. That power differential created the necessary condition for the West to expand across the globe. The motive to expand is multivariate, with motives originating in rational capital accounting as a necessary part of that motivational complex.

It is therefore not correct to believe that capitalist industrialization spreads by promises of wealth and the political freedom to enjoy it. These things come later at best, and therefore cannot be causal factors in that expansion. Another force is more prominently at work: the compulsion on latecomers in the development process to catch up in wealth and power with those who developed first, the alternative being destruction at the hands of those who developed first. In the international system, the struggles for wealth and for power are thus reunited. Both come together in the compulsion on latecomers to catch up in production power as a strategy of survival for society (Sen 1984).

Whether or not the process of development is able to raise the world's population to the mass consumer way of life now enjoyed by most people living in the rich part of the world is open for debate (for an optimistic answer, see Simon 1995), but is at best questionable.[24] At present, with that prospect further away than ever, concentrated production power in the hands of a few has produced material abundance for a decreasing proportion of world population and led to the discovery of relative poverty by the rest.[25] Improving the human condition clearly is not a part of the intention of those who carry on the development process across the globe. That is why the process of development operates as a causal force over which humans have no control (Schmookler 1984, 1993).

3.5 *State and Market Forces in the Industrialization of East Asia Diversity in Development*

3.5.1 *Performance by Japan and China after the Arrival of the West*
In the mid–nineteenth century, China and Japan were approximately at the same time forcefully inserted into the international system by the United Kingdom, France, and the United States. With the Chinese peasant population most likely somewhat poorer at that time than the Japanese, the level of material living in both countries is believed not to have been essentially different.

In the early 1980s, however, per capita income in Japan (in exchange rate dollars) surpassed that of the United States (World Resources Institute 1996: 164).[26] In its recent summary "Poverty in China: What Do the Figures Say?" the World Bank estimated that about one-third of the Chinese population lives in poverty

($1 or less a day).[27] Why and how did Japan so effectively respond to the challenges coming from abroad? Why were the more numerous and politically more centralized Chinese not successful? Why did Communist successor governments that did try to catch up engage society in such destructive experiments?[28] Why did the Communist government in 1978 begin to introduce capitalist institutions to agricultural production, followed by the coastal strategy of development?

At the end of the eighteenth century in China, the Manchu rulers proved unable to renovate the political system (for a world systems point of view, see Moulder 1977).[29] To appease the British, the Chinese court replaced its functionaries in the southern harbors of the country who had set British opium stores alight.[30] During the Taiping Rebellion, the emperor accepted help from British troops, which had earlier plundered and then set fire to his summer palace, against its own rebellious peasantry.[31] The landed nobility and the state bureaucracy, who did not have an independent power base in society and were unable to find a coalition partner outside the peasantry against the court, cooperated with that policy.

In Japan, power fragmentation created opportunities for vertical alliances between daimyo (lords), samurai, and the emperor against the Shogun (the military overlord who controlled most of the country, though by no means all of it), from which the modernizing coalition of the Meiji Restoration emerged (Powelson 1994: Chapters 2–4). In Imperial China, a modernizing coalition, united by the will to expel the foreigners by catching up in production power, did not come forward. Elite power concentration at the court led to paralysis.

Japan is perhaps the only independent progenitor of capitalist industrial development outside the Euro-Atlantic world.[32] After being challenged from abroad, and the elites observing the fate of imperial China, a modernizing and nationalist coalition emerged in 1868 from the country's fragmented political system.[33] Appealing to the emperor and pushing aside the Shogun, the coalition of social forces around the Meiji Restoration set as the top priority for the country the expulsion of the foreigners. How? The slogans of the new government expressed it well: by becoming rich, by becoming militarily strong, and by honoring the emperor, that is, by cultivating nationalism. To achieve these aims, the Meiji government began to impose upon Japanese society a program of reform deliberately calculated to meet the challenges coming from abroad as effectively as possible.

Governments in Japan during the Meiji period helped to build production power by removing or softening the impact of three bottlenecks to any late industrialization:

1. Capital scarcity, to be eased by intersectoral resource transfer and the creation of urban-countryside growth linkages. In Japan, agricultural production had already experienced substantial commercialization of land, labor, and produce

before Captain Perry first stepped ashore in 1853.[34] The Meiji government in Japan found ways to generate a high level of savings in an agrarian society, which requires high interest rates and stable prices, as well a way to induce a high level of investment by offering low rates of interest to enterprises willing to invest in production for the international market (for tax reform interacting with the promotion of agricultural production, see Beasley 1995: 61ff.). Right from the beginning of the Meiji period, agricultural policy played a crucial role as a generator of savings and of labor power for industrialization.[35] To press agriculture into the service of industrialization requires investment in agriculture to increase productivity in that sector, which is a precondition for the continuous outflow of labor and capital to the industrial sector. In Northeast Asian industrializers, industrialization has not been decoupled, as in colonial commodity producers of Southeast Asia, from commercializing the agricultural sector. Rising incomes in agriculture provide demand for locally produced industrial goods. To prevent rising incomes from being spent on imports requires either import control or control of access to domestic trade channels. With border control lost under the Treaty Port Regime of 1858 and 1866, imports flooded the market, resulting in an escalating balance of trade deficits in 1871. After being stripped of tariff protection, Japanese leaders found new methods to reduce imports: preventing foreign traders from getting access to trade channels between port cities and the countryside. Suppression of consumer demand for imported products is still a feature of the way the Japanese economy is run.

Between savers in the countryside and private investors in cities stood the government as an aggregator of savings and as an allocator of investment funds. Up to now, the selective access to credit favoring core companies producing and exporting trademarked consumer products is a feature of the Japanese economy.

2.   The bottleneck of balance of trade deficits and the loss of control over the overseas part of the trade channel under the Treaty Port Regime. In 1858 and 1866 Japan was forced to open up the economy for foreign traders, who appropriated extraterritorial rights. Under that regime, Japan was unable to levy import duties higher than 5 percent, leading to booming imports paid for by the outflow of gold and silver. Between 1853 and 1881 precious metals worth 200 million yen left the country.[36] In 1887 nine-tenths of external trade was handled by foreigners.

The increase in U. S. silver output (until 1897 Japan was on a silver standard) and the change to the gold standard in the 1870s by Western countries effectively depreciated the yen, boosting exports (the country moved to gold in 1897 in order to borrow abroad).[37] The war indemnity imposed on a defeated China helped to provide relief in the balance of trade.

To boost exports, an undervalued exchange rate is required. To import raw materials, capital goods, and technology, an overvalued exchange rate is helpful, though at the risk of stimulating imports of advanced manufactured consumer goods for the elite.

To achieve these contradictory ends, Japanese governments used multiple interest rates and subsidies to produce the same effects as multiple exchange rates (viz., to allocate foreign currency to successful exporters at cheap yen rates). After World War II, in 1949 the U.S. government, in order to revive trade, set the dollar-yen exchange rate at 360:1. Japan resisted pressure to revaluate its currency against the dollar until the collapse of the Bretton Woods system in 1971 made it inevitable.

3.   Governments shielded fledgling industries from more advanced imports, yet exposed domestic producers of advanced manufactured consumer products in export industries to competition on the world market.[38] By expanding into the Pacific, the Western powers induced Japan to participate in the struggle for colonies. In the 1870s and 1880s Japan tried to mete out the same sort of treatment to Korea, Taiwan, and China that the Western powers had in mind for Japan — though with a difference. The origin of Japanese economic involvement in Taiwan and Korea sprang from national security concerns (viz., the need to create a protective bulwark against the Western powers that were active in the region).[39] War with China evolved in 1894, with Russia in 1904, and again with China from 1931–37 until the end of the Pacific War.

When Taiwan and South Korea became colonies of Japan in 1895 and 1910, respectively, a new sort of colonial state apparatus was superimposed on an agricultural system. In some respects, Korea's agricultural system at that time may be compared with the one of the *ancien regime* in prerevolutionary France. In colonial Taiwan and Korea, the peasantry was not "separated" from the land in order to create empty space for plantations. Korean absentee landlords were firmly tied to agricultural production by making them responsible for crop size, taxation, and policing rebellious peasantry. In Taiwan, which did not have a centuries-old absentee landlord class, the Japanese relied on monetary incentives to channel already commercialized peasants into cultures desired by the colonial government. The creation of a precise cadastre registered the land rights of farmers, which further stimulated commercialization. A modern and efficient system of taxation was put in place, weights and measures were unified, and a stable monetary system was set up.[40] The colonial government invested in harbor construction and other infrastructure. State agencies initiated foreign trade and mobilized the private sector.

To reduce the foreign exchange cost of sugar imports into Japan, the colonial government in Taiwan designated sugar and, due to their low labor cost, textiles as fit for import substitution. Taiwanese tariff-protected sugar competed successfully with sugar produced in Japan itself. Government revenues from the sugar consumption tax were reinvested in the colony itself, not in mainland Japan. Price discrimination against foreign shipping companies brought transport within the sphere of the island's economy. The sugar industry, organized in large-scale plantations, however, was in the hands of Japanese companies. To the reduce revenue loss due to rice imports (Japan first became a net rice importer in the mid-1890s) Taiwan was developed into an exporter of rice. The Japanese introduced the most up-to-date agricultural practices (new seed varieties and fertilizer, crop rotation, and multicropping). New methods of cultivation required education and training.

After World War I, Taiwan became an exporter of rice. Whereas the sugar industry was the preserve of Japanese companies, commercial rice production was in the hands of Taiwanese farmers working on land they owned. Food security in the Japan–Korea–Taiwan triangle improved, whereas in the colonial monsoon region outside Japanese control, the population increase between 1921 and 1935 began to outstrip the growth of rice production. Japanese colonization ensured postwar food self-sufficiency until U. S. food exports began to destroy that in the 1980s.[41] When Japan moved to war, Taiwan was intensely developed as an industrial base. The public sector in Taiwan remained the core of the country's industrial development until the 1980s. Up to the late 1960s, the agricultural sector would remain the largest foreign exchange earner.

In Korea a crueler Japanese regime also introduced elements of modern administration, a monetary system, a rail network, and education. In 1940 about a quarter of a million Koreans were employed in metal working and chemical factories in Korea, another million in manufacturing jobs in Manchuria. However, for political reasons the landowner class survived the annexation period. Japan's colonization of Taiwan and Korea had a developmental *intent* as well as a developmental *impact*.

4. Production-oriented Industrial Capitalism in Postwar Northeast Asia

Following Lazonick (1991) one could view as "collective capitalism" the extension of the planning of the industrial division of labor on the work floor across legally distinct firms, whose activities coalesce. Accordingly, proprietary firms are integrated in networks or enterprise groups, each one dominated by powerful industrial/commercial/financial enterprises or "core companies," which take the lead in planning, using a hierarchical chain of "satellite" firms as subcontractors.

An enterprise group of cross-stockholding companies creates opportunities for a cooperative *investment strategy* across legally independent enterprises and for cooperation in R&D projects. Lifelong employment of top personnel in core companies plus rewarding them according to seniority up to the middle management level, as well as collective rewards as part of normal income (bonuses), induce cooperation and loyalty. Loyalty reduces monitoring costs, exploits knowledge about production available at all levels of personnel, facilitates industrial learning by reducing the fear of being exploited, and reduces coordination costs in decentralized organizations (Sable 1994: 231–74).

In the United States, legal ownership does constrain cooperation between firms in getting access to inputs and in distributing output. In corporations in North America, management easily sheds workers, and management itself has no loyalty to the firm beyond the short-term cash nexus. Monitoring costs are high in companies in which workers are treated as a variable cost. In companies in which the threshold of inclusion is drawn just below top management and technical specialists, the knowledge relevant to production available in the work force below the threshold is not tapped. Shareholders have likewise no long-term interest in the health of the company. Loyalty, which mobilizes work energy and binds it to the company, is difficult to achieve in a system held together only by money. The time horizons of all participants are therefore short.

In Japan, companies achieve a competitive advantage by building organizational capabilities and by improving human capital for core companies. Such companies shift cost structures instead of optimizing within market-determined cost structures. Indeed, from the 1890s onward, Japan moved from importing textiles to exporting textiles, competing in the Chinese market successfully with British producers. British exports of cotton goods declined as a percentage of world exports from 82 percent in 1882/1884 to 28 percent in 1936/1938. Downward flexibility of wages in the United Kingdom, to which the British work force has been exposed again since the Thatcher government, hindered entrepreneurs from moving to more capital intensive sectors such as electrical goods, automobiles, and chemical industries.[42] Between 1914 and 1937, Japan's cotton textile industry achieved competitiveness in the world textile economy. By the mid-1930s Japan had become the largest exporter of cotton piece goods. Textiles remained the largest item in the balance of trade of the country until the mid-1950s, when heavy industry products like ships displaced textiles and light industries as the largest export earners. In the 1970s, computers and telecommunication equipment became important to the economy. In that decade, the Japanese economy passed the threshold in production power that U. S. postwar planners had had in mind for the country. In the 1980s and 1990s the heavy industry sector was replaced by automobiles, electronics, and other technology-intensive goods like aviation products, new materials, medical equipment, and numerical machine tools, competing worldwide with U. S. enterprises (for the history of sectoral change in Japan's economy until the Pacific War, see Howe 1996; for postwar industrial development and how it has been achieved, see Johnson 1982, 1995).

Through a "governed-market" approach to catch-up development, the Northeast Asian economies have been able to surmount the barriers to entry by benefiting from industrial learning enjoyed by enterprises from first-industrializing countries. Industrial learning as a barrier to entry results from the fact that experience gained in production, as measured by the size of past output, is a factor that decreases unit cost.[43] Industrial learning is a factor of growth internalized into the economy. Industrial learning as a source of efficiency in production became more widely known due to the Dutch economist Verdoorn.[44] A trade implication of industrial learning for producers in developing countries is that enterprises in first-industrializing countries have, despite high wage levels, a cost advantage in production and thus a competitive advantage in export markets. Government intervention helps to bridge the difference in unit cost.

Production-oriented industrial capitalism is required in order to profit from first-mover advantages. Production-oriented industrial capitalism is based on capital ownership by home entrepreneurs. Japan and the Northern NICs got access to foreign technology by licensing and by reverse engineering. Japan and the NICs thus separated capital ownership from access to technology. Entrepreneurs in these countries have remained in control of the capital stock, which is reflected in the low level of penetration of these economies by foreign entrepreneurship.

In 1980, enterprises from Japan owned 4 percent of the world stock of foreign direct investment (FDI); in 1990, their share had tripled to 12 percent. FDI in Japan, however, remained flat at 0.6 percent in 1980, and 0.5 percent in 1990. In 1996, this ownership amounted to 0.5 percent, whereas Japan's share of FDI decreased somewhat to 10 percent. Between 1980 and 1994, FDI in Japan as a percentage of GDP remained constant, at a level of between 0.3 and 0.4 percent; the share foreign investors contributed to the capital stock of the economy decreased during this period from 0.2 percent in 1990 to 0.1 percent in 1994.

The fact that foreign entrepreneurship cannot give effective competition to domestic producers provides the Japanese government with a powerful tool to harmonize the national and the international market. Domestic consumers may be taxed via price rises for the benefit of investment and for price setting by exporting enterprises. If the yen appreciates, domestic consumption may be increased by lowering effective consumer prices in order to prevent surplus capacity and price increases on export markets.

The Japanese auto industry may be called upon as an example of how protection helps to break into markets in which enterprises from first-industrializing countries have traveled far down the learning curve. Japan's automotive industry is the single most significant new entry in the world's passenger car market, producing in 1990 one out of four of the world's cars, half of which were exported. That success was not achieved by free trade. Beginning with car imports in the 1930s, the Automotive Manufacturing Industry Law of 1936 banned foreign production, compelling GM and Ford to close plants in Japan. That law required all vehicle makers to be licensed. Only Toyota and Nissan were licensed. In 1949, the domestic market was effectively closed for car imports to be followed in 1950 by closure of Japan to foreign producers. Import tariffs remained in place until 1978, two years before Japan surpassed U.S. assemblers as the world's largest passenger car manufacturing country. Nontariff barriers survived until the early 1990s. In 1960 Japanese car manufacturers exported and marketed under their own brand names 7,013 vehicles worldwide; in 1988 the number had increased to 4,431,890 units (Ruigrok and van Tulder 1993:327–29). In Japan, foreign entrepreneurship has been unable to capture from Japanese producers the overseas part of the trade channel, as they have done in the economies of Southeast Asia.

The achievement of industrial success by governing market forces did not prevent Japan in the summer of 1996 from joining the United States[45] and the E.U. (which at present protects its own auto industry against Japanese imports) in protesting the Indonesian government's decision to build and protect a national car industry.[46] None of them are eager to see a new entry in the already over-crowded world market of passenger cars. All three share an interest in preemptive exports by domestic assemblers to the fourth most populous country of the world.

Until 1960 both Korea and Taiwan could be described as agroexporters. In 1960, 86 percent of South Korea's and 73 percent of Taiwan's exports were accounted for by primary products, mostly farm goods destined for Japan. The turn to export-oriented industrialization came with the reduction of U.S. aid to both countries at the end of the 1950s. The 1960s was the decade of export-oriented industrial success, beginning with textiles and garments. When Nixon reoriented United States foreign policy toward China, South Korea moved to import substitution again by developing — against World Bank advice — steel, shipping and chemical industries. In the 1980s and 1990s, automobiles and computers for export brought the economy into more complicated sectors.

Like Japan, South Korea has in the 1990s become an important source of investment capital. However, South Korea itself has strictly limited the operation of foreign entrepreneurship in its domestic economy. In 1980, South Korea was host to 0.2 percent of the world's FDI capital stock; its share had increased to 0.3 percent in 1990. In 1980, its enterprises had invested $142 million abroad; in 1996 Korean companies owned production facilities abroad to the extent of well over $1 billion. FDI stock in South Korea remained throughout the 1980s at a level of between 1.8 and 1.9 percent of GDP. It was after the building up of basic industries that foreign investment as a share of GDP increased in the 1990s to 3.3 percent. In South Korea, foreign investors have contributed a decreasing share to the capital stock of the economy: from 1.4 percent in the 1980s to 0.6 percent in 1994. FDI stock in Taiwan between 1980 and 1994 has hovered between 4.7 and 6.6 percent of GDP; the contribution of foreign investors to the capital stock of the economy has remained constant at a level between 3.8 and 2.4 percent in the same period. Consequently, Japanese, South Korean, and Taiwanese entrepreneurs obtained access to the complete value-added chains of their traded manufactured goods.

In a world of sequential industrialization, the build-up of production power is for latecomers the pillar of national survival. Development is therefore considered to be too important to be left to the vagaries of the market (Tyson 1995: 137).[47] Late-industrializers who have been "opened up" for trade by force "naturally" move out of necessity toward the production, innovation, and capital accumulation view of industrial capitalism. Japan has been so restrictive in attracting foreign capital because its policymakers were "pre-occupied with the question of building an independent nation invulnerable to imperialist aggression from the West" (Shin 1996: 91). It is precisely success in realizing this aspiration that seems to hurt, if not to insult, American and E. U. trade officials. Indeed, demand suppression for imports follows from the logic of security via the building of production power. For successful catch-up industrializers, commercial rivalry with first-industrializers borders therefore on strategic competition.

It comes as no surprise that Japan is the only developed major economy in the world that has a surplus in its balance of trade with all of its major nonoil trading partners and has avoided dependence on foreign investors. Since the defeat of its army in World War II, the country has sharply reduced import exposure (Kojima 1997: 4).[48] It now prevails over a larger foreign currency reserve than any other government.

The United States, on the other hand, has experienced since the 1970s the reverse process of integration into the world economy. In 1950, U. S. merchandise exports accounted for 3.6 percent of GDP; in 1990 its export ratio had increased to 7 percent. The 1970s was the crucial decade: the export ratio doubled from 4.2. to 8.3 percent. However, if U. S. GNP is disaggregated for industries whose goods enter into international trade statistics, and export ratios are calculated as percentages of output produced by these industries, the export ratio increased from 8.9 percent in 1950 to 14.1 percent in 1970 to 31.1 percent in 1990. Exposure of the U. S. tradable goods sector to international competition thus sharply increased after 1970 (Irwin 1996: Table 1).

It should be further noted that the United States as an importer has outstripped integration of the American economy as an exporter. The reason is that in American society production power is geared to consumption, which is reflected in the low savings rate of society.[49] In turn, the consumption level in the United States is causally linked to the entrepreneurial success of presidential candidates in the vote market. Consumers in the United States have as importers since 1980 taken out of the world economy almost $1.5 trillion more than U. S. producers have contributed to it. The implication is that the U. S. balance of trade deficit will not disappear if Japan "opens up" for U. S. imports.[50] In fact, says Moran, "the greatest threat to America's power in the international system is 'made in the USA.'" To finance U. S. overconsumption, Germany and Japan have accumulated more than $1.5 trillion in claims on U. S. productive assets (Moran 1994).

Since World War II, the United States has been accustomed to being the forerunner in the development process. It is at present the mirror image of Japan, the catcher-up in production power. Due to the fact that the consumption level of the forerunner is partly financed by the catcher-up, the United States and Japan hold each other in a mixed-motive embrace. In that sort of game, each side is exposed to the temptation to suffocate the other, but only at great damage to itself. For the first time in its history in the international system, the United States no longer has the option to either withdraw from the world or to dominate it (Kissinger 1996). In American politics, securing consumption has become the road to political success for presidential candidates. For a presidential candidate to propose to reduce domestic consumption to production for the home market plus what the country's exports buy in terms of imports, is recipe for failure. For this reason the United States is involved in a crusade to "open up" markets world-wide.[51] For the Japanese government, the accumulation of claims on the U. S. economy is a tool for obtaining the nation's security. Its elite therefore is unwilling or may be unable to increase consumer spending on imports. The remarkable outcome therefore is that the hegemonic currency of the dollar can operate as long as it is supported by the yen. The potential for instability of this relationship is located in the fact that the yen's role as a support for the international role of the dollar postpones reforms in both societies. However, U. S. trade negotiators want it both ways: to reduce the U. S. deficit in the overall balance of trade by imposing on Japan numerical import targets. Trade conflicts between both countries no longer deal with tariffs. The objective of each of these economic giants has become to secure its domestic institutions for the production and distribution of wealth against the onslaught of the other.

During the cold war, development policy and performance in Northeast Asia was strongly shaped by U. S. postwar planning and security policy (for detailed information on resource transfer to Japan during the Korean War, see Hayes et al. 1987: Chapters 2 and 6).[52] In that period of time, the United States helped reconstruct Japan's production power up to the level of a second-rate economy. Japan greatly profited from the Korean War, and South Korea and Taiwan benefited from the war in Vietnam.[53] For the cold war era, the outcomes of development policies by the governments of Japan, Taiwan, and South Korea thus have to be studied for their continuous interaction with U. S. security policy.

The security objective of the Northern NICs of catching-up has indeed been achieved. South Korea, earning in 1960 1.74 percent of the per capita income of the United States, substantially reduced the gap in per capita income in 1995 by earning 36 percent of U. S. per capita income (in exchange rate values). The development performance of Taiwan and South Korea is superior to countries in Southeast Asia. Indonesia's relative position in 1994, after almost thirty years of successful industrialization under the new order government, was essentially what it was in 1960.[54] Yet South Korea and Indonesia have achieved since the 1980s about the same level of industrialization, as measured by the share of industry in GNP. Both economies have large export sectors.

Latin American economies confirm that industrialization alone, though necessary for production power, is not sufficient for catching up. In the 1970s and 1980s, that region achieved levels of industrialization comparable to Northeast Asian NICs. However, Latin American economies experienced, on average, negative growth in real per capita income throughout each year of the 1980s, whereas Northeast Asian NICs experienced sustained high growth rates in real per capita income during that period.

4.1 Northeast Asia's Success and Neoliberalism in the West

Schumpeter saw in the status-leveling, rationalizing, and secularizing impact of industrial capitalism on Western societies a move away from nineteenth-century liberalism toward social democracy. The social transformation in East Asia is a movement in the opposite direction: the focus is on the spread of industrial capitalism into the most populous region of the world.

However, the effects of capitalist industrialization in East Asia feed back into developed countries. Indeed, as East Asia's share of the manufacturing exports of developing countries increased from less than 10 percent in 1965 to over 45 percent in 1988, the region also moved into the position of being the most important trading partner of OECD countries outside the developed core as well as the most important host of OECD foreign entrepreneurship. The result of the linking of these unequally developed regions is, among others, the importation into developed countries from East Asia of a "purer" form of industrial capitalism than the welfare capitalism of the 1960s and 1970s.

It is not amazing, therefore, that Schumpeter's conception of representative democracy as an intraelite bargain (Held 1987: Chapter 5) has since the 1970s made its comeback in Western polities.[55] Power fragmentation, which is inherent in the international system, and the creation of linkages between its unequally developed parts have made democracy in Western countries safe again for the capital accumulation drive to move into social preserves previously exempted from it.[56] The retreat of the welfare state in the 1980s and 1990s is reflected in increasing income inequality in industrialized countries since the mid-1970s/early 1980s and in wage competition between them.

In the 1990s, with liberal democracy restored, the free enterprise system in the first-industrialized countries has resumed its pre–World War I role of being an expansive, quasi-governmental, and discipline-providing structure that essentially operates beyond the control of elected governments. These effects also demonstrate that instead of living in a society moving toward social democracy, we are experiencing a new wave of capitalist expansion, creating upheaval in world society. Schumpeter missed the international link in his prediction cum fear that capitalism in Europe and the United States was giving way to social democracy.

Under conditions of rapidly falling costs of transport and communication, manufactured goods may be produced in locations far removed from consumer markets. Since the application of the microelectronics revolution to manufacturing, which began in the late 1970s with the robotization of Japanese automobile manufacturing, the knowledge content of capital goods and consumer durables has been increasing. The more recent application of computer technology to design, marketing, and servicing has eroded the role of value added in manufacturing. New materials have reduced the metals content of manufactured products. The role of value added through design, advertising, and retailing surpasses for many products the cost of metals, wages, and manufacturing. As Taylorist mass production recedes, the styling of consumer products becomes more important. In other words, the demand side penetrates the manufacturing part of the value-added chain. The technology for designing, marketing, and servicing of branded products gets more strongly interconnected and located into one decision-making center. Under these circumstances, manufacturing is not necessarily the most profitable part of the production process.

Competition at the technological frontier between enterprises from the United States, Japan, and the E. U. has in these circumstances created an incentive to relocate labor-intensive manufacturing processes to Southeast Asian economies. For example, Nike makes expensive athletic shoes in Indonesia with workers earning $38 per month, retail outlets like Walmart and Sears have their expensive skirts made in Bangladesh by women working 60 hours a week for $30, reducing labor cost to 4 cents per shirt.

To improve competitiveness in global markets for domestic enterprises under these conditions, governments of Japan, the United States, and the European Commission promote the relocation of production processes at the end of the product cycle to industrializing Third World countries. Competition between triad members at the top of the product cycle is causally linked to their competition for production sites in East Asia. The response by the American government is de jure: the creation of treaty-based free-trade/free-investment areas. Japan's response is de facto (viz., the creation of production alliances across East Asia). The Mediterranean Policy of the European Union[57] and Japan's investment-aid expansion in Southeast Asia are examples of asymmetric regionalization driven by global competition in products in early stages of the product cycle.

It is not a new departure in international relations for governments of developed countries to allocate to less developed economies the production of labor-intensive processes. Lord Brougham recommended to governments in 1816 to compensate producers for initial losses "in order, by a glut, to stifle in the cradle those infant manufactures in the United States which the Napoleonic War has forced into existence." Free trader Cobden desired to abolish Britain's Corn Laws in order to prevent others from catching up in production power and thus posing a threat to Britain's monopoly of exporting manufactured products (Reinert 1996: 26). The Northern NICs have in the cold war era, and partially due to it, been able to prevent the United States "by the glut" to "stifle in the cradle" infant industries (ibid.: 25). Since the cold war, to "stifle by a glut" has become a declared U. S. commercial policy objective.[58]

Since the end of the cold war[59] the market approach to development has become the weapon of First World elites to "open up" industrializing economies in the region for preemptive exports of manufactured goods, of food products (Bello and Cunningham 1994: 445–58), of telecommunications, information, and financial services (Kantor, as quoted in USIS 1996a).[60] The objective of OECD governments therefore is for complete liberalization of Third World countries for First World investors. Predictably, Western trade policy toward the region has become more contentious. Since the winding down of the cold war, the United States's commercial policy no longer fits into its global security policy. Domestic audiences hurt by import competition can no longer be bought off by national security arguments. It is not surprising therefore that the number of antidumping orders filed by U. S. trade authorities against foreign producers has strongly increased, from 4 in the 1960–70 decade to 118 in the 1986–90 half-decade. The number of countervailing duty orders increased from zero in the 1960–75 period to 37 in the 1986–90 half-decade (Eckles 1995: Table 8.1).

In Northeast Asia, U. S. trade authorities under the Clinton administration have reoriented trade policy toward the new objective of leveling the state-market machinery responsible for success in catching up in production power and preventing its further spread. The barter version of industrial capitalism shows up in this struggle as an ideological tool. It is not difficult to understand why that is the case.

In the production-based version of an industrial market economy, governments of late-industrializing countries have little choice but to help to build up and protect the production power of enterprises. In the market-based approach to the spread of international capitalism, on the other hand, these societies, if their leaders are insightful enough, make the transition voluntarily to industrial capitalism due to the universal attractions of wealth and the superior allocative efficiency of markets. Accordingly, free markets spread voluntarily, to the benefit of all. If governments of late-industrializing countries in East Asia would come to their senses, they would open up their markets voluntarily for the importation of advanced manufactured consumer products and foreign entrepreneurship, respectively. In the colonial era, markets had to be opened by guns. In the modern era, wise rulers in Third World countries, acting upon the interest of their society, now see the reason why.

The propagation of the free trade doctrine by developed countries has its roots therefore in the progressivist view of history in which first-industrializers give the law to the rest of mankind. "No nation has the right to refuse to hold inter-course with others," the first U. S. consul to Japan told the Japanese. After having industrialized behind high tariff walls, President Wilson proclaimed that "our flag is the flag of humanity." Since Wilson, the U. S. conviction of being the spearhead of human progress has radicalized foreign policy. The truth in all these endeavors was probably best formulated by Morgenthau (1967: 9), that in international politics, self-deception dominates the relationship between speech and the brute facts of behavior to a degree that may defy the understanding of even the best psychologist.

Western governments in their trade policy toward industrializing China and Southeast Asia therefore tend to act upon the presupposition of "no more Japans." To incorporate industrializing Third World economies at the low end into the value-added chain of the international industrial division of labor, American trade policy under Clinton and E. U. external policy have taken a unilateral, a bilateral, and a regional free-trade/free-investment direction. In Southeast Asia, the United States is promoting free trade in the name of "open regionalism" in Asia-Pacific Economic Cooperation (APEC).

In Northeast Asia, the United States's trade policy has taken a unilateral and a bilateral market-opening turn. The short-term objective is to impose import targets on Japan and South Korea.[61] The long-term objective is to redirect Japan toward a U. S.-style of corporate capitalism and an indebted consumerist society, which would deprive its economy of its sting.

5.   Southeast Asia

Countries in Southeast Asia have not repeated the development performance of Japan and the Northern NICs. In Southeast Asian economies, import substitution is not complete; it does not extend to capital goods industries and knowledge-intensive production processes. These economies add new knowledge to produc-tion in the form of imported machinery and foreign entrepreneurship, despite high savings levels. To better understand why both subregions differ, one may compare colonial Southeast Asia with pre–Civil War United States. In the South, the British textiles revolution induced a cotton slave economy that imported manufactured products from England, creating in its elite an interest in free trade. In the industrializing North, on the other hand, manufacturers sought (and ultimately got) protection and a mercantilist type of government intervention in the building of industries. The industrial North won the battle.[62] In Northeast Asia, the "cotton South" was preempted by indigenous governments. In colonial Southeast Asia, however, "the cotton South" won. In the colonial past, the governments of Europe shoved off on colonial economies the production of noncompeting agricultural primary commodities, but maintained control for their own firms over the means of transport, insurance, processing, branding, and retail parts of the value-added chain.

The separate status of Southeast Asian economies is reflected in the role of foreign entrepreneurship. In Indonesia, Malaysia, and Thailand, FDI stocks as a percentage of the GDPs of these countries dramatically increased in the 1980–94 period. In Indonesia the foreign investment stock increased from 14.2 percent in 1980 to 36.6 percent in 1990, back to 26.5 percent in 1994. The country's boom in the export of manufactured products is closely related to the expansion of FDI. In 1980, the share of manufactures in total exports of Indonesia was less than 3 percent; between 1983 and 1990 the manufacturing share in exports jumped from 6 to just over 40 percent. In Malaysia, the FDI stock increased from 24.8 percent of GDP in 1980 to 46.2 percent in 1994; FDI stock in Thailand as a share of GDP tripled from 3 percent in 1980 to 10.1 percent in 1994. The suppression of local entrepreneurship by colonial powers and the privileges accorded to expatriate traders helps explain why foreign entrepreneurs are so important in Southeast Asia.

Data suggest indeed that industrialization in Southeast Asia has not restored a balance between the demographic and economic weights of the region. In 1990, the ASEAN-4 countries (Indonesia, Malaysia, Philippines and Thailand) with 5.62 percent of world population produced 1.27 percent of world GDP. Japan, on the other hand, with 2.2. percent of the world's population produced in that year 13.54 percent of world GDP; South Korea accounted in that year for a share of 1.12 percent of world GDP, produced with 0.77 percent of the world's population. In terms of shares of world exports of merchandise trade in 1995, South Korea and Taiwan rank twelfth and fourteenth on the list of the world's top twenty exporters; none of the ASEAN-4 countries belongs to that list.

It may be argued that FDI reduces the time required for an economy to develop an ability to produce sophisticated consumer goods for home and export markets. The time-compressing role of FDI may be illustrated by the computer sector in Malaysia. That country manufactures and exports advanced hand-held personal computers. However, the technology for producing them, the trademark, marketing, and retail remain in the hands of the Phillips Corporation, which has distributed the production of parts for its hand-held computers throughout the world. Training people in Malaysia to handle equipment producing these machines does not give them access to knowledge of how to produce that equipment. Backward links to domestic entrepreneurship are weak. The country is unable to further improve the technology incorporated into these machines.

However, the transport sector in Indonesia demonstrates that backward linkages of FDI may be rather strong and beneficial. In Indonesia a transport revolution occurred in the oil boom years of the 1970s. Since the 1970s the number of registered motorcycles, buses, and commercial vehicles increased twentyfold. Transport opened the countryside, and helped to focus agricultural producers on their main task by providing them with access to inputs produced elsewhere and by opening access to education and to health services.

Time compression in the capacity to produce advanced manufactured goods comes at a price, which includes:

1. Incomplete import substitution and loss of control over the most profitable parts of the value-added chain of exports. Instead of relocating branches of industry, production processes are spatially distributed across the development hierarchy on the basis of their knowledge content.

2. Local capitalists get locked into the international division of labor as dependent subcontractors producing labor-intensive parts or assembling parts imported from abroad, using imported capital goods. To add knowledge to production from imported capital goods does not provide access to that knowledge, nor the capability to advance knowledge production. Reverse engineering is one of the most effective channels of technology transfer, but becomes more difficult as technology becomes more complex.

3. As technology becomes more complex, the gap between training in the use of imported machinery and training to produce machinery increases. Reliance on foreign direct investment and on subcontracting to local firms may be considered as manufacturing equivalents to raw material suppliers from an earlier epoch in their history.

Without doubt, first-industrializers have an interest in other countries joining the international division of labor. However, these governments have no interest in seeing others reduce the distance between them. As technology becomes more complex, start-up costs increase, learning curves become steeper, and production runs get shorter. The microelectronics revolution is making manufacturing less material and more knowledge-intensive, and service provision less personal and more integrated into the manufacturing process. Foreign enterprises and home governments will for these reasons become reluctant to transfer advanced technology. To transfer advanced technology to competitors would deplete the production power of the home economy.

The upgrading of the economies of developed countries is reflected in the rise of labor productivity in manufacturing. Between 1960 and 1994 the manufacturing sector in developed countries reduced its employment share from about 25 to 18 percent. However, the share manufacturing contributed to GDP in constant prices remained flat, at a level of about 22 percent.

5.1 The Rise of a Regional Economy

After the sharp revaluation of the yen in 1985, Japan's investment in manufacturing in East Asia increased tenfold from about $500 million in 1985 to about $5 billion in 1994. However, as far as supplying the home market is concerned, Japan continues to rely on home production. Japan's FDI in the region goes together with a substantial trade surplus with the host region. In addition to boosting Japanese exports of capital goods and high-tech intermediate products, overseas production generates an export trade of finished products to the markets of the United States and the European Union. Japan's FDI in the region is supported by official development aid. Aid disbursement correlates in time and space with shifts in the distribution of investment capital.

In East Asia, productive capital is distributed among participants of unequal size and with unequal power in business networks (Irwan 1995). Japanese, South Korean, and Taiwanese and overseas Chinese business networks since the mid-1980s have been spanning the East Asian region (Lim 1983). Capital flows and production networks connect offshore East Asia with southern coastal China, Hong Kong, Taiwan, Indonesia, Thailand, Singapore, Malaysia, and the Philippines, leading to a more coherent economic region. Japanese production and trading networks are one part of the network that binds the region together. Chinese networks of cooperating firms are another part of the region's production network.

In East Asia, China presently is the largest host country of FDI. Overseas Chinese are the most important source of that capital. Between 1978, when reform in China started with agriculture, and 1994, total Chinese exports as a percentage of GDP increased from around 6 to 24 percent (World Bank 1996: Table 13). Total FDI increased in the same period from less than $1 billion in 1979 to about $38 billion in 1995, which is about equivalent to the annual inflows of all developing countries in the first half of the 1980s (United Nations Conference on Trade and Development 1996: 53). In other words, the foreign sector of the Chinese economy is transforming and financing the transition from Maoist autarchy to incorporation into the world economy (Weidenbaum and Hughes 1996: Chapter 1). Hong Kong is the source of and gateway for foreign capital entering China, with expatriate Chinese, Taiwanese, and Singaporeans the most important Asian sources of foreign capital. Altogether "offshore China" accounts for about three-quarters of the origin of FDI entering China.

The extension of networks of production and trade into China is driven by the desire to get access to still cheaper labor and by the apparent ability of the Chinese government to discipline the work force during the transition to a market economy.[63] However, capital entering China has a strong regional concentration. The result is unequal development within China, which has set off an unprecedented migration of impoverished peasant families to the coastal south of the country.[64]

Guangdong Province, which neighbors Hong Kong, attracts well over one-third of the FDI entering China. In 1980, three areas in this province were designated as Special Economic Zones (SEZs), with one SEZ in neighboring Fujian province. In 1984, fourteen other coastal cities obtained SEZ status, to be followed by the designation of Hainan Island as a SEZ in 1988 and part of Shanghai in 1990. In its wake, manufacturing relocated by businessmen from Hong Kong is creeping north along the coast and its river mouths.

The ethnic Chinese in Southeast Asian countries form rather small minorities, except for Singapore. Their minority position in demographic respect is in stark contrast, however, to the disproportionately large share of capital wealth they control in these countries (East Asia Analytic Unit 1995). In the case of Indonesia, Irwan (1995: Table 3.1) refers to figures indicating that the Chinese, making up between 2.8 and 4 percent of the population, control between 70 and 75 percent of the capital assets of the economy. Of the seventeen richest businessmen in 1993 in Indonesia, twelve were ethnic Chinese. The rapid rise in the 1990s of two conglomerates controlled by sons of former president Suharto has not basically changed the predominance of the ethnic Chinese in Indonesia's economy.

The position of the Chinese minority in Southeast Asian countries as the preeminent traders and financiers originates in the destruction by colonial invaders from Western Europe of the trading networks of Arabs, Indians, Malays, the Bugis, the Makasars, and the Javanese. In Imperial China, the development process could not profit from the overseas trading networks. For most of its history, traders were expelled to the inaccessible coastal south of the country (Seagrave 1995: Part 1). In China and in ex-colonial Southeast Asia, the entrepreneurial class has to be nurtured by state power. The state and the armed forces, functioning as the womb of entrepreneurship, dissociate the industrialization process from productivity as well as from the development of liberal institutions.

The predictable result of the wealth-cum-political exclusion of what began as expatriate Chinese traders has often been discrimination, official pressure upon them to assimilate, and mob violence. In the colonial past, the Dutch could not live without the Chinese intermediaries, which did not prevent the application of violence against them.

Minority status and being a target of discrimination and repression compel intense cooperation from victims in clans, families, and dialect group networks of mutual protection. Outsider rejection of the Chinese minority is more complete in cases in which class opposition, religious differences, and ethnic differences coincide. Where religious differences are absent, as in Thailand and the Philippines, rich Chinese seem to enjoy their wealth more at ease than in Indonesia. The tragic situation of overseas Chinese minorities is probably best reflected in the statement of one of them that "real life lies elsewhere, though exactly where it lies is difficult to say."[65]

6. The Bust: Destruction Without Creation

The geographical spread of industrial capitalism has been conceived in this chapter as resulting from competition between domestic arrangements for group survival. These arrangements are tested in the international system for their capacity to generate production power and are assumed to be selected for survival and spread on that basis. Plan-rational, production-oriented capitalism is one these "domestic arrangements."

Production-oriented and barter-oriented approaches to catch-up development have different roles of the banking sector and its relation to enterprises and to the government. In Northeast Asian developing economies, the financial sector has the task of financing industrial expansion at lower than market rates.[66] As noted above, Japan's industrial expansion is "plan-rational." Managers, in cooperation with government ministries, extend the scope of planning of the industrial division of labor within companies across the boundaries of legally independent enterprises. The banking sector, in cooperation with the insurer's role of the government, is therefore capable of extending the time horizon in financing industrial expansion across the learning curves of interrelated enterprises. Debt financing at lower than market interest rates in setting up industries is part and parcel of production-oriented capitalism as practiced by industrial latecomers in Northeast Asia.

In Japan and South Korea, debt financing has helped induce a lopsided industrial structure. Alongside a few very large enterprises operate numerous very small enterprises. Preferential access to capital and credits (credit subsidies, tax rebates, public enterprises producing intermediate goods required by private industry down stream) favoring very large companies has caused this dual industrial structure. To allocate massive amounts of capital to giant industrial enterprises violates the prescription of the barter-oriented theory of industrial capitalism to allocate capital in labor-abundant societies in the labor-using direction (Yamamura 1995: 120).

Due to credit financing, late-industrializing economies tend to close off the financial sector for external participation. Japan began to open its financial sector for foreign participation in the early 1980s. At that time, due to the slowdown in economic growth since the mid-1970s, corporate demand for domestic investment credit declined, investment opportunities abroad increased, leading to deregulation of the financial sector. Thus, Japan liberalized exchange controls to profit from overseas investment opportunities when it became a creditor nation.

Financing industrialization in ex-colonial Southeast Asia is different. In Northeast Asia, preferential access of companies to credits is geared to productivity, which is tested by export success. In Southeast Asian economies, preferential access of enterprises to credit depends on preferential access of their top management to patrons in the state apparatus. Both subregions differ in state strength. First, as noted above, the indigenous bourgeoisie is less developed in Southeast Asian countries. Second, Southeast Asian economies deregulated the financial sector without having substantially reduced the gap in productivity.[67]

South Korea avoided reliance on foreign entrepreneurship, but banks and enterprises did borrow substantial amounts of money abroad to finance industrial expansion. Unlike Southeast Asia, that money is invested productively, with export success as the test. In the 1990s South Korea's current account is for all practical purposes in equilibrium: GDP grows at about 8 percent, as in the 1980s, its inflation rate is comparatively low, and its level of indebtedness is one the lowest in the developing world. The *won* was not pegged to the dollar. Why then the bust? Due to a crisis in liquidity: state and business managers of the Korean financial system overplayed their hand by borrowing too much in the short term relative to the country's foreign currency reserves. The system collapsed when foreign holders of the *won*, anticipating its depreciation, began to sell the currency and thus created a self-fulfilling prophecy. If the present bust in South Korea originates in the way in which the financial sector has been institutionally geared to finance catch-up industrialization, we have in this system also the cause of increasing monetary volatility when industrial capitalism spreads around the world. The creation of new centers of capital accumulation and credit creation deprives the sitting monetary hegemon of its capacity to run the international financial system.

In Schumpeter's analysis, business cycles originate in inventions, which create new opportunities for investing businessmen. In his theory of the business cycle, the dynamics of investment (investment accelerator) and of spending (income multiplier) in the real sector plus the failure of governments to smooth out the cycle by countercyclical monetary and fiscal policies could be blamed for the instability.

For developing countries, a macroeconomic policy crisis is a more usual cause of financial instability. When governments run large budget deficits and then print money to finance them, inflation rates increase beyond nominal interest rates. This is followed by capital flight, current account deficits escalating out of control, and a collapse of the currency on the exchange market. This is the classical way for a developing country to end up in the hands of the IMF. However, a macroeconomic policy crisis in developing countries hardly comes alone, as terms of trade commonly deteriorate prior to the macroeconomic policy crisis.

The present financial crisis in Southeast Asia is of a different sort. It has been called a crisis in financial stability. A crisis in financial stability originates in the private sector, however with the proviso that the environment in which the private sector operates is largely shaped by government policy.

The crisis in financial stability in Southeast Asia evolved as follows. Between 1992 and 1996, capital inflows from Japan and Western Europe (Germany in particular) in the form of bank lending and portfolio investment overwhelmed the inflow of foreign direct investment. In Indonesia alone, banks from the United States, the United Kingdom, and Japan have a claim of $60 billion, $23 billion of which is accounted for by Japanese banks. Portfolio investments boost bank deposits. Between 1992 and 1996, net inflows as a share of host country GDP doubled. Banks work on a fractional reserve basis between liabilities (deposits) and assets (reserves and lending). Bank lending therefore increased by a multiple of direct investment capital inflows. Due to capital imports, domestic investors in these countries continued borrowing from banks in local currencies at low U. S. and extremely low Japanese interest rates. Neither industry nor the service sector was capable to absorb that amount of money. Financial institutions therefore began to invest in real estate instead in export production. Banks thus exposed themselves to the risk of currency depreciation. When exports decreased and the balance of payments began to deteriorate, foreign investors began to withdraw investments and share prices began to fall.

In early March 1997, stock market prices in Thailand began to decline. When the government defended the fixed exchange rate by selling foreign currency, foreign currency reserves became depleted. On July 2, 1997, after spending billions of U. S. dollars on the defense of the baht, the Thai Central Bank felt compelled to let its currency float. It soon lost 60 percent of its precrisis value. The collapse of the Thai baht set off a chain reaction affecting Malaysia and Indonesia, whose precrisis achievements and problems are largely similar to those of Thailand. Ultimately, the crisis reached South Korea, whose government decided to let the *won* float on November 17, 1997, which led to a loss of 50 percent of its value.

To use a military analogy, if currency speculation is the trigger and the Thai real estate collapse the ignition, the loading of the barrel consisted of borrowing appreciating dollars on the short term abroad by the domestic banking system and by competitive bank lending in local currency to investors in the home economy. When the exchange rate collapsed, debtor banks could no longer pay off their dollar and yen debts. Productive enterprises with dollar debts could no longer pay off their debts from local currency receipts, causing technically bankruptcy even if they were profitable on the home market.

The origin of the crisis in financial stability in Southeast Asia lies in the decision of governments taken in the early 1990s to peg the national currency to the dollar without assuring that their rates of inflation did not go beyond the rate of inflation in the United States and Japan. Fixing exchange rates between a strong and a weak currency is doomed to failure if inflation rates differ.[68]

In the summer of 1995, the dollar sharply increased in value against the yen, against major European currencies, and against the Chinese yuan, which had devalued in late 1994, resulting in overvalued Southeast Asian currencies.[69] Consequently, exports from these countries priced themselves out of the markets of Japan, China, and Western Europe. As Southeast Asian exports became more expensive, economic growth began to slow down, increasing current account deficits. When investors began to withdraw investments, share prices began to fall.

The crisis in financial stability in Southeast Asia implies a failure of governments to mediate successfully between national and international monetary systems.[70] When a national government mediates, it operates as a revolving door between the national and the international system. Depending on the pressure put upon each side of the door, the government of a powerful state may seek relief for a national problem by imposing domestic change upon a weakling beyond its borders. A government of a less powerful state may solve an international problem by imposing its costs on domestic society. The U.S.-Korean trade disputes over food trade may serve as an example. The U.S. government, under pressure from its subsidized farmers and food producers-exporters, is pushing on the door from the outside to get access to a country with rapidly growing incomes. The Reagan administration imposed upon security-dependent South Korea a diet change in favor of food imported from the United States. South Korea gave in to American wishes, to the disadvantage of its farmers, as part of its international security policy.

The massive inflows of portfolio investments and foreign bank lending reported above allow us to draw three conclusions:

1. Foreign capital comes in when it is least needed. Rates of saving and investment were high throughout the region before the crisis hit. Private capital owners from abroad came in to feed upon an already prepared dish, not to help create that dish.
2. Private foreign capital leaves when it is most needed to prevent collapse. By fleeing when it is most needed, foreign capital has helped create a carcass out of a booming regional economy.[71]
3. Financing catch-up industrialization by bank credits works on conditions that it is geared to productivity and the closure of the financial sector until the moment when the catching-up process has been completed.

The IMF recipe for East Asian economies is geared to solving the macroeconomic policy crisis mentioned above. A macroeconomic policy crisis is a crisis of overspending. The IMF's prescription is therefore to reduce imports by deflating the economy. Accordingly, the institution imposes budget cuts (reducing government subsidies for basic necessities as food, cooking oil, and fuel) and prescribes a restrictive monetary policy, and thus high interest rates and further deregulation. In other words, the recipe is to push these economies into a recession. The conclusion from application of this prescription to East Asia is that Western banks, via the IMF, are able to privatize profits made from growth not of their own making, and in bad times to socialize losses partly of their own creation. Bankers are assumed to know the creditworthiness of their borrowers best, but knowing they can be bailed out permits them to shift the burden of recapitalization to the taxpayer. The IMF approach implies that the financial aid it provides will be spent to repay loans to Western and Japanese banks, not on imports.

In the Korean case, the IMF seems to pursue the more radical objective of changing the country's highly successful production-oriented capitalism toward a market-oriented one. This aim is reflected in the IMF's detailed prescriptions to the government on how to reorganize relations between businesses, between enterprises and banks, and between the government and the economy. For years, U. S. trade officials complained bitterly about limited access for American exports and investors to Japanese and South Korean markets.[72] In the case of Japan, these officials try to exploit the Asian crisis to "open up" the Japanese market for Southeast Asian and their own exports.

The overall conclusion from this episode is that the problem of finding out who is in trouble is in politics decided not on the basis of causation but on relative power. In other words, the IMF gives the hot potato of domestic adaptation to the weaker party.[73]

Why did China escape from the turmoil? In 1994, the Chinese government de facto devalued the national currency by setting the exchange rate at 8.3 yuan per dollar, though the rate of economic growth has been declining since 1992. Since 1994 China's capital market has been open to foreign participation only in the current account of the balance of trade; transactions in the capital account are, with the exception of limited foreign participation in the Shanghai and Shenzhen stock markets, closed to foreigners. The national currency is therefore not fully convertible. That provides shelter against hot money and currency traders. It does not solve the problem of nonperforming loans, which are estimated by the Chinese government to be $120 billion. The most important source of foreign capital in China are the offshore Chinese. In present circumstances, they will have less to invest abroad. The question therefore is whether or not the yuan will further decline as Chinese shares in export markets are exposed to renewed competition from Southeast Asia. East Asia's least developed economies, with large export sectors, are therefore exposed to competitive currency devaluation and competition in the offering of tax breaks to foreign investors in search of cheap labor, lax environmental standards, and a government capable of imposing discipline on the work force. That is precisely where foreign investors and governments of developed countries want to have these economies. None of them are waiting for new entrants into the markets of advanced consumer products like autos, electronic equipment, computer chips, telecommunications equipment, and banking/financial services in the early-middle part of the product cycle. "No new Japans" summarizes best what Western business leaders have in mind for new upstarts in Southeast Asia.

Vietnam and Myanmar, too, have closed their capital markets and have thus been able to escape from foreign speculation. These economies are among the poorest in the region. The richest and most open economies of Japan, Hong Kong, and Taiwan have been least affected by the onslaught of the world money market. It is precisely the rapidly growing Southeast Asian economies with a tradition of politically motivated state influence on the provision of credit and a liberalized capital market that have been most affected.

It is ironic that the transition of Southeast Asian economies toward manufacturing may have made them more vulnerable to sudden collapse. In Schumpeter's analysis of the business cycle, overexpansion of industrial production during upswings saddles manufacturing enterprises with unsold stocks, making investment unprofitable. Industrial sector production in East Asia has become the most important employer. In the economies of developed countries, on the other hand, employment shifted after 1970 from manufacturing to services.[74] Usually services cannot be stocked and are in continuous demand. Demand for services and their production is therefore less vulnerable to steep upturns and downturns (Webber 1997).

What lies ahead for Southeast Asian economies? As noted above, the import content of Southeast Asian exports is high. The devaluation of their currencies will thus not translate into an equal competitive advantage on export markets to the same degree. Despite their industrial transformation in the past decades, Southeast Asian economies have not really been success stories in terms of reducing the economic distance between themselves and the developed countries. As I discussed in Section III, countries in the region did not start from the same baseline. The potential of Southeast Asian economies to catch up is large. Their organizational capacity to do so is not. Further growth in the niche in which they are now located depends on enlarging that space by a further restructuring of developed economies. Insofar as Southeast Asian economies did catch up, they achieved success in natural resource– and minerals-based technology in which energy cost, the cost of low-skilled labor, and iron, steel, and other metals form a substantial part of unit cost. In these kinds of products, design, manufacturing, marketing, and retail are performed in separate departments. This is the reason why these functions are distributed across countries at different levels of development.

In electronic consumer products, in data and image processing equipment, in telecommunication products and related services, the design, product development, component production, assembling, quality control, and customer-interactive marketing and retail have in technical terms become integrated. For catching up in these sort of products, installing state-of-the-art technology in manufacturing is not enough.

7. Conclusions

1.   After World War II, American enterprises surpassed enterprises in Europe and Japan in production power. During World War II, the United States had produced itself into a position of hegemony. During the first decades of the cold war, enterprises from the European Union and Japan caught up in production power. The 1970s were the crucial decade of transition toward a new national, regional-international alignment of social forces.

Wartime production by private corporations but on state orders explains the U. S. surge in labor productivity during the war years. However, during the cold war, American enterprises could not fully exploit their advantage in external markets. American security policy allowed many exceptions to market openings created by multilateral tariff reductions in GATT between the Geneva Round (1947) and the Tokyo Round (1973–79). The external tariffs of the European Community and domestic protection in Japan, South Korea, and Taiwan are the most important of these exceptions.

2.   During the decades of the 1970s and 1980s, enterprises from Europe and Japan caught up in production power with firms from the United States. In the 1980s and 1990s, enterprises from the United States, the European Union, and Japan are competing at the edge of the technological frontier in the world markets. In these decades the multilateral tariff negotiation process has begun to falter and trade disputes have become more numerous.

3.   In that sort of world, first-industrializing countries impose free trade on less developed economies and protect their own production power against competitors. At the end of the product cycle, enterprises from first-industrializing economies outsource labor-intensive production processes. The result is the creation of a linkage between restructuring the economy of developed countries and capitalist transformation of East Asia by export-oriented industrialization in which foreign capital plays an important role. In the more open world economy of the post–cold war era, industrializing developing countries therefore get, on the supply side, imports of advanced consumer products designed and retailed by enterprises from first-industrializing economies. Unless protected and subsidized, local production will be preempted by imports. On the demand side, high-income countries shape consumer preferences in low-income countries in favor of their own export sector.

4.   The tools required for catching up find little sympathy in developed countries. Policymakers in developed economies are under pressure to promote and to adapt society to upgrading the domestic economy by relocating labor-intensive production processes to low-wage overseas production zones in the Third World. The direction and speed of economic change in Southeast Asia is therefore shaped

by the restructuring policies of developed countries. Not one of these economies, however, has been able to catch up substantially in production power with developed countries.

Notes

1. China is now the largest importer of sugar and cooking oil in the world and will soon become the largest importer of cotton and wheat. Economies in Southeast Asia are competing with China's low production cost, leading to displacement of exports in developed country markets.

2. In 1995, 30 percent of Latin America's exports went to pay for principal and interest on its debt, an increase of 5 percent over 1990; in sub-Saharan Africa indebtedness increased from 226 percent of exports to 270 percent in 1995; in the Middle East and North Africa, indebtedness rose in that same period from 110 to 137 percent of exports; in East Asia and the Pacific, indebtedness decreased from 107 to 83 percent during the period.

3. "[I]t is forgotten that each of the tens or hundreds of thousands of societies which have existed side by side in the world or succeeded one another since man's first appearance, has claimed that it contains all the meanings and dignity of which human society is capable…and its claim has in its own eyes rested on a moral certainty comparable to that which we can invoke in our own case" (Strauss 1966: 58).

4. The building of the Jalan Raya Pos in Northern Java by the Dutch is a good example of the destructive impact on local communities of being linked to the external world by outsiders.

5. Cultural elements now easily diffuse across societies, creating the false impression of increasing diversity and choice.

6. Agrarian-aristocratic empires satisfy the conditions Marx elaborated for what he called the "Asiatic mode of production."

7. Rural insurgencies in Thailand, the Philippines, Malaysia, and Indonesia after independence continued to orient militaries inward (McVey 1992).

8. The United States, apparently preferring the dismemberment of Indonesia to its slide into communism, used air power against government army troops repressing the regional army rebellion in 1957 in Sumatra (Prados 1986: 130–44; see also Kahin and Kahin 1996); U. S. subversion was not limited to Indonesia. Since the publication of the *Foreign Relations of the United States, 1958–1960,* Vol. 19, 1996, the story of the Tibetan rebellion in Lhasa of 1959 has to be revised as well (U. S. Department of State 1996). The document contains numerous references to CIA operations before the March rebellion, in conjunction with Taiwan's Special Operations Unit, coordinated by Indian intelligence. Western countries tend to protect — in the name of human rights — a traditional theocracy living off submissive and illiterate peasants but overlook the contribution the United States has made to Chinese repression.

9. The last Indian families were hunted down in the southern tip of Argentina in the late nineteenth century; in contemporary Mexico the hunt seems to be on again; a slow-motion killing process has been under way in the Amazon throughout the twentieth century.

10. Is it just a coincidence in timing that Western governments began to practice human rights diplomacy toward Third World governments after colonial powers had transferred to independent governments the dirty task of development?

11. Japanese colonialism in Taiwan and South Korea differs from Western colonialism not in its brutality but in its developmental impact. The Japanese, in a hurry to take colonies when the Western powers moved into the region, promoted economic development to make the colonies strong against the West.

12. Burnham's work is a constant reminder of the fact that resource availability in a country is irrelevant for its development; the decisive fact of industrial capitalism is that resources are brought together as a result of the single-minded pursuit of capital accumulation via sales to customers.

13. I am grateful for Reinert's willingness to share with my department several of his manuscripts in draft form.

14. In Weber's study of industrial capitalism, the economy is conceived to be a part of politics. Political maneuvering by oligopolistic business leaders is part of the process of the creation of market opportunities, of getting access to and of excluding others from these opportunities. Schumpeter and Weber were more than contemporaries. Rejecting the general equilibrium of the circular flow model of the exchange theory of markets, in which profits dwindle to zero, both shared the same preoccupation with the question of the origin of value and of profit and its role in the development process.

15. However, small companies at the bottom of the hierarchy are used as shock absorbers for setbacks in foreign markets. These companies, with substantially lower pay levels and without lifelong employment, maintained the competitiveness of top companies producing and selling trademarked products in foreign markets.

16. At the firm level, there is little or no empirical evidence of first-moving enterprises staying ahead forever. Societies that industrialized first, however, have so far stayed ahead. Despite the spread of industrialization outside the core region, despite world communication, the explosive growth in trade and investment between developed and developing countries, the postwar period displays at the world level widening income disparities. The systemic process of continuing divergence at the world level is compatible with a Pareto distribution process. Accordingly, sequential development is a process of serial appropriation of development opportunities in which those who come first take a random part of the most rewarding options; those who follow have to build upon what has been left behind.

17. The unit of analysis should be the enterprise in its social setting, not either one or the other.

18. Societies and their enterprises that compete in production power at the technological edge are not necessarily market interdependent. For example, in the 1990s the United States spent about 2 percent of its national income in Japan. Precisely because Japan has caught up in production power with the United States, it has been able to prevent a high level of import penetration by American firms. Due to the size of these economies relative to their external sector, living standards in each of the triad members is basically determined by the growth of productivity of the home economy, not by relative success in export markets.

19. The beleaguered Red Army received, among others, 12,161 battle tanks and other armored combat vehicles, 32,200 motorcycles, 11,075 railroad cars, 112,293 submachine guns, 15,000 aircraft, over 2.5 million tons of petroleum products, 16 million pairs of boots, and a half-pound of food per war day for each Soviet soldier (Mueller 1989: 82–83).

20. For research on alternative processes that may produce the strong observed correlation between the level of per capita wealth in a society and its having a democratic political system, see Przeworski (1997).

21. The issue of designing a conceptual framework in the study of development is of tremendous importance for subsequent analysis. By choosing an appropriate cultural framework, one could

study differential economic performance by ethnic groups in the Asian region, linking values to success.

22. However, it is in my view incorrect to believe that Japan is, with respect to the relationship between business and government, in a different category than Western democracies. Following Weber, in production-oriented capitalism there is no neat distinction between the enterprise and the market. A score of studies of business elites in Western societies have come up with findings not very different from Japan. However, it may be true that the myth of separation between government, bureaucracy, and business helps to legitimize representative democracy.

23. It is highly unlikely that its collapse will bring a transition to stable democracy. Territorial collapse or military dictatorship seems more likely. Comparative studies of revolution in the Northern Hemisphere lead to the conclusion that mass mobilization interacting with a split at the top is required for revolution. A split at the top occurs when the elite sees it as impossible to reproduce for their children their own status and level of living. The disturbing thing in Indonesia is the absence of an alternative leadership capable of rejuvenating the economy and polity. It is for these reasons unlikely that the United States will enforce the IMF reform program.

24. The U. S. Senate, which represents about 5 percent of the world's population, a population that annually uses about 8 tons of the oil equivalent of fossil energy per capita, thereby producing a world share of 22.9 percent of the carbon emissions in the half-decade from 1990 to 1995, voted 95 to 0 not to sign any treaty emerging from the conference on climate change in Kyoto, December 1997, "unless the protocol or other agreements also mandates new specific scheduled commitments to limit or reduce greenhouse gas emissions for developing parties." In that same five-year period, each American produced 5.3 tons of carbon, each Chinese 0.7 tons. International industrial capitalism allows those who come first to development to capture, appropriate, and commodify in markets divisible common pool resources, as well as to spoil the common property resources of nature. Even the most ardent supporter of the private car in America will oppose privatization of the costs imposed by exhaust fumes. Solar energy may be the way out. However, no one has set in motion a plan to find a solution. To build an artificial shelter within nature for the world's population may be a process of entrapment instead of a process of sequential development.

25. An Indian from French Canada brought to France in 1776 is quoted as having said: "May the devil take you. Why then have you taken me from my country to show me that I am poor? Never in my whole life would I have known that without you. In my forests I knew nothing of riches or poverty. I was my own king, my master and my servant. And you have cruelly torn me from this happy state, to teach me that I am a miserable creature and a slave" (Pagden 1993: 32). Due to the revolution of mass communication and export penetration of poor areas by Western consumer products, the requirement of direct on the spot observation and comparison is no longer required for the discovery of relative poverty.

26. In purchasing power parity dollars, Japan was trailing the United States in 1992 by about $2,000.

27. The bank reduced its purchasing power parity (PPP) estimate of per capita income in China in 1994 from $2,500 to $1,800.

28. Recent estimates of the number of people perishing from hunger during the Great Leap Forward are around 40 million, with several million more suffering from continual hunger (Becker 1996; see also Rummel 1991: 248–49).

29. Moulder defends the view that preincorporation China and Japan were basically similar. Accordingly, Japan developed so rapidly because, due to warfare among the major powers and their expansion elsewhere in the colonial world, the country escaped colonization. China's lack of development, by contrast, is ascribed to external domination. However, preincorporation elites of both countries had very different views of the outside world. Japan sent its last tribute

mission to China in 1549. The fact that this practice was stopped implies that Japanese imperial tradition had changed to interstate competition, in which withdrawal was a viable option for the islands. The Chinese people, on the other hand, did not have the concept of the "state," or the "country." These notions first emerged in the vocabulary of the May Fourth Movement of 1919, when students discovered that Western powers in Versailles had handed over Germany's possessions in China to Japan.

30. In the late nineteenth–early twentieth century, Western governments and their companies were the world's great drug barons. Poppy cultivation in Bengal was intended for opium exports to Asian markets. Discouraging opium use in India itself, the East India Company, in order to balance its trade with China and to recover its own costs, directed opium exports to the Chinese market. Despite the protests of the Chinese government, which prohibited the importation of opium in 1799, profits from opium exports to China increased from just over half a million pounds in 1811 to over seven and half million pounds in 1871. It would not be until 1906 that Britain agreed to gradually reduce its exports to China. Only first-comers in a partially industrialized world have the privilege of earning money with impunity from encouraging addiction outside their own borders.

31. Britain wanted to maintain the Manchus in power to extract further concessions from it; it feared that the overthrow of the dynasty would result in anarchy, hurting its trade interests. However, protecting the prey in order to exploit it better helped to unleash a level of chaos the British had not anticipated (Gregory 1969: Chapter 7).

32. For an extensive documentation of Japan as an outsider, instead of being part of a systemic process, see Powelson (1994: esp. Chapters 2–4).

33. Captain Perry's mission had the aim, at that time unpublished, of preventing British naval dominance in the Far East and South Asia, which, if unchallenged, would have allowed Britain, as Perry wrote to President Fillmore, "to have the power of shutting up at will and controlling the enormous trade of those seas." Major power competition is still today a causal force in the international expansion of industrial capitalism.

34. Perry's men could therefore report about the "the high cultivation of the land everywhere… the innumerable thrifty villages," and "the sense of beauty, abundance, and happiness which everyone delighted to contemplate" (quoted in Howe 1996: 78–79).

35. The nationwide post office system as a collector of savings should be mentioned.

36. In Imperial China, the outflow of silver to pay for opium produced by the British East India Company undermined the monarchy's financial basis.

37. For Britain, the gold standard prevented the pound from depreciating as British export performance began to fail and the exporting of capital allowed trade to be unbalanced. Consequently, without the compensating fall in the value of the pound, quantity adjustment replaced price changes.

38. This is the big difference from the protection of new industries in Latin America. Import substitution protected indefinitely producers of well-established manufactured consumer goods sold on home markets.

39. Two remarkable events may demonstrate the legitimacy of past aggression by first-comers relative to the violence used by latecomers. The Blair government recently succeeded in wringing out of the Japanese government an apology for its World War II aggression against British colonies. The same government intends to wage war against Iraq for its possession of weapons of mass destruction, whereas the British themselves may have taught Saddam the effectiveness of those weapons in the 1920s. In the 1920s Britain used poison gas against the Kurds in a very liberal way, leveling 1,365 out of 2,382 dwellings in 79 Kurdish settlements

in oil-rich parts of the country. Sir Arthur (or Bomber) Harris learned the art of carpet bombing in the 1920s in Iraq. To further discredit British human rights policy, Harris has recently been saved from oblivion by a monument in London inaugurated by the British monarchy (see also McDowall 1997). Imagine if comparable things had occurred in Japan, with the emperor inaugurating a statue for Japanese experimentation with biological weapons in Northern China!

40. A principal reason for the decline of the state in Africa after the fall in commodity prices in the 1980s is revenue dependence of the government on export taxation. European powers did not take the trouble to develop a system of taxation.

41. One may expect that U.S. farmers will suffer from the economic downturn in South Korea. Maybe a regional food market will be put in place as demand is relocated to currency-depreciated countries of the region.

42. In Western Europe, Germany entered the industrialization process in these more modern sectors. It thus could avoid competition in manufacturing sectors in which firms from first-industrializing England had already established themselves. For that reason, the German case does not satisfy Akamatsu's model of late industrialization in all respects.

43. Another factor is technological: most capital goods industries have a minimal efficient size below which unit cost increases. Technological advance itself is produced at decreasing cost.

44. Verdoorn, studying U.S. war production during World War II, observed that unit cost decreased as production size of mass-produced equipment as planes, tanks and ships increased.

45. The United States itself industrialized between the end of the Civil War and World War I behind very high tariff walls and other protectionist devices.

46. It is highly unlikely that the Indonesian government will achieve in the foreseeable future the level of state capacity needed to lift indigenous car manufacturers into the world market. Apparently foreign producers and their complaining governments thought otherwise.

47. What is true for high-tech sectors for governments of developed countries is true for late-industrializers for any industrial sector: "Technology intensive industries clash with the assumptions of free trade theory in several ways. Costs tend to fall and product quality tends to improve over time.... A nation's comparative advantage is less a function of its national factor endowments and more a function of strategic interactions between its firms and government and the firms and governments in other nations. In such industries, comparative advantage is created, not endowed by nature" (Tyson, as quoted in King 1995: 137). The Clinton administration, in which Tyson served as chairperson of the Council of Economic Advisors, had this to recommend to leaders of emerging Asian markets: "[T]he principle of free trade and investment has been critical to the past and present economic miracles of the Asia Pacific; history makes clear that to stand still is to risk backsliding into protectionism; the Asia Pacific has no choice but to move forward" (Asia-Pacific Economic Cooperation Secretariat 1994: 3).

48. In the 1909–29 period, average import dependence was about 20 percent of national income; between 1950 and 1993–94, import dependence was halved from about 12 to about 6 percent. All other advanced economies increased their import dependence after World War II. Postwar U.S. import dependence increased between 1950 and 1994 by 21 percent annually to a level of 12.2 percent in 1994, providing a market outlet for Japan and other catch-up industrializers in East Asia. Japan's nonoil import dependence decreased 10 percent annually over the same time period. After World War II, the Japanese government prohibited the importation of manufactured goods, instead deciding to build a "full set" of manufacturing industries, limiting the importation of intermediate goods wherever possible, particularly after the oil shocks.

49. Between 1970 and 1996, the percentage of disposable income saved by Americans oscillated downward from about 9 percent in 1970 to 4 percent in 1996. Household debt as a percentage

of disposable income rose from 67 percent in 1980 to 89 percent in 1996 (*Economist*, 30 August 1997, p. 34).

50. That belief is an example of the fallacy of composition; the balance of trade is determined by savings rate, taxation level, level of government expenditures, and investment, thus by domestic variables alone.

51. Balance of trade deficits do occur despite low oil prices and despite devaluation of the dollar from its Bretton Woods value.

52. See the section on the "Kennan restoration" in Bruce Cumings well-known article on the matter.

53. South Korea contributed, however, per capita more troops to battle than the United States.

54. In 1960 Indonesians earned in exchange rate value 1.16 percent of the U. S. per capita income; in 1994 that percentage had increased to 3.4 percent.

55. TNCs are able to escape the rich countries hard-won labor standards by transferring production to countries with labor conditions resembling those of the past.

56. Legalization of the market for sexual services may serve as an example of government-created opportunities for enterprising businessmen.

57. "[E]ven if it is reinforced by the establishment of a barrier-free internal market, the Community will not be able to withstand competition from the two main strategic areas of America and Asia unless it extends its economic area and market. To create this European strategic area, the Community will have to turn to its neighbors.... In the Mediterranean, the Community must rapidly make up for lost time: the Mediterranean is now a focus of U. S. and Japanese trade, investment, economic aid, and above all, technological colonization" [for the European Union, see Economic and Social Committee (1997), quoted in Parfitt (1997: 869)].

58. As says former Undersecretary for Trade Garten: "The Clinton Administration has concluded that it does no good to call for a truce in government support to firms.... [T]he only choice now is a reluctant one to play the game as hard as the others so far as most kinds of supports go, including financing, high level trade missions, and political intervention by ambassadors, cabinet members and even the president" (Garten 1995: 58).

59. "The days of the cold war, when we sometimes looked the other way when our trading partners failed to live up to their obligations, are over. National security and our national economic security cannot be separated" (Commerce Secretary Ron Brown, as quoted in USIS 1996b).

60. "With the largest population on earth, traders for 150 years have dreamed of tapping the Chinese market. Businessmen in the nineteenth century dreamed of adding an inch to the shirt of every Chinese. Today, we dream of putting a cellular phone in the hands of every Chinese" (Barchevsky, as quoted in USIS 1996).

61. With great success in security-dependent South Korea, but without much effect in Japan, which finances U. S. trade deficits.

62. The United States industrialized behind very high tariff walls and other protective policies. It denies late-industrializing countries in East Asia the chance to do the same.

63. Taiwan and Hong Kong, by transferring to China the low-skill, labor-intensive parts of their production for export to developed country markets, replicate the Japanese pattern.

64. In the 1996–97 period, 35.9 million rural migrants found work in cities (*South China Morning Post*, 16 December 1997).

65. However, to be in a marginal position may also be a source of tremendous strength, independence, and initiative; the status of being between two cultures may help to explain the release

of energy and its channeling to the acquisition of wealth as a method to reduce uncertainty of identity and threats from other humans.

66. Schumpeter simply defined capitalism as "that form of private property economy in which innovations are carried out by means of borrowed money, which in general, though not by logical necessity, implies credit creation" (quoted in Heertje 1981: 174).

67. In PPP terms, Southeast Asian economies are catching up; in exchange rate values they have not.

68. In 1997, the inflation rate in Indonesia was 10 percent, in Malaysia 4.1 percent, in Thailand 7 percent, and in South Korea 4.3 percent, all above the U.S. and Japanese rates.

69. In guilders, the baht, the rupiah, and the ringgit began to lose value from July 1997 onward.

70. The concept is used by Mcfarlane, governor of the Reserve Bank of Australia, speaking on the economic crisis to Australian business economists, in Sydney, December 4, 1997. I am grateful to Jacob Meesters, Director of the Section Monetary and Economic Policy of the Dutch Central Bank, for providing me with a copy of McFarlane's speech.

71. To help create such a carcass is, according to standard Western practice, not a violation of human rights — only the consequences of the crisis are denoted as such. Western enterprises are now feeding upon the carcass by picking out pieces of flesh at sharply reduced local currency rates.

72. Mickey Kantor, the U.S. trade representative: "The time has come to expand the scope of trade rules to encompass trade-distorting domestic policies that are not currently dealt with in a trade context" (1995: 1).

73. That weaker party, however, is growing in power. Status quo powers causing the dissatisfaction of rising powers is the classic mechanism of the power transition — war linkage in power transition theory. In the past, when the United Kingdom and the United States expanded into the Pacific, they prevented Japan and Germany from doing the same (de *Soysa et al. 1997*).

74. In the OECD economies, total employment in manufacturing decreased between 1970 and 1994 from 28 to 18 percent. Even so, the share of manufacturing in GDP remained unchanged (in constant prices).

References

Abramowitz, M. (1994). "The Origins of the Postwar Catch-Up and Convergence Boom." Pp. 21–52 in *The Dynamics of Technology, Trade and Growth*, edited by J. Fagerberg et al. Brookfield, MA: Edward Elger.

Amsden, A. (1989). *Asia's Next Giant. South Korea and Late Industrialization*. New York: Oxford University Press.

Asia-Pacific Economic Cooperation Secretariat (1994). *Achieving the APEC-Vision. Free and Open Trade in the Asia-Pacific*. Second Report of the Eminent Persons Group, Singapore.

Beasley, W. G. (1995). *The Rise of Modern Japan. Political, Economic and Social Change since 1850*. New York: St. Martin's.

Becker, J. (1996). *Hungry Ghosts. China's Secret Famine*. London: John Murray.

Bello, W. and S. Cunningham (1994). "Trade Warfare and Regional Integration in the Pacific: The U. S., Japan and the Asian NIC's." *Third World Quarterly* 15(3): 445–58.

Burnham, J. (1941). *The Managerial Revolution. What Is Happening in the World*. Westport, CT: Greenwood.

Collins, R. (1986). *Weberian Sociological Theory*. New York: Cambridge University Press.

Cumings, B. (1984). "The Origins and Development of the Northeast-Asian Political Economy: Industrial Sectors, Product Cycles and Political Consequences." *International Organization* 38(1): 1–40.

de Soysa, I. et al. (1997). "Testing Power Transition Theory Using Alternative Measures of National Capabilities." *Journal of Conflict Resolution* 41(4): 509–28.

Diamond, J. (1997). *Guns, Germs and Steel. The Fates of Human Societies*. New York: Norton.

Dixon, C. (1991). *Southeast Asia in the World Economy. A Regional Geography*. Cambridge: Cambridge University Press.

Drooglever, P. J. (1978). "The Netherlands Colonial Empire: Historical Outline and Some Legal Aspects." Pp. 104–65 in *International Law in the Netherlands,* Volume I, edited by H. F. van Panhuys et al. Alphen aan de Rijn: Sythoff.

East Asia Analytic Unit (1995). *Overseas Chinese Business Networks in Asia*. Department of Foreign Affairs and Trade, Commonwealth of Australia.

Eckles A. E. (1995). *Opening America's Market. U. S. Foreign Trade Policy since 1776*. Chapel Hill: North Carolina Press.

Garten, J. E. (1995). "Is America Abandoning Multilateral Trade?" *Foreign Affairs* 74(6): 50–62.

Gregory, J. S. (1969). *Great Britain and the Taipings*. London: Routledge & Kegan Paul.

Gurr, T. R. (1993). *Minorities at Risk. A Global View of Ethnopolitical Conflict*. Washington, DC: United States Institute of Peace.

Hayes, P., et al. (1987). *American Lake. Nuclear Peril in the Pacific*. Harmondsworth: Penguin.

Heertje, A. (1981). *Schumpeter's Vision. Capitalism, Socialism and Democracy after 40 Years*. Amsterdam: Insinger, Willams and Cie.

Held, D. (1987). *Models of Democracy*. Oxford: Polity Press.

Hirschman, A. O. (1962). *The Strategy of Economic Development*. New Haven, CT: Yale University Press.

Hirschman, A. O. (1978). "Exit. Voice and State." *World Politics* 31: 90–107.

Howe, C. (1996). *The Origins of Japanese Trade Supremacy. Development and Technology in Asia from 1540 to the Present*. Chicago: Chicago University Press.

Inglehart, R. and M. Carballo (1997). "Does Latin America Exist? (And Is There a Confucian Culture?): A Global Analysis of Cross-Cultural Differences." *Political Science and Politics* 30(1): 34–46.

Irwan, A. (1995). *Business Networks and the Regional Economy of East and Southeast Asia in the Late Twentieth Century*. Ph. D. dissertation, State University of New York at Binghamton.

Irwin, D. (1996). "The United States in a New Global Economy? A Century's Perspective." *American Economic Association* (Papers and Proceedings May): 41–46.

Johnson, C. (1982). *MITI and the Japanese Miracle: The Growth of Industrial Policy*. Stanford, CA: Stanford University Press.

Johnson, C. (1995). *Japan. Who Governs? The Rise of the Developmental State*. New York: Norton.

Kahin, A. R., and G. McT. Kahin (1996). *Subversion as Foreign Policy. The Secret Eisenhower and Dulles Debacle in Indonesia*. New York: Free Press.

Kantor, M. (1995). "Review and Outlook." P. 1 in *Trade Policy Agenda and 1994 Annual Report of the President of the United States on the Trade Agreements Program*, edited by B. Clinton. Washington, DC: U. S. Government Printing Office.

Kautsky, J. (1982). *The Politics of Aristocratic Empires*. Chapel Hill: University of North Carolina Press.

King, P. ed. (1995). *International Economics and International Economic Policy. A Reader*. New York: McGraw-Hill.

Kissinger, H. (1996). "The New World Order." Pp. 173–81 in *Managing Global Chaos. Sources of and Responses to International Conflict*, edited by C. A. Crocker et al. Washington, DC: United States Institute of Peace.

Kojima, K. (1997). "A Conundrum of Decreased Import Dependence in Japan." *Hitosubashi Journal of Economics* 38: 1–20.

Lane, R. (1966). "The Economic Meaning of War and Protection." Pp. 382–98 in *Venice and History. The Collected Papers of Frederick C. Lane*, edited by a committee of colleagues and former students. Baltimore, MD: John Hopkins University Press.

Latouche, S. (1996). *The Westernization of the World. The Significance, Scope and Limits of the Drive towards Global Uniformity*. Cambridge: Verso.

Lazonik, W. (1991). *Business Organization and the Myth of the Market Economy*. Cambridge: Cambridge University Press.

Lim, L. et al., eds. (1983). *The Chinese in Southeast Asia*, Vol. I: *Ethnicity and Economic Activity*. Singapore: Maruzen Asia.

McDowall, David (1997). *A Modern History of the Kurds*. London: Tauris.

McVey, R. T., ed. (1992). *Southeast Asian Capitalists*. Ithaca, NY: Cornell University Press.

Moran, T. (1994). "An Economics Agenda for Neorealists." *International Security* 18(2): 212–15.

Morgenthau, H. (1967). *Politics among Nations. The Struggle for Power and Peace*, 4th edition. New York: Alfred Knopf.

Moulder, F. V. (1977). *Japan, China, and the Modern World Economy. Toward a Reinterpretation of East Asian Development ca. 1600 to ca. 1918*. New York: Cambridge University Press.

Mueller, J. (1989). *Retreat from Doomsday. The Obsolescence of Major War*. New York: Basic Books.

Newman, S. (1991). "Does Modernization Breed Ethnic Conflict?" *World Politics* 43(3): 451–78.

Pagden, A. (1993). *European Encounters with the New World. From Renaissance to Romanticism*. New Haven, CT: Yale University Press.

Parfitt, T. (1997). "Europe's Mediterranean Designs: An Analysis of the Euromed Relationship with Special Reference to Egypt." *Third World Quarterly* 18(5): 865–81.

Powelson, J. P. (1994). *Centuries of Economic Endeavor. Parallel Paths in Japan and Europe and Their Contrast with the Third World*. Ann Arbor: Michigan University Press.

Prados, J. (1986). *President's Wars: The CIA and Pentagon Covert Operations since World War II*. New York: Morrow.

Przeworski, A. and F. Limongi (1997). "Modernization. Theories and Facts." *World Politics* 29(2): 155–83.

Reinert, E. (1996). "The Role of the State in Economic Growth." Paper prepared for the conference The Rise and Fall of Public Enterprises in Western Countries, Università Bocconi, Milan.

Reinert, E. (1997). "Exploring the Genesis of Economic Innovations: The Religious Gestalt-Switch and the Duty to Invent as Preconditions for Economic Growth." *European Journal of Law and Economics* 4: 233–83.

Reinert, E. (1998). "The Other Canon: The History of Renaissance Economics." Paper prepared for the International Economic History Conference (draft version), Seville, August.

Ruigrok, W. and R. van Tulder (1993). *The Ideology of Interdependence. The Link between Restructuring, Internationalization and International Trade.* Ph. D. dissertation, University of Amsterdam.

Rummel, R. J. (1991). *China's Bloody Century. Genocide and Mass Murder since 1900.* New Brunswick, NJ: Transaction.

Sable, C. S. (1994). "Learning by Monitoring: The Institutions of Economic Development." Pp. 231–77 in *Rethinking the Development Experience. Essays Provoked by the Work of Albert O. Hirschman,* edited by Lloyd Rodwin and Donald A. Schon. Washington: Brookings Institution.

Schmookler, A. B. (1984). *The Parable of the Tribe. The Problem of Power in Social Evolution.* Boston: Houghton Mifflin.

Schmookler, A. B. (1993). *The Illusion of Choice. How the Market Economy Shapes Our Destiny.* Albany: State University of New York Press.

Schumpeter, J. (1976). *Capitalism, Socialism and Democracy,* London: Allan and Unwin.

Seagrave, S. (1995). *Lords of the Rim. The Invisible Empire of the Overseas Chinese.* New York: Bantam.

Sen, G. (1984). *The Military Origins of Industrialization and of International Trade Rivalry.* New York: St. Martin's.

Shin, J. (1996). *The Economics of Latecomers. Catching-Up, Technology Transfer and Institutions in Germany, Japan, and South Korea.* London: Routledge.

Simon, J. L. (1995). *The State of Humanity.* Cambridge: Blackwell.

Strauss, C. L. (1966). *The Savage Mind.* London: Weidenfeld and Nicolson.

Suryadinata, L. (1997). "Democratization and Political Succession in Suharto's Indonesia." *Asian Survey* 37(3): 269–80.

Tyson, L. D. (1995). "Managed Trade: Making the Best of the Second Best." Pp. 129–59 in *International Economics and International Economic Policy. A Reader,* edited by Philip King. New York: McGraw-Hill.

U. S. Department of State (1996). *Foreign Relations of the United States, 1958–1960,* Vol. 19. Washington, DC: U. S. Government Printing Office.

United Nations Conference on Trade and Development (1996). *World Investment Report 1996.* New York: United Nations.

USIS (1996a). "Kantor Says Bribery and Corruption Impeding U. S. Business." March 6. Washington, DC: Author.

USIS (1996b). "Remarks of Secretary Brown to International Trade Group." March 26. Washington, DC: Author.

USIS (1996c). "USTR Barchevsky 5/21 Remarks to PBEC Conference." May 21.

von Haberler, G. (1954). *The Theory of Free Trade with Its Applications to Commercial Policy,* 3rd edition. London: William Hodge.

Wade, R. (1990). *Governing the Market. Economic Theory and the Role of Government in East Asian Industrialization.* Princeton, NJ: Princeton University Press.

Webber, S. (1997). "The End of the Business Cycle?" *Foreign Affairs* 76(4): 65–82.

Weidenbaum, M. and S. Hughes (1996). *The Bamboo Network: How Expatriate Chinese Entrepreneurs Are Creating a New Economic Superpower in Asia.* New York: Free Press.

World Bank (1996). *World Development Report 1996.* New York: Oxford University Press.

World Resources Institute (1996). *World Resources 1996–1997.* New York: Oxford University Press.

Yamamura, K. (1995). "The Role of Government in Japan's 'Catch-Up' Industrialization. A Neoinstitutionalist Perspective." Pp. 102–32 in *The Japanese Civil Service and Economic Development,* edited by H.-K. Kim et al. Oxford: Clarendon.

CHAPTER 2

Singapore, a Global City-State into the Twenty-First Century?

Philippe Régnier

This chapter reviews the past and current conditions of Singapore's prosperity in order to identify some possible factors sustaining a global city-state into the twenty-first century. The author argues that the economic rise and success of Singapore as a newly established independent city-state in 1965 is neither an isolated accident of history nor a "miracle" of development.[1] But it may be compared to the various destinies of city-states worldwide throughout the centuries, even if that particular form of state organization seems to have declined sharply during modern times.[2]

1.   The Birth and Development of Singapore as a City-State

The island-emporium and later city-state of Singapore is the modern and post-modern successor of a long series of flourishing city-states in Southeast Asia during precolonial and colonial times. Therefore, a number of specific structuring factors have shaped the economic birth and existence of Singapore as a city-state, like its predecessors in the region, and possibly like other city-state systems in various other parts of the world.

1.1   *A Long Tradition of Commercial Emporia in Southeast Asia*

There has been an uninterrupted succession of commercial emporia in Southeast Asia belonging to a system of intraregional and international relations that is more than two thousand years old. The Republic of Singapore inherits its functions precisely from this succession of state organizations based on the typical economic structures of an emporium. In relation to Singapore and its regional environment, there is a remarkable continuity over the centuries of certain forms of state power and the interaction between them, and this helps us to evaluate and compare the transformations that have taken place in recent times (Cowan 1968).

When Singapore was founded in 1819, this did not represent either an artificial creation by the British colonizer or an isolated phenomenon in the history of the region where, on the contrary, sea-based emporia have appeared down the ages. A glance at the map of Southeast Asia makes it clear how great is the geostrategic importance of the Strait of Malacca linking the Indian Ocean and the South China Sea, which would confer great maritime and commercial power on any form of state organization capable of controlling this pivotal zone.[3] At least since the second century A.D., this attribute has caused a series of state organizations, definable as maritime commercial emporia, to emerge and then disappear in the vicinity of the strait. Singapore is only the latest in this series. Clearly, this type of occupation of coastal and maritime space is not peculiar to Southeast Asia, since other great sea routes throughout the world have given birth to renowned examples of the same phenomenon such as Venice and the medieval Hanseatic ports in Western Europe.

The existence of commercial emporia on the southern coastline of Southeast Asia is remarkable in that throughout history they have flourished alongside state organizations of another kind: those based on agriculture. These, in contrast to the emporia, which control maritime trade, dominate the interior, that is to say, the vast hinterlands on either side of the strait: the Malay Peninsula and the Indonesian Archipelago, but particularly Java and Sumatra (Evers 1984). This intraregional dichotomy has continued in the region since ancient times right up to ASEAN today. The difficult coexistence of these two types of states has produced an unstable equilibrium that exerts a pervasive influence over the nature of economic and political relations within the region. This has been the case before, during, and since the colonial era.[4] The resulting ties of natural economic complementarity (agriculture and commerce) and interdependence (in the political sphere among others) can be a possible source of conflict between the sea-based emporia, which are open to the region and to the world, and their neighbors, whose internal order is largely based on agriculture. Confrontations at various levels were the unavoidable destiny of the first historical empires in the region — Srivijaya and Majapahit — just as they affected Singapore and Malaya much later when they were ruled by the British and the Dutch East Indies during colonial rule: the two rival colonial systems competed keenly with one another.

The economic relationship that subsists today between the commercial and industrial emporium of Singapore and its two immediate partners, Malaysia and Indonesia, is unquestionably a result of this powerful legacy from the past.

The history of Singapore did not begin when the British installed themselves there in 1819, but much earlier when the Malacca sultanate was created in the early fifteenth century. The extent of trading activity in the island of Tumasik was mentioned around the 1490s, when Paramesvara, prince of Palembang, was taking refuge there so as not to submit to the rule of Majapahit. He founded the new emporium of Malacca a few years later. Temasek or Tumasik is the ancient name of the isle where modern Singapore was founded in the nineteenth century. You can still identify the name today: Temasek Holdings is the biggest public holding controlled by the Singaporean government, and has various investments both in local firms and overseas.

Like Raffles much later, Paramesvara's geostrategic instinct caused him to establish himself at the entrance to the Malacca Strait. Inheriting the attributes of Srivijaya, Malacca became a major new commercial power at the very heart of the Malay world, and was the true forerunner of Singapore.[5]

In the fifteenth century, the sultanate expanded on an unprecedented scale. Having become the chief trading center in Southeast Asia for Arab and Chinese merchants (the latter being supported by the presence of armed Chinese fleets), it drew its wealth from its activity as an entrepôt for spices and other rare and sought-after products of the region — and likewise for similar products from abroad.[6] This international meeting-place, which the British faithfully imitated in the nineteenth century, was a forerunner of the organization of Singapore.

This last great emporium of the precolonial age fell to the assault of Albuquerque in 1511, and like the fall of Srivijaya this event is highly instructive concerning the life-cycle of this type of state. As with its predecessors, Malacca's wealth and its very viability were fragile. Among Malacca's internal weaknesses, the lack of cohesion in its ruling elite was inevitably dangerous for a trading city that faced mounting external threats — a lesson taken to heart by those ruling Singapore today. At the beginning of the sixteenth century, the absence of a system of hereditary succession — and the rivalries this caused in the sultan's court — was aggravated by the fickleness of the foreign traders. Whether residing permanently or only transitorily in the sultanate, these were ready to offer their loyalty unreservedly to any newcomer who could show naval or military superiority. In any event, the beneficiaries were the Portuguese.

The external weaknesses were mainly structural. Having no agricultural base, Malacca was dependent for most of its food supplies on Java and Siam, and the sultanate was therefore in no condition to withstand a Portuguese blockade from the sea. After the sultanate fell, the Portuguese succeeded in revitalizing the economy of Malacca by making it one in a series of staging ports: Hormuz, Goa, Ceylon, Amboina (today Ambon in Indonesia), and Macau. For more than a century, Malacca continued to enjoy a solid prosperity by imposing taxes on the numerous vessels that passed through the strait.

Like Batavia and Singapore in the nineteenth century, Malacca was an essential link between Europe, India, and the South China Sea, used successively by the Portuguese, the Dutch (from 1641), and the British (from 1824), and administered by a captain-general under the authority of the viceroy in Goa. A similar structure was used by the British, who administered Singapore from Calcutta.

2. The Rise of Early City-State Systems

Throughout history, economic systems have been created, with their centers in great mercantile capitals like Venice, Genoa, Lisbon, Bruges, Amsterdam, and London, but with vital chains of warehouses, of which certain links were in Southeast Asia. One world economy — i.e., "an economically autonomous piece of the planet, essentially self-sufficient and with its external links and its trade conferring an organic unity upon it" (Braudel 1979) — followed another in succession.

Whether one is talking of Venetian and Arabic powers turning to the riches of the East, or the Portuguese and Dutch colonial empires exporting the model of the first European maritime centers, or the British empire built on a string of trading posts extending from the Mediterranean to Southeast Asia and China, each of these world economies has strewn the great sea routes — their nervous systems — with local emporia of which the latest to appear in the Malay world was Singapore.[7]

With the passage of time, these world empires were replaced by "world cities," entities whose entire vocation was international — as subsidiary centers and staging posts in a process of wealth accumulation, through which the main currents of goods, capital, news, and human talent flowed. Singapore, at once a world staging post (formerly for the business of the British empire and today for that of Japan, the United States, and Europe) and a regional center (of the Malay world and, today, of ASEAN), is hemmed in by a hierarchy of zones in varying stages of economic development, which — to varying degrees — trade with it. The whole ensemble constitutes a regional economy tending in the direction of a form of integration of its own, while at the same time taking its place in a world economy that largely transcends national frontiers (Wallerstein 1980).

Beyond all these concepts and the specific nature of Singapore, it may be said that the regional space and the regional division of economic activities are organized between a major urban metropolis (a powerful magnet for regional development), secondary cities (other emporia and regional communication centers), and peripheral zones (remote and relatively inaccessible agrarian hinterlands little affected by the rise of the regional metropolis and its satellites).

3.   The Founding of Singapore and the Expansion of a New Emporium

Penang was the first emporium to be founded by the British in 1786, but it was too far from the Malacca Strait to have the advantages required vis-à-vis the Dutch colonial competitors.

On January 28, 1819, Raffles, who was familiar with the legend of Tumasik, and could appreciate its remarkable geostrategic position, disembarked at Singapore. After involving himself in a succession dispute in the sultanate of Johore, he negotiated an agreement that permitted him to establish a trading port on the island. The inspiration for Raffles's commercial ambitions came both from the ancient emporia of the region and from Britain's contemporary imperial ambitions. He wrote in 1819 to the governor-general in Calcutta: "What Malta is in the West, that may Singapore become in the East." From that time onward, the status of the island closely reflected its economic rise.

The economic history of Singapore could be summarized in an impressive series of statistics and achievements. Its rapid growth recalls the development of the earlier emporia, and prefigures that of the independent republic from 1965 onward (Hall 1985: 60).

In 1825–40, the sheltered deep-water harbor established itself as a rendezvous for large European merchant vessels and the boats of Chinese and other local owners, the former with goods from India (textiles, arms, opium) for redistribution in the region, and the latter with spices, silks, tropical woods, tea, and tin.

Raffles and his successor Crawfurd founded in Singapore a free port that was destined to loosen the trading monopoly of Batavia and attract the greatest possible number of traders of all nationalities (Buckley 1902; Hall-Jones 1979).

The existence of a free port and a policy of laissez-faire gave an immediate stimulus to Singapore's mercantile economy, to which the island's demographic evolution bore eloquent witness: from 15,000 inhabitants in 1824 to more than 50,000 in 1850 (the village seen by Raffles in 1819 had a population of about 150 fishermen). In the 1830s, fully half of the goods carried through the Strait of Malacca also passed through the control of the island authorities, and Singapore enjoyed a corresponding boom. The volume of this traffic was swollen by the opening up of China. Thus, Singapore, with no significant manufacturing industry until 1959–63, made its mark on the economic scene in the region purely through its dynamic performance in the commercial and tertiary sectors.

As regards communications and transport, the opening of the Suez Canal in 1869 gave a boost to steam navigation, and Singapore became the premier staging post in Southeast Asia, providing water and coal, and docks, unloading jetties, and repair yards capable of handling several dozen ships at one time. The traveling time from London had been halved, and numerous shipping lines established service on the island. The telegraph played a part in this revolution:

links with Batavia and Calcutta were inaugurated in 1859 and 1870, respectively. From then on, commerce in Singapore grew in tandem with the development of communications.

Even if Singapore had to yield pride of place to Hong Kong where exchange with China was concerned, its trade still made progress with forty-three agency houses (twenty were British), handling most flows of goods after 1846. Banks and chambers of commerce, both European and Chinese, made their appearance, and thus were born the local financial empires with branches reaching throughout the whole region.

In the late nineteenth century, the colonization of the Malay Peninsula (1874–09) continued Britain's uninterrupted territorial growth in the region, and Singapore became the outpost for London's financial interests involved in the exploitation of the tin and natural rubber production of the interior. To coal storage in the port was now added petroleum, for which the demand grew steadily during the First World War.

In the years following the First World War, Singapore failed to recover its former prosperity. Being dependent on a British economy weakened by four years of conflict in Europe and then by the effects of the economic crisis of 1929–32, its recovery was long delayed. However, a large-scale program of public investment went some way at least toward mitigating the bad turn events had taken. In order to guarantee the security of the British possessions in Southeast Asia and to respond to Japanese expansionist tendencies, the imperial conference that took place in 1921 decided to build a powerful naval base in Singapore. The project was completed twenty years later, just as air transport was coming fully into its own: Singapore's airport was opened in 1937. Right up to 1965–70, these infrastructural installations continued to be a major center of activity, and reinforced Singapore's position as a regional and international crossroads.

4.   The Stakes for Survival and Stability

Rapid, externally conditioned economic development and then a sudden and usually definitive decline due to external changes have characterized the rise and fall of many commercial emporia. Like Srivijaya and Malacca, ancient Tumasik — destroyed by the intervention first of Siam and then of Portugal — was not immune to this historical law. The example of Singapore, in its turn, raises similar questions to those presented by the fate of its vanished predecessors.

Many observers since the early nineteenth century have believed the basis and modus operandi of this little colony to be transitory. The threat posed by the Dutch became less immediate after 1824, but a fear inspired by the opening of other free ports in Southeast Asia and in the Far East (notably Hong Kong), and by the possible building of a canal across the isthmus in southern Siam, took its place. However, these factors had the effect of stimulating Singapore's development.

The absence of agriculture because of insufficient space and of industry because no work force or vocation for manufacturing existed bred anxiety: Singapore's dependence on the outside world and on imports was considered excessive and therefore a danger (Fisher 1964: 147). The absence, too, of any military base (except the modest Fort Canning, built in 1860) to reduce its vulnerability as an island, together with internal disorder (caused by the weak interventionism of the authorities in public housing, by financial red tape, and by the Chinese secret societies whose machinations long remained unchecked), added to this first wave of anxiety about the viability of Singapore. Of course, the formidable economic expansion of the second half of the nineteenth century swept these doubts away (Turnbull 1977: 92, 155, 332).

However, if certain doubts were removed with the passage of time — with the help, especially, of the building of the British naval base and the growth of a more diversified socioeconomic system — others remained. These were of a kind that are inherent in the conditions that influence the destiny of commercial emporia, and in Singapore's case they have reappeared throughout its history. This fact is well illustrated by the Japanese occupation and the difficult years around the time of independence.

Despite new port fortifications built in haste (1932–41) and the presence of two of the mightiest capital ships of the Royal Navy, Singapore should not have been viewed by the British in isolation from its external environment. On February 15, 1942, the pearl of the British Empire fell to the Japanese without a struggle, and this event proved to be a bitter demonstration of the fragility of Singapore. Another lesson came from the fact that the Japanese placed Syonan (or Singapore) at the very center of their "Coprosperity Sphere" in Southeast Asia (1942–45).

Again, the years immediately before independence (1959–65) offer another example of the nature of the challenge that can imperil the survival and viability of the emporium. When Britain granted Singapore an autonomous status in 1959, this marked the starting point of a new period of disturbance against the backdrop of the anticommunist state of emergency (in force since 1948) and the riots of 1956, which had seriously threatened the internal security of the island. In 1961, the moderate wing of the People's Action Party (PAP) led by Chief Minister Lee Kuan Yew had to face a new onslaught from the left. Fearing a victory of the Communists, the prime minister of Malaya proposed to merge Singapore in a great federation of Malaysia. Malaysia, which came into existence in 1963, seemed to provide Singapore with the framework for a new stability, internally and externally.

However, as history showed, the respite did not last long, as the island was again at the mercy of political developments that could have destroyed or jeopardized its flourishing economy (Boyce 1968; Wilson 1972; Morrison and

Suhrke 1978). The policy of confrontation with Malaysia pursued by President Sukarno of Indonesia from 1963 till 1966 left deep scars among Singaporean leaders, who became acutely conscious how economically and politically vulnerable the island was to any hostile move by a neighbor country.

The separation of Singapore from Malaysia and its later independence on August 9, 1965, intensified the problem of the city-state's survival to a degree unprecedented in its entire history since 1819.[8] The small new republic now found itself called upon to take up the most formidable challenge of its entire existence, and without any delay. Now that it was politically independent but none the less inseparable from its traditional hinterland — namely, Indonesia and Malaysia — how were its economic validity and development to be guaranteed? How would these neighbors be able to accept this little sovereign Chinese enclave in the very heart of the Malay world?

This was the big question, straddling politics and economics, to which those in charge of Singapore's destiny strove tirelessly to find an answer from August 9, 1965 onward.

5.   The Success of the Systemic Organization of a City-State

The observation of the reconfirmed prosperity of independent Singapore in less than thirty years after the shocks of 1963–65 suggests that the systemic organization of the city-state in economic, political, and social terms has shaped strong domestic and external assets in order to adopt a niche strategy in regional and international relations.

5.1   *The Objective of Economic Revitalization and Sustainable Prosperity of Independent Singapore*

In 1965, nobody except one Dutch economist (Winsemius, who later became a permanent advisor to Lee Kuan Yew) bet on the economic viability of an independent Singapore. Therefore, the legitimization of the PAP regime depended much on the theme of economic survival, which became the leitmotif regulating all domestic and external activities of the city-state.

The relative decline of traditional entrepôt trade had to be replaced by a new strategy of industrialization (Huff 1994: 273–99; Rodan 1989: 85–188, 207–15). In the absence of an existing local class of private entrepreneurs, a vast manufacturing and tertiary sector could be achieved by the mobilization of substantial foreign investment (70–80 percent of today's GDP) and of a significant public sector.

Since the early 1980s, Singapore has been able to become a regional and worldwide crossroads of high-tech manufacturing and service activities. High annual rates of growth (8–10 percent on average), rapid gains in productivity, competitiveness ranking among the highest in the world, standards of living higher than Italy and United Kingdom are among the best performances leading to a strict and continued national mobilization for sustainable prosperity (Murray and Pereira 1996: 1–9, 152–68; Toh and Tan 1998: 3–40).

Such a mobilization of a small insular society, which served both the establishment of a strong state and a highly dense network of transnational corporation headquarters, could not have been possible without the implementation of a specific systemic organization of the city-state. This system aims at reducing its various structural vulnerabilities (as proved throughout history) and at overplaying its strongest assets (leadership and good governance of limited human resources).

5.2 Struggling for Survival and Total Mobilization of Society: Cornerstones of Nation-Building

Since 1965, the PAP leaders have initiated mobilization campaigns involving the whole population in the name of the necessary struggle for national survival (Chan 1971; Morrison and Suhrke 1978; Onn 1978; Mauzy 1984: 196–204). This permanent effort for the defense of the emporium and its unflagging ability to adapt to outside events got quickly transformed into something of the nature of a national ideology. The syndrome of extreme vulnerability found a determined will among the Singaporean leaders to mobilize the island society using methods that, in some respects, are reminiscent of campaigns and mass rallies in China.[9]

After the crisis of 1963–65, the PAP continued to keep up an atmosphere of psychosis, in direct relation to the perpetual challenges of unpredictable external events: the communal violence in 1969 throughout the Malay Peninsula, the British military withdrawal from Singapore in 1971, the oil crisis in 1973–74, the Vietnamese expansion after 1975, the rise of protectionism, and the international economic recession that affected the region from 1978–80 onward. The concept of survival became the linchpin of Singapore's internal cohesion and of its intangible independence, endlessly repeated in its foreign policy.[10]

The comprehensive range of external conditions that have allowed the island emporium to develop are far beyond its own control, and Singapore has to work endlessly to lessen the numerous risks threatening its survival. Beyond its initial economic development, which was mainly due to large-scale foreign investment, and its political security, which was tightly bound to its regional environment, its primary strategy is to multiply all kinds of interdependencies through the city-state in order to become, and remain, useful and even indispensable to most actors on the regional and international scene. But it is also obvious that such a small state as Singapore will never be able to claim any significant influence on the pattern of world and even regional affairs.

In all of this there is just one certainty: The mobilization and fully coherent organization of the island society is probably Singapore's only major independent resource.

The citizens of Singapore are first and foremost social beings, and their quest for excellence and the attainment of their maximum potential as individuals corresponds to the greater objective of making society also work to its greatest capacity. The working of every cog reflects the incessant struggle for survival: the social atmosphere produced is one of institutionalized urgency. And in order to anticipate any trouble or threat that could be damaging to the city-state's prosperity, the authorities and the whole population must always know where the "devil" is likely to come from.

Sociologists could share with political scientists the analysis of the two interdependent factors that determined the appearance in Singapore of a *dirigiste* government driven by the will to mobilize all the potential strength of the island society. The fragile geopolitical situation of the city-state, arising from the gross disproportion between its physical size and the immeasurable challenges to its survival, required a governing team whose first task would be to make the emporium permanently viable, and to obtain that goal, an optimally organized and rationalized society was needed in the domestic sector. On the other hand, there is a clearer correlation between this task and the smallness of the population, its concentration within an area smaller than that of a large European metropolis, the absence of any significant agricultural hinterland, and the existence of a dense urban-type communications network within the island, making it possible to supervise the actual impact of any government decision with a minimum of delay: an island space of this kind makes the process of national integration much easier, and enhances the effectiveness of governmental measures adopted for the promotion of social mobilization.

In view of the grave crises of 1957–65, the PAP probably had no choice but to make sure that it controlled every facet of social activity on the island. Its aim was thus to remove all elements of potential uncertainty and all internal weaknesses in society, which a destabilizing force from outside could exploit. Parallel to the most judicious possible management of external dependencies and of unforeseeable circumstances, the slogan of a "rugged society" launched by the PAP made it clear that the survival of the city-state depended on the cohesiveness of its society and the infallibility of its government (Busch 1972: 33–34; Morrison 1976: 230; Neville 1980). This strategy is all the more indispensable because until 1965 any notion of state and nation had been lacking in an island populated by immigrants of different ethnic origins, who had never even considered the possibility of an independent Singapore. Lee Kuan Yew took up this theme when he declared on July 13, 1965: "I would say that our best chance lies in a very rigorously organized society. There is no other outcome. Numerous small societies like ours have survived.... [W]hat is necessary is a highly disciplined, determined and educated society, ready to work hard. Create such a community and you will see it survive and prosper for thousands of years" (Josey 1968: 486–87; see also Lee 1981: 1; Tan 1981: 11).

6. Monopoly of Power and *Dirigisme* in the Name of Social Welfare

6.1 *Authoritarian Economic and Social Planning*

After 1963–65, the first generation of PAP leaders concentrated all power in their hands. They had just eliminated the main Communist-inspired opposition force, the Barisan Socialis, and now cultivated their image as the only political force able to tackle the dangers of stagnation or decline immediately after independence. Society had to yield to the absolute priority of the emporium's survival, and thus to the particular political entity — the PAP — which was its incarnation. The party's cohesion, discipline, centralization, and professional skills were indispensable if the vulnerability of such a small territory was to be overcome.

The economic successes achieved in the first years after independence rallied a large majority of the population to the regime, and it was a powerful incentive to the PAP to be able to implement whatever measures it judged appropriate for Singapore's development: hence the installation of a form of *dirigisme* and authoritarian planning. Economic growth and social transformation materialized so rapidly during the 1970s that the PAP's electorate and a majority of Singaporeans became convinced of the "genius" of their prime minister and his government. The PAP has justified its monopoly of power up to the present time by the need to consolidate the city-state's initial achievements; by denying itself the right to commit errors; by finding the optimum solution to every one of the challenges that have to be faced periodically; and by refusing to allow any questioning of the political order. The PAP has identified itself as the guarantor of stability and prosperity.[11]

The centralization and consolidation of power by the PAP and its predilection for long-term action are the essence of Lee Kuan Yew's own political philosophy. Ever since his historic speech to the Malayan Forum in London in January 1950, Lee does not seem to have deviated from certain golden rules like pragmatic socialism, the rejection of Communism, multiracialism, and a mode of government in which the leading figures are men inspired by a lofty view of the role of public authority, to the service of which they are completely devoted. The decisive role of the small group of friends who have been close to Lee since the start of the PAP, and have been able to respond with tremendous success to the initial crises and challenges on both the internal and external fronts, could only lead to an extreme centralization of power, where all important decisions, political and social control, and the instruments of national mobilization are in the hands of the prime minister and his closest advisers.[12]

6.2 The Building of a Technocratic State

The government of Singapore is based on a technocratic state apparatus. The strong and coherent PAP elite is composed of senior civil servants and politicians, all carefully selected for their education and competence — and most of them are inspired by a true personal devotion to Lee Kuan Yew and his closest colleagues (Chen 1975; Chen 1974; Chen and Fawcett 1979; Shaw 1977). Lee himself estimated in 1967–68 that the ruling elite consisted of about two hundred individuals, assisted at the managerial and operational level by two thousand others. "If", he added, "you kill the 200 at the top and the 2,000 at the base with a single blow, you will have destroyed Singapore."

To have the freedom to put a planned welfare society in place of the nonegalitarian laissez-faire policy of colonial times, and to establish a charter for political stability leading to economic and social development, the PAP has considerably reduced both the possibility of social conflict and the resistance of the traditional elites. Government action and keeping the PAP in power do not depend so much on the leadership's capacity to respond to individual or particular demands from the island society; the PAP government promotes its own perception of the city-state's overall interests, both internally and externally. The decision-making process has thus become, over the years, more "administrative" than "political" (Crouch 1984: 13–23; Quah, Chang, and Seah 1985; on the more recent period, see Chua 1995: 9–39, 169–202).

The depoliticization of Singapore's citizens was made possible by the elimination of the Barisan Socialis (the political party to the left of the PAP) and the consequent absence of an organized opposition, as a center of trade unionism and of social and public expression. An obvious redistribution of the fruits of economic growth has also taken place, improving the collective social well-being of the population — the local human resources are the only capital that truly belong to a small city-state.[13] Such a redistribution of wealth has favored the rise of a numerous middle class but may have brought less benefit to the grass-roots workers, who accepted low wages until the 1980s and have thus made an enormous contribution to the rapid industrialization of Singapore. However, a majority of the population — the somewhat materialistic Chinese — have seemed well satisfied with the island's economic success and the spectacular improvement in their living standards over a span of less than twenty years.

At the top level of society, the political influence of old traditional business has also declined significantly. The slowdown of the entrepôt trade and the diversification of the economy have made necessary a rather large and interventionist state administration, which is more independent from the traditional Chinese commercial and banking community and from the old colonial business interests than it was before 1965. The private sector is dominated today by foreign and transnational companies whose activities usually embrace world markets and which therefore rely on looser political contacts and interaction with individual government administrations — in this Singapore is no exception (Quah 1978; You and Lim 1984: 295–98). Furthermore, the integrity of Singaporean civil servants and politicians has been elevated to the status of a dogma: this was the achievement of the first generation of PAP leaders, who included only a very few businessmen. The city-state has been among the countries where institutionalized large- or small-scale corruption is least prevalent. Remembering the troubled times of David Marshall's or Lim Yew Hock's governments in the mid-1950s, Lee Kuan Yew was persuaded that any development of corruption would undermine the foundations of the city-state's success and its international reputation. Power is also highly personalized. For Singaporeans of Chinese descent, Lee is a symbolic leader and guide in the loyalist and Confucianist sense of personifying the philosophy of good government, and any functional sense of his position as prime minister and now senior minister has only a secondary ranking in the Chinese collective mentality. He has revealed a political character different from what one might expect from such a brilliant politician, educated in Britain and exposed to Western legal systems and the concept of parliamentary democratic rule. His conception of power seems to be derived partly from Chinese tradition, based on the conviction of a certain superiority of the East to the West; he sees the West as going through a period of decline and decadence. He is attached to the one-party system related to a so-called purely "Asian" concept of political power and social management. This goes so far as to reproduce in Singapore a form of nepotism not unknown in other parts of Asia. Lee Kuan Yew's son Brigadier-General Lee Hsien Loong has been propelled to the front of the political stage, and could become Lee's successor after Goh Chok Tong has served as a transitional prime minister in the 1990s.

Lee cannot be described as an ideologue, but the mobilization of Singaporean society — given its exceptional geopolitical situation — was the result of his gift of persuasion. The psychosis of the critical period 1957–65 and the first economic successes of the postindependence years made this all the more persuasive (Goh 1981b: 3). Without using the whole panoply of means of coercion found in most other states of the region or in authoritarian regimes elsewhere — but keeping open the possibility of using the Internal Security Act at any time — the PAP quickly earned the reward of massive support and trust from the population. Under the banner of a so-called democratic, nondoctrinaire socialism, its actions have been based on several simple underlying precepts (Goh 1972; Nair 1976a, 1976b, 1982).

First, external challenges of various kinds justify a permanent attitude of pragmatism and adaptability. Political dogmatism can result in paralysis when there is a need for action, and those in power should be able to revise their decisions if circumstances change. Second, through state authoritarian rule and intervention the appropriate responses could be found for national cohesion and for the reform of a society originally created to serve the interests of the colonial power. The authority of the virtuous government depends on the willingness of its citizens (the majority of whom are Chinese) to give their collective support to those who provide them with stability, employment, housing, and social services, and these citizens might feel less attracted to individual freedoms as these are understood in parliamentary democracies (Gosling and Lim 1983:Volume 2, p. 280). Third, the system of social mobilization places a high value on work, effort, ingenuity, and talent — once again, the quintessential characteristics of the Chinese immigrant. In addition, it guarantees equality of duties and rights to all citizens, regardless of race, religion, or social class, and here the divergence between theory and practice is certainly less evident in Singapore than it is elsewhere in the region. Finally, the construction of the Singaporean state produces technocrats who identify with the ideal of Confucianist ethics; in other words an administration that cares above all that the population should conform to the rules of good social conduct defined by the elders (Lee Kuan Yew and the first generation of PAP leaders). A Chinese cultural tradition of the mandarin type contributes to this regulation of daily life and of morality, which the great majority of Singapore's people have seemed to accept so far.

7.   A "Guided Democracy"? Prioritization of Political Stability

Maintenance of political stability at any price, the controlled expression of any opposition, strict definition of social relations — these are some of the elements that best describe the PAP regime.

According to Singapore's leaders, internal fragility is a luxury that the city-state cannot afford, except at the risk of sinking into decline or disappearing altogether; the social and political stability of the small republic, and of its neighbors, is seen as the best guarantee of long-term economic development and an indispensable element in the stability of the whole region. The stability of Malaysia cannot be separated from that of Singapore, and the social cohesion of the city-state could act as a safety valve in the event of serious troubles erupting in its immediate neighborhood, as occurred in Malaysia in 1969.

The primacy accorded to stability dominates the political life and social order of the island: Singapore has adopted a constitutional system close to the British model but limited by numerous restrictions implemented by the regime. As he explained in a well-known speech at London's Royal Institute of International Affairs in 1962, Lee Kuan Yew does not believe that it is possible to transpose parliamentary democracy pure and simple to Asia (Josey 1973: 46–53; Vasil 1984: 71–90). At the end of the colonial period, civilian society had first of all to undergo a structural change to enable independence to become viable — in a way that would be credible both within and outside the island-state.

Are the majority of Singaporeans, being Chinese, less interested in individual political freedoms than in the ability of the government to assure them of a noticeable improvement in their living standards? It is open to anyone to believe or to disbelieve this analysis, but it is the philosophy of government that the PAP would have them accept, and that Lee Kuan Yew seems to have put into practice in a fairly reasonable and socially beneficial way, although the same philosophy has brought some other regimes to the threshold of dictatorship.[14] The emporium's chronic vulnerability, its delicate geopolitical position, and the very serious domestic political disturbances from 1957 to 1963 left the PAP governing team with probably almost no alternative but to go into high crisis management and form a kind of supreme command, as in the army, at least in the first years after independence.

Did this reaction, amply justified at first, have to become institutionalized in an authoritarian style of government right up to the 1980s and perhaps even into the 1990s? Opinions differ. For some, the ideology of the permanent struggle for survival reflects the very real dangers that punctuate the life of any emporium; for others, it only symbolizes the PAP's determination to stay in power by promoting its paramount ideology into something almost sacred.

7.1 Control of the Opposition

The elimination of the most radical opponents by applying special emergency measures in 1961–63, and the vigilance of the authorities against any signs of their reemergence, discourage would-be detractors of the regime. The permanent need to defend the viability of the emporium and consolidate the economic and social success that were possible after 1965 motivated the rejection of every sign of opposition, which has been systematically accused of risking the very basis of the city-state's prosperity and stability.

Each time it has had the chance to express itself through elections, about a quarter of the electorate has refused to give its endorsement to the PAP, but the political groups that the PAP had to face were and still are divided. Both the numbers of activists they can mobilize and the financial resources they can command are modest. None of them can appear very credible or constructive as long as the PAP government continues to be seen as the architect of three decades of remarkable economic and social development.

Periodically — and tirelessly — the PAP launches vigorous attacks against even the most embryonic show of opposition thought, rightly or wrongly, to be connected somehow with the procommunist agitation of the preindependence period, which those in power believe to be still latent today. Subsequently, the PAP has also started to enforce some legal restrictions against the foreign press. Some newspapers and periodicals like *Asian Wall Street, Asiaweek* and *Far Eastern Economic Review* have been accused of interfering in Singapore's domestic politics, and their circulation has been occasionally suspended or limited within the city-state.

7.2 *Control of Social Relations — Labor*

Up till 1961–63, Malayan trade unionism was associated with the anticolonial independence struggle, but had also fallen very much under the influence of the Malayan Communist Party. The official demise of the Barisan Socialis after 1961–63 and the end of its representation in Singapore's parliament was inevitably followed by a depoliticization of local society and a lessening of conflict in social relations: on these possibly depended the success of the island's early industrialization strategy, based as it was on labor discipline and modest wages in order to attract substantial foreign investment. To safeguard its viability at this stage, the city-state could neither afford any political disorder as in the period before independence nor disruptive British-style trade unionism (Pang 1982).

The National Trade Union Congress (NTUC), which in 1965 replaced the Singapore Association of Trade Unions with its strong links to the radical left, became from that time onward a mere suborganization of the PAP as the party in power. Possessing no freedom of action in the normal spheres such as wage negotiation, it sought to fill the void in developing various social services for the work force, e.g., cooperatives, transport, insurance, and travel. These restrictions on the social rights of labor seem to have been generally accepted by a majority of the active population for as long as the PAP has been able to get rid of unemployment (since 1971–73), to keep inflation very low, and to activate important social programs that are accessible — and of benefit — to all: public housing, public health, schools, and higher education.

Any disagreement with this new social system has been met with extreme inflexibility by the government. In 1969, workers in the naval dockyard slowed down production in a bid to retain their right to work overtime — Lee Kuan Yew did not hesitate to fire them all, citing charges of sabotage and high treason. In 1974, agitation once again flared up in this sector and received the support of the University Students' Union: arrests, trials, and sanctions swiftly halted this supposed emergence of a new left wing. Certain trade union leaders had made a show at the time of opposing the government's *dirigisme* in industrial relations:

a reform in 1978 opened control of the NTUC to non–trade unionists (in other words, to PAP cadres), and the NTUC secretary-general Devan Nair was endowed with a power of veto over the appointment of future trade union leaders, sector by sector. The NTUC and its affiliated unions have become powerless to defy political decision-making. Lim Chee Onn, a young technocrat who was appointed to head the NTUC in place of Devan Nair in 1979, had to face this reality: in 1983 his rise was abruptly terminated when the government did not hesitate to dismiss him and appoint Ong Teong Cheong as his successor.[15] Another example was the authoritarian freezing of wage rises between 1985 and 1988. It was imposed by government decision following rapid wage rises in 1980–83 and the economic recession of 1984–86, to the dissatisfaction of many people.

7.3 The Urban Milieu

The drive to discipline and unify the whole of society is also found in the urban environment of the city-state itself. Before 1965, professional associations and Chinese secret societies had maintained sharp divisions between ethnic groups and social classes. After independence, their place was taken by some 175 Community Centers and some 300 Residents' Committees (consultative committees of citizens) (You and Lim 1984: 315–38).

These committees, with permanent members nominated by the PAP, are the expression of "democratic centralization" of power rather than direct participation by the masses in the management of local and national affairs. They are firmly established in the HDB (Housing Development Board) public housing districts, which provide homes for 75 percent of all Singaporeans.[16] They perform many civic and social activities, and play a role in the circulation, interpretation, and implementation of the PAP's decisions. As grass-roots units for the controlled organization of society, they influence the social atmosphere and thus people's reactions. But their basic task is to cultivate in the population a strong identification with the fundamental values and rules for the island's survival and viability.

8. Internal and External Security: The Affirmation of a National Identity

An emporium obviously does not have a national or "state" identity of its own. It is an economic entity, artificially established in an alien territory and totally dedicated to its international, outward-looking vocation. Singapore was in no way predestined to become a sovereign state, and in its unique situation the PAP had few models to turn to for inspiration as to how best to make its independence truly effective. Rapid and sustained economic success was probably the only way to build up some kind of functional autonomy for such a special territory.

Having to govern a very heterogeneous society of immigrants without a common language, culture, or political allegiance, the PAP could not in the long run rally the population under the "welfare state" banner alone. Planning social order through material well-being does not necessarily lead to a national cohesion that no power can destroy — i.e., to a code of collective values with which the whole population can voluntarily agree to identify. In the view of Lee Kuan Yew and his close cabinet friends, the struggle for survival, guided democracy, and redistribution of growth had to serve as a key investment in the future in order to forge a national identity, a Singaporean citizenship.

8.1 *Multiracialism as the Cornerstone of the Singaporean Nation*

The creation of a multiracial society is first and foremost an objective linked to internal security and stability. It also reflects the concern to make Singaporean society resistant to any new wave of communalist agitation in or from Malaysia. Any attempt at oppressive domination of the Malay minority in the island (15 percent) by the Chinese majority would be unacceptable to both Indonesia and Malaysia, and Singapore is very well aware of the acute anti-Chinese sensitivities of its two neighbors and their desire to protect the Malay populations and culture (Benjamin 1975; Busch 1972). Finally, a frank and ambitious multiracial policy should be able to create a broad social consensus among the population at home, and somehow to challenge the communalist discrimination that it sees being practiced in Indonesia or Malaysia. Multiracialism has become one of the major components of Singapore's efforts at national integration (Clammer 1985: 107–17).

Building a genuine multiracial society is a long and difficult process. If the Indian minority, small in numbers but strong in professional achievements, is relatively well integrated into the island society, the Malays find themselves much more marginal: this is one major structural problem delaying genuine social cohesion, and it is far from being resolved.

8.2 *Multiracialism in the Symbols of the Nation*

In creating a multiracial island society, Singapore has used both classic symbols of the nation-state and other key instruments of national cohesion, notably education and defense. All the national symbols — starting with the flag, the colors of which are inspired by those of its two neighbors — try to consolidate the city-state's multiracial identity and to counterbalance the preponderance of the Chinese in favor of the ethnic minorities. Of the four official languages, Bahasa Malaysia figures as a sort of "national" language because of its use in the Singapore anthem, which is not translated into the other local languages.

The Chinese have been deliberately underrepresented in the government departments that contribute to the manufactured image of Singapore conveyed to the outside world. Malays are particularly numerous in the police, the army, and the judiciary; however, following the communal troubles of 1969, the government barred access for the Malays to key positions in the army and police; the PAP and the Chinese majority were unable to tolerate the idea that national security could be challenged by minority communalism.

8.3 *Education and Multiracialism*

It is truer in Singapore than in most other countries that the future depends on the young generation. More than half the population are under thirty-five years old, and more than a quarter are still receiving education or training of some kind. Education is one of the government's priorities and is the most important budget after defense.

The maximization of its human resources and skills — the island's only asset — has a double dimension. First, there is the economic dimension, which is related to the necessarily rapid development and growth in the 1970s and 1980s, and is also linked now with the current transition to advanced services and high technologies. There is a political dimension through the inculcation, from primary school onward, of the essential national values as a guarantee for the long-term survival and secure viability of the city-state.

8.4 *Multilingualism and National Cohesion*

Multiracialism and multilingualism have evolved in a single direction, namely, toward neither communism nor communalism of Chinese inspiration, but an integration of all citizens trying to lead to a true Singaporean national identity.

Bilingualism was introduced in schools in 1966. The core of instruction — at least 70 percent — is in English, which, unlike the three other languages, has no ethnic flavor; it creates a more egalitarian means of communication between all Singaporeans, and of course is indispensable as a means of fulfilling the emporium's international vocation. On the other hand, each citizen's mother tongue and its Asian cultural backing are not neglected: here the policy is to preserve a sense of Asian identity and self-expression for all, and to resist or reject certain so-called decadent aspects of Western society transmitted by the English language and media.

The PAP has always considered it too dangerous and destabilizing in a plural society to leave the definition of the official languages and the content of education subject to communalist politicization. Through the promotion of bilingualism, the PAP set itself the task of tackling the ascendancy of Chinese dialects and of Chinese education imparted by institutions traditionally close to the Communists like Ngee Ann College and Nanyang University (closed in 1980). The PAP also wanted to play down the overly strong Chinese image of Singapore on the regional scene.

A certain anglophile assimilation has, to some degree and in different ways, been accepted by each ethnolinguistic group, and a kind of Singaporean identity has started to emerge. More recently, the PAP has tried to restore some of the values and virtues of Confucian society, and to modernize them, especially among the young, in order to counterbalance the rapid moves toward a materialist Westernization, which has been brought on by meteoric economic growth.

8.5 *Multiracialism and Meritocracy*

The prosperity of Singapore depends on the best use being made of its human resources and on the high quality of its rulers. The deliberate elitism of Lee Kuan Yew and his government team has been but one application of their strategy of social mobilization to ensure survival for the emporium. The system of "meritocracy" puts a premium on the social opportunities open to all citizens according to their intellectual skills and capacity for hard work; they can achieve high professional and social standing regardless of their ethnic, cultural, or religious background.[17]

The universalization of compulsory primary and secondary education, and the great increase in high-level university departments and specialized training programs, combined with exceptional economic growth and full employment, have produced a well-educated generation of young people and dynamic new elites. However, even if it is impossible not to admire the policy and performance of the PAP and the results achieved in barely three decades, the system of meritocracy has been questioned by many foreign observers, especially since the authorities tried to initiate a kind of "brain planning" for the future. By giving preference to methods of assessment and selection of intellectual capacity based on some American systems of testing, sometimes as early as primary school, and by insisting on the priority of education and professionalism, the educational machine has been producing a new generation of high-quality graduates (almost all in economics and technology), but has often forgotten that academic knowledge and intelligence do not always go together. At the top levels of both the government administration and the national enterprises, the problem is quite similar: brilliant young technocrats are called on to succeed gradually — through a stage-by-stage period planned in advance — to those figures of the first generation who were the architects of independence and of the first two decades of Singapore's "economic miracle." Goh Chok Tong, who became vice premier in 1984 and is now prime minister, is one of those technocrats who often address Singaporeans as if they were an administrative council. No one has been able to see in him, so far, more than the makings of a transitional prime minister after Lee's resignation in November 1990, and all eyes turn insistently toward Lee's elder son, who occupies the post of deputy prime minister.

Meritocracy, as the expression of the best possible form of social organization, runs the risk of branching off into rigid elitism if it has to depend on a uniform mold for education and individual promotion.

9.   The Ultimate Leap for Survival: From Military Defense to the Concept of Total Defense

A well-equipped and structured defense does not automatically mean an absolute guarantee of Singapore's survival if conflict should occur: specialists in strategic studies are unable to state clearly how far an island territory of 620 square kilometers can be genuinely capable of defending itself or engaging in an armed dispute without the possibility of receiving a mortal blow at a very early stage of the conflict (Josey 1968: 180).

9.1 *Internal Security: Multiracialism and National Defense*

Rigorous national military service and the parallel existence of a reserve corps of men up to fifty years old contribute to a decisive mixing of ethnic groups and cultures in all postings and grades, and foster a spirit of multiracialism and tolerance. All young males are obliged to serve between twenty-four and thirty months. National service generally has to be completed before one enters higher education, and it molds the young generation through the ideology of Singapore's permanent mobilization as a condition of survival and sustainable prosperity. At the end of his term, each serviceman receives a certificate that is, in a sense, also a certificate of good citizenship, before taking full responsibility for the future development of the city-state.

The reservists and those holding senior rank in the army are those whose concern is to preserve national cohesion, and they perform a function of social discipline largely derived from the example of the Swiss army. As in other ASEAN countries, senior military figures are sometimes called upon — like Lee Kuan Yew's own son, who at one time ranked third in the army staff — to assume important national responsibilities outside the military sphere, and when this happens they have to retire from the service. The presence of numerous reservists in the economic, political, and social life of the city-state is seen as a supplementary guarantee of internal stability that would enable it to weather any period of external uncertainty.[18]

9.2 *External Security: Defense by Deterrence*

Right after independence, the burden of defense fell squarely on the city-state as Britain announced its impending military withdrawal: Goh Keng Swee was given the task of organizing a credible defense to serve the island's fledgling sovereignty, and to be used as a catalyst in the process of nation-building.

Goh Keng Swee had to move rapidly and effectively, but he also had to avoid too great a strain on the vulnerable economy of that time. In 1967, he opted for a system of conscription and reservists and turned for assistance to Israeli and Swiss advisers. In less than ten years (1967–75) the Singapore Armed Forces (SAF) were operational on land with AMX 13 tanks, by sea with twelve patrol boats and missile-launching vessels, and in the air with its first squadron of Hawker Hunter fighters. Until 1971–2, defense represented nearly 40 percent of the government's annual budget and 11 percent of the gross national product.

Faced with such formidable difficulties as its extreme vulnerability (1942 was an ever-present memory), the initial hostility of its neighbors, the British military withdrawal, and the loose structure of the ANZUK (Australia/New Zealand/United Kingdom) security agreement, Singapore concentrated its efforts on building up as credible a policy of deterrence as possible.[19] With a capacity for the lightning destruction of any potential aggressor launching a first strike, and a citizen-soldier system operating throughout the whole population, Goh Keng Swee could demonstrate that the price of aggression would be too high.[20] He used the image of a "poisoned fish," which the attacker would have to swallow before being able to set foot on the island. Besides, the enormous destruction that would be caused by any massive attack on Singapore's dense urban environment would nullify the very thing coveted by any potential enemy — the wealth of the city-state. Thus any major attack could only aim at the complete destruction of Singapore; otherwise it would be pointless.

Without sufficient resources or territory to resist a sustained attack or siege, the city-state has consolidated its strategy of deterrence by means of repeated qualitative upgrading. By opting for ultramodern equipment and rigorous training to compensate for the negligible size of its geographical and human base, the city-state has become an impressive military-industrial center in the region.

9.3 *Singapore's Emergence as a Military-Industrial Focus at the Heart of ASEAN*

With its army of 50,000 and a pool of 200,000 reservists — more than in Malaysia or the Philippines — Singapore has scored some outstanding achievements in terms of military preparedness in the context of the ASEAN region. With a defense budget higher than that of the Philippines or New Zealand, the city-state stands on an equal footing with Sweden or Switzerland and among the ASEAN countries, making the highest contribution per inhabitant. Because it is an island, its major means of deterrence is the air force, which is very close to the capacity of its Thai counterpart, and can also benefit from a strong local civil aviation industry. Here Singapore has combined the sophistication of its defense with its strategy to develop high-tech industries, and it has already become a center for light arms procurement and for maintenance and repair services for military hardware.

At regular intervals the city-state, recalling its neighbors' criticism of its military cooperation with Israel, declares that there is no case for a "siege city" strategy, and that its defense system is not directed against its ASEAN partners. The spirit of detente was reaffirmed on a number of occasions, both by various leaders in Malaysia and by numerous prominent figures in Singapore. However, the introduction of the concept of "total defense" gives an impression that Singapore has lately moved in the opposite direction. But this new slogan is perhaps designed more to reinforce internal cohesion than to convey mistrust of the outside world.

9.4 The Struggle for Survival as a Sacred Cause: Total Defense

Taking the civil-military defense systems of Switzerland, Sweden, and Israel as its inspiration, the PAP has launched since the mid-1980s a campaign of social mobilization that, under the slogan "total defense" intends to muster the entire population and every single sector of activity in the event of any acute external crisis. In order to mobilize all Singaporeans within twenty-four hours, five areas of action are identified. First, military defense would continue to be based on conscripts and reservists, and information about the Singapore Armed Forces would be fed to the public from primary school onward. Second, civil defense would be concerned in case of war with the dead and wounded, and with large-scale material destruction. Tight organization would be needed in view of the high density of the urban areas and the small area of the island. Third, economic defense would mean not only mobilizing the whole machinery of industrial production in case of war, but also shaping in peacetime a strong linkage between all the civil and military applications of each branch of economic activity. There are several possibilities of precise application to be distinguished here: easy conversion of civil infrastructures to military uses, development of high technology in arms procurement; and the exercise of civil responsibilities by the highest-ranking officers. Fourth, social defense should guarantee the internal invulnerability of Singapore by uniting the population around the dominant values affecting daily life and citizenship in the city-state, values with which most citizens should be able to identify. And, finally, psychological defense should protect the young from dogmatic ideology and subversion (mainly from Communism), from the potential danger of certain imported Western values, or from overdependence on material comfort and welfare. When Rajaratnam declared in November 1984 that every Singaporean had to be prepared to face new crises because these would be certain to arise in the future, he touched on the quintessential theme of survival and viability for the emporium city-state.[21]

The launching of the concept of total defense has coincided — not entirely by chance — with the onset of an important political and social transition for the city-state. Numerous challenges have arisen, and have duly been magnified by the PAP to suit its long-term ambitions. These challenges are the ever-present themes of current political debate: the conditions of sustained economic growth, the political succession by the younger generation and the selection of new cadres, and the emergence of a legal opposition with the right of free expression. Total defense is a new global instrument serving the permanent mobilization of society. It is also highly symptomatic of the political philosophy of the PAP, for whom not only the survival of the city-state but also its own retention of power are seen as inseparable.

10. Toward a New Challenge: The Financial Crisis of 1997–98

Since its early signals in Thailand in mid-1997, an unpredicted financial crisis has rapidly spread all over Southeast Asia. Singapore has felt the winds of the regional storm, but has not been severely hit like its neighbors. Similarly to Taiwan in Northeast Asia, the Chinese-dominated city-state has proven so far that its economic and social fundamentals were resilient. However, Singapore could catch a bad cold if the region continues sneezing. Real contamination could be derived from the neighbors' uncured illnesses.

Contrary to Thailand, it remains to be seen how Malaysia can recover without any intervention of the International Monetary Fund: current policies could favor inflows from local and external overseas Chinese capital — including from Singapore — but could also dangerously threaten the fragile economic and social equilibrium of a multiethnic and multicultural nation built up since the adoption of the new development policy of the early 1970s.

Scoring 65 percent of the votes in the parliamentary election of 1997, the People's Action Party (PAP) has been able to reverse its gradual decline since the end of the 1980s, and the legitimacy of Prime Minister Goh Chok Tong has therefore been consolidated during his second mandate. But most fears in Singapore focus on giant Indonesia, next door. The abysmal financial crisis has led to economic and social turmoil, which was not politically addressed by the old dictatorial regime of President Suharto. The worst enemy of Indonesia would be a chaotic and violent domestic situation sending destabilizing waves to Singapore and the whole region. It happened in the 1960s and could happen again.

Notes

1. This terminology is derived from the famous June 1993 World Bank report, *The East Asian Economic Miracle*.

2. During the second half of the twentieth century, only a few city-states were left throughout the world. Many previous ones have disappeared, and even the most prosperous one in East Asia, namely, Hong Kong, has become a full part of China.

3. "In retrospect it can be seen that any dominance exercised over the Strait of Malacca had been derived from a position of economic strength located either on the east coast of Sumatra or on the west coast of the Malay Peninsula" (Leifer 1978: 8).

4. "The continuing theme of an unstable and changing balance between the influence of a policy based on a populous and agricultural Java, on the one hand, and that of the commercial and maritime power of a rival system in or near the Straits area on the other, can be observed throughout the colonial era as before it" (Cowan 1968: 9; see also Watson and Smith 1979).

5. "The state based on maritime commerce reached its fullest development after the establishment of Malacca around 1400. The models of Srivijaya and Majapahit clearly inspired the founder of the last precolonial trading empire, just as the example of Malacca was later to serve the Portuguese and their successors" (Williams 1966: 47).

6. "Malacca thus appeared, at the end of the XVth century, as the capital of a sort of trading empire in which Muslims of all races were the agents. It anticipated the future role of Singapore" (Dupuis 1972: 28; see also Reid 1984).

7. "In a strategic sense the parallel with the Mediterranean sea later in the century is suggestive, and the series of British footholds at Penang, Singapore, Labuan and Hong Kong may be compared with Gibraltar, Malta, Suez and Aden" (Fisher 1964: 85).

8. "For me it is a moment of anguish because all my adult life I have believed in the merger and unity of these two territories." Lee Kuan Yew, Radio broadcast at midnight on August 9–10, 1965.

9. "Singapore's survival is the paramount concern of the PAP rulers. Everything else, including political norms, have [*sic*] to be subordinated to that" (Vasil 1984: 143).

10. See Lee (1965) and Thompson (1966); "Viability is not a simple or absolute concept, but a relative quality, which varies and fluctuates with circumstances" (Paul 1973: 387).

11. Goh (1981a: 4, 8); and see *Straits Times*, 12 August, p. 23; 20 December 20, p. 25, 1984).

12. The expulsion of the young secretary-general of the NTUC, Lim Chee Onn in April 1983 and the dismissal of the president of the republic, Devan Nair in April 1985 give further support to this contention.

13. "For such a small state, the goal of flexibility to external changes has meant the internal centralisation of power and control by one aggressive political party, and the close control of labour demands to ensure the continued attractiveness of Singapore to foreign capital" (Beaulieu 1975: 276).

14. "It would probably be more correct to say that most Singaporeans of Chinese descent are much less interested in democracy than they are in humanistic reasonable government by a leadership elite" (Lee Kuan Yew as quoted in Josey 1968: 605).

15. "If the union leadership challenges the political leadership, the political leadership must triumph, if necessary, by changing the ground rules to thwart the challenge" (Lee Kuan Yew, *Far Eastern Economic Review*, 30 November 1979).

16. The 75 percent of Singaporeans, mainly of modest or middle incomes, who have acquired HDB apartments on preferential terms (Chen 1983: 315–38).

17. The concept of meritocracy was invented by Rajaratnam in 1970 — (see *Straits Times*, 13 April and 10 May 1970).

18. "If Singapore suffers a major economic crisis and the present PAP second leadership fails to overcome it, then an alternative to the PAP government under the tutelage of the military could become possible" (Chen 1983: 195).

19. "The nightmare that haunts even the Singapore leaders of today...is that one day they may wake up to find that they have been asked to go to Collyer Quay to hand over the city to an Indonesian admiral, or to the Johore Causeway to hand over the keys to a Malaysian general" (Wilson 1975: 78–79).

20. Singapore speaks of the "poisoned shrimp" system of deterrence — (*The Mirror*, 8 January 1968).

21. "There must be threats, and there will always be threats because history has always been of threats. So most important is...take precautions long before the threat becomes unmanageable.... One lesson that Singaporeans must learn is please, don't build a philosophy that the world is fine, that it consists of saints, and therefore let's have a good life" (Rajaratnam in *Straits Times*, 20 November 1984).

References

Beaulieu, P. (1975). *Singapore: A Case Study of Communalism and Economic Development.* Seattle: University of Washington Press.

Benjamin, G. (1975). *The Cultural Logic of Singapore's Multiracialism.* Departmental paper. Department of Sociology, Singapore National University.

Boyce, P. (1968). *Malaysia and Singapore in International Diplomacy.* Sydney: Sydney University Press.

Braudel, F. (1979). *Civilisation matérielle, économie et capitalisme,* 15–18 s., volume 3: *Le temps du monde.* Paris: Armand Colin.

Buckley, C. B. (1902). *Anecdotal History of Old Times in Singapore (1819–1967).* 2 volumes. Singapore: publisher unknown.

Busch, P. A. (1972). *Political Unity and Ethnic Diversity: A Case Study of Singapore.* New Haven, CT: Yale University Press.

Chan, H. C. (1971). *Singapore: The Politics of Survival, 1965–67.* Singapore: Oxford University Press.

Chen, G. W. H. (1974). *The Social Bases of Political Development and Integration: The Case of Singapore.* Eugene: University of Oregon.

Chen, P. S. J. (1975). *Elites and National Development in Singapore.* Departmental paper. Department of Sociology, Singapore National University.

Chen, P. S. J., ed. (1983). *Singapore Development Policies and Trends.* Singapore: Oxford University Press.

Chen, P. S. J. and J. T. Fawcett (1979). *Public Policy and Population Change in Singapore.* New York: Population Council.

Chua, B.-H. (1995). *Communitarian Ideology and Democracy in Singapore.* London: Routledge.

Clammer, J. (1985). *Singapore: Ideology, Society and Culture.* Singapore: Chopmen.

Cowan, C. D. (1968). "Continuity and Change in the International History of Maritime Southeast Asia." *Journal of Southeast Asian Studies* 9: 1–11.

Crouch, H. (1984). *Domestic Political Structures and Regional Economic Cooperation,* Singapore: ISEAS.

Dupuis, J. (1972). *Singapour et la Malaisie.* Paris: French University Press.

Evers, H.-D. (1984). *Traditional Trading Networks of Southeast Asia.* Saarbrücken: Verlag Breitenbach.

Fisher, C. A. (1964). *Southeast Asia, a Social, Economic and Political Geography.* London: Methuen. George, T. J. S. ([1973] 1984). *Lee Kuan Yew's Singapore.* Singapore: Eastern University Press.

Goh, C. T. (1981a). *Collected Speeches.* Singapore: Government of Singapore.

Goh, C. T. (1981b). *Collected Speeches,* Volume 5. Singapore: Government of Singapore.

Goh, K. S. (1972). *The Economics of Modernization.* Singapore: Asia Pacific Press.

Gosling, L. A. P. and L. Lim, eds. (1983). *The Chinese in Southeast Asia.* Singapore: Maruzen Asia.

Hall, K. R. (1985). *Maritime Trade and State Development in Early Southeast Asia.* Honolulu: University of Hawaii Press.

Hall-Jones, J. (1979). *An Early Surveyor in Singapore: John Turnbull Thomson in Singapore, 1841–1853.* Singapore: National Museum.

Hill, M. and K. F. Lian (1995). *The Politics of Nation Building.* London: Routledge.

Huff, W. G. (1994). *The Economic Growth of Singapore.* Cambridge: Cambridge University Press.

Josey, A. (1968). *Lee Kuan Yew.* Singapore: Times International.

Josey, A. (1973). *Singapore, Its Past, Present and Future.* Singapore: Eastern University Press.

Lee, K. C. (1981). *Collected Speeches,* Volume 5. Singapore: Government of Singapore.

Lee, K. Y. (1965). "Survival for Smaller Nations." Speech at National Press Club, Canberra, March 16.

Leifer, M. (1978). *Malacca, Singapore and Indonesia.* Alphen aan den Rijn: Sijthoff & Noordhoff.

Mauzy, D., ed. (1984). *Politics in the ASEAN States.* Kuala Lumpur: Marican.

Morrison, C. E. (1976). *Southeast Asia in a Changing International Environment: A Comparative Foreign Policy of Four ASEAN Member Countries.* Baltimore, MD: Johns Hopkins University Press.

Morrison, C. E. and Suhrke (1978). *Strategies of Survival, the Foreign Policy Dilemmas of Smaller Asian States.* New York: St. Martin's.

Murray, G. and A. Pereira (1996). *Singapore, The Global City-State.* New York: St. Martin's.

Nair, D. (1976a). *Tomorrow, the Peril and the Promise.* Singapore: NTUC.

Nair, D. (1976b). *Socialism That Works...The Singapore Way.* Singapore: Federal Publications.

Nair, D. (1982). *Not by Wages Alone.* Singapore: NTUC.

Neville, M. W. (1980). *Singapore, a Disciplined Society.* Auckland: Heinemann.

Onn, W.-H. (1978). *The Economics of Growth and Survival.* Singapore: NTUC.

Pang, E. F. (1982). *Education, Manpower and Development in Singapore*. Singapore: Singapore University Press.

Paul, E. C. (1973). *The Viability of Singapore: An Aspect of Modern Political Geography*. Berkeley: University of California Press.

Quah, J. S. T. (1978). *The Origins of the Public Bureaucracies in the ASEAN Countries*. Departmental paper. Department of Political Science, Singapore National University.

Quah, J. S. T., H. C. Chang, and C. M. Seah, eds. (1985). *Government and Politics in Singapore*. Singapore: Oxford University Press.

Reid, A. (1984). "Trade Goods and Routes in Southeast Asia, c. 1300–1700." SPAFA workshop paper, Jakarta.

Rodan, G. (1989). *The Political Economy of Singapore's Industrialization*. London: Macmillan.

Rodan, G., ed. (1993). *Singapore Changes Guard*. New York: Longman.

Shaw, K. E., ed. (1977). *Elites and National Development in Singapore*. Tokyo: Institute of Developing Economies.

Tan, T. (1981). *Collected Speeches*, Volume 4. Government of Singapore.

Thompson, G. G., ed. (1966). *Singapore's International Relations*. Singapore: Education Board.

Toh Mun Heng and Tan Kong Yam (eds.) (1998). *Competitiveness of the Singapore Economy*. Singapore: Singapore University Press World Scientific.

Turnbull, M. (1977). *A History of Singapore, 1819–1975*. Kuala Lumpur: Oxford University Press.

Vasil, R. K. (1984). *Governing Singapore*. Singapore: Eastern Universities Press.

Wallerstein, I. (1980). *Le système du monde du XVe s. à nos jours*, volume 1: *Capitalisme et économie-monde, 1450–1640*. Paris: Flammarion.

Watson, W. and R. B. Smith (1979). *Early Southeast Asia: Essays in Archaeology, History and Historical Geography*. London: Oxford University Press.

Williams, L. E. (1966). *Southeast Asia, a History*. New York: Oxford University Press.

Wilson, D. (1972). *The Future Role of Singapore*. London: Oxford University Press.

Wilson, D. (1975). *East Meets West: Singapore*. Singapore: Times Printers.

You, P. S. and C. Y. Lim, eds. (1984). *Singapore: 25 Years of Development*. Singapore: Nan Yang Zhou Lianhe Zaobao.

CHAPTER 3

Growth and Planning in an Asian NIC
The Singapore Development Model[*]

W. G. Huff

1. Introduction

"Whatever one may say about the World Bank (1993) *East Asian Miracle report,*"
D. Rodrik observed, "this study has made it very difficult for any reasonable
person to argue that there was little government intervention in East Asian
countries" (1997: 413). However, the nature of intervention and its degree remain
a matter of controversy. That debate is of particular interest to Caribbean countries
since, like Singapore, having small populations and extremely open economies,
they have not infrequently been advised to follow the Singapore development
model. In light of such advice it is useful, first, to understand more fully the
Singapore model of economic development.

The present chapter therefore has two main purposes. Although few could
doubt the importance of outward orientation for Singapore, an island of just 3.2
million people in 1996, with trade (imports+exports) normally about 350 percent
of GDP, one purpose of the chapter is to analyze in the context of Singapore an
aspect of the Asian newly industrialized country (NIC) experience still subject
to disagreement: the mix between active government policies and market forces.
I argue that the Singapore model featured a strongly interventionist government
and planning, which went well beyond the World Bank's (1993) "market-friendly"
approach to include "market replacement." In Singapore, decisive departures from
the price mechanism and a domestically managed regime allowed capitalism to
work. As Singapore's *Strategic Economic Plan* observed, "Economic planning
has played a very significant role in the development of Singapore for more than

*   I owe thanks to the editors of this book for comments on an earlier draft. Research was supported
by a grant from the British Academy Southeast Asia Programme, and data collection by a grant from
the Scottish Economic Society, which are gratefully acknowledged.

thirty years" (Singapore, Economic Planning Committee 1991: 14). If anything, Singapore, often cited as the "most successful of the four 'Asian dragons'" (Giordano and Kato 1993:S.01), is in harmony with Keynes's (1980: 386) conclusion that planned development is the "more efficient" alternative. Singapore exemplified a rational *dirigisme* "which combines plan and market in a creative partnership" (Nolan 1990: 59).

Second, the chapter attempts to unravel Singapore's development model since political independence in 1959 and the election of the People's Action Party (PAP), the only party to have held power in independent Singapore. A distinctive feature of the Singapore model was government control over wages and labor. This allowed three further features of the model to emerge. First, a small economy like Singapore's can usefully be thought of as able to tap a perfectly elastic supply of capital at a given world rate of profitability. Wage control was important in maintaining the required rate of profit. Second, fundamental to the Singapore model was that capital came in the form of direct foreign investment and gave rise to almost complete multinational enterprise (MNE) dominance in the manufactured export sector. Third, labor-intensive jobs created by MNEs allowed Singapore to utilize surplus labor and rapidly ended unemployment. Full employment, combined with Singapore's rising labor productivity, enabled the government to force a high level of domestic saving. This was, in turn, mobilized to build superb infrastructure. Infrastructural facilities, fiscal incentives, and Singapore's location on the world's main East-West communications route combined with low wages as independent variables explaining MNE investment. In Singapore, multinationals contributed substantially more than in the other three Asian NICs — South Korea, Taiwan, and Hong Kong — to the high investment ratios and rapid capital accumulation characteristic of all four countries.

The Singapore model resembled South Korea's and Taiwan's, although not Hong Kong's, in the strong government control exercised over the price mechanism in key economic sectors. Industrialization in Singapore, however, occurred under more restricted labor supply conditions than in the other Asian NICs, including Hong Kong, where between 1945 and 1955 massive labor inflows caused a population increase of about 400 percent, with continued rapid growth into the mid-1960s (Szezepanik 1958; Chow and Papanek 1981). Its split with Malaysia in August 1965 allowed Singapore, constituted as an independent republic, effectively to close its borders and regulate labor flows. Like Hong Kong, but in contrast to South Korea and Taiwan, by the 1980s Singapore had turned to internationally traded services as the most dynamic component of the economy. Singapore's unusually strong locational advantage was vital to its becoming a major world exporter of services, which even by 1992 were almost equivalent in value to Switzerland's (GATT 1993). The republic's "natural resource" of location and uniqueness as a city-state have particular relevance to the Singapore model's likely replicability.

The chapter is structured in seven further sections. Section 2 reviews Singapore's macroeconomic performance. Sections 3 and 4 focus, respectively, on the manufacturing sector and economic planning. In Section 5, the Singapore model is further disaggregated by examining financial and business services. Section 6 analyzes the relationship between macroeconomic policy, planning, and economic development. Section 7 tries to assess the effect on Singapore of the East Asian financial crisis, which started in 1997. In conclusion, the chapter comments on the Singapore model's relevance to the Caribbean as well as to development theory.

2.   Macroeconomic Performance

Between 1960 and 1996, Singapore's real gross national product (GNP) increased nineteenfold. Singapore advanced from the world's thirty-third highest per capita income in 1965 to rank eighth by 1995, ahead of France, the Netherlands, and Sweden (World Bank 1984, 1997). Infant mortality and life expectancy in Singapore are, respectively, among the lowest and highest in the world. Full employment has obtained since 1973 and absolute poverty is virtually nonexistent. Gini coefficients for individuals were around 0.46 in the mid-1980s (Lim and associates 1988: 401–2; Islam and Kirkpatrick 1986). Yet even with income per head of US$26,730 in 1995, Singapore has not fully achieved developed-country status. Accordingly, Singapore is not officially classified as a developed country (World Bank 1997: 215). The justification for this, explored below, is part of a wider strategy of heavy reliance on foreign companies and workers; in 1996, 32.2 percent of GDP accrued to non-Singaporeans, i.e., neither citizens nor permanent residents (Singapore, Department of Statistics 1997: 55).

Five characteristics of Singapore's economy immediately attract attention: sustained rapid growth; sharply increasing export orientation; exceptionally high saving and investment; low inflation; and fundamental structural transformation. These are indicated here, and discussed at length in subsequent sections.

At the end of the 1950s, Singapore's per capita income was already higher than almost anywhere in Asia and over one-third of the United Kingdom's (Benham 1957, 1959; Silcock 1959). Furthermore, from 1960 to 1966, real GDP increased at an annual average rate of 6.4 percent (Table 3.1), largely due to government expenditure on infrastructure and protected, import-substituting industrialization in the context of Singapore's union with Malaya to form Malaysia. In 1959 the Economic Development Board was set up as "the spearhead for industrialization by direct participation in industry" and building necessary infrastructure (Singapore, Economic Planning Unit 1964: 37; see also Singapore

Table 3.1: *Singapore Macroeconomic Indicators, 1960–96 (%)*

	1960–66	1966–69	1960–69	1970–79	1980–89	1990–96
Annual real GDP growth rate	6.4	13.6	8.7	8.9	7.1	8.3
Annual inflation rate[a]	1.1	1.1	1.1	5.6	2.7	3.2
Saving ratio[b]	6.7	18.2	11.5	28.8	40.6	47.7
Investment ratio[b]	17.5	24.8	20.7	40.5	41.8	36.4

[a] GDP inflator.

[b] The saving ratio and investment ratio are defined, respectively, as gross national savings and gross capital formation divided by gross domestic product. All variables are in real terms deflated by the GDP deflator.
Sources: Singapore, Department of Statistics (1988, 1993b, 1994, 1997), Singapore, Ministry of Trade and Industry (1994, 1997).

1961; O'Connor 1966). Heavy government developmental expenditure, which included the Board's new industrial estate at Jurong, created a base for future export-oriented industrialization, although it yielded little in either industrial production or exports until at least the mid-1960s (Goh 1970; Singapore, Economic Planning Unit 1964). In the latter half of the 1960s a resurgence of Singapore's historic role as a trade and service center for the surrounding region provided the main impetus to growth (Goh 1970: 10–11; Singapore, Ministry of Finance, Trade Division 1970: 3), while by 1967 manufactured exports also began to contribute significantly to GDP. A doubling of growth during the 1960s, together with infrastructure and institutions established in that decade — the Economic Development Board and its offshoots, the government-owned Development Bank of Singapore and Jurong Town Corporation — provided a foundation for Singapore's continued expansion. During the 1970s, and again from 1980 to 1990, real GDP more than doubled, with a similar increase in the 1990s.

From 1970 to 1979, manufactured exports became the engine of Singapore's growth. The proportion of direct manufactured exports to GDP rose from 12.7 percent in 1966 to almost half in 1979 and 57.0 percent in 1995.[1] Indicative of the export-led nature of growth in manufacturing is that from 1967 to 1995 while real manufactured output grew at an annual average rate of 11.0 percent, real direct exports of manufactures grew considerably faster at 13.9 percent (Singapore, Economic Development Board 1992, 1997).

High savings and investment characterized Singapore's economic development. The PAP government enforced state-directed abstinence, and the saving ratio (Table 3.1), under 10 percent for most of the 1960s, averaged 29 percent in the 1970s and over 40 percent from 1980 — the world's highest. From the start, the government decided on a high investment ratio as "the paramount need...in an economy which wants to expand its basic wealth at a fast rate, a target like 20 percent or more should be aimed at" (Singapore 1963). In fact, the investment ratio was sustained at over 40 percent during the 1970s and 1980s

(Table 3.1). However, domestic saving explained only a part of Singapore's high investment, which relied heavily on direct foreign investment by MNEs. Indeed, between 1980 and 1990, Singapore was the largest single less-developed country recipient of direct foreign investment, and received almost 13 percent of all such investment in developing countries (United Nations 1992). Direct foreign investment has continued to grow strongly in the 1990s.

Development in Singapore occurred with low inflation, remarkable for an economy already chronically short of labor by the late 1970s (Table 3.1). The increase in the GDP deflator was 2.6 percent or less during twenty of thirty-five years, and exceeded 5 percent in only eight years, despite high world inflation and Singapore's very open economy.

Table 3.2: *Singapore GDP (1990 Market Prices) and Employment by Industrial Sector, 1960–96*

	1960	1969	1979	1992	1996
GDP[a]					
Total ($m)	5,891.7	12,497.1	30,613.7	77,353.8	109,787.1
Agriculture & quarrying (%)	3.8	2.7	1.5	0.4	0.2
Manufacturing (%)	16.6	23.2	29.4	27.6	27.4
Construction & utilities (%)	7.0	10.7	9.1	6.8	10.1
Commerce (%)	24.6	22.9	19.4	18.2	18.4
Transport & communications (%)	8.8	7.2	11.6	14.7	13.5
Financial & business services (%)	14.0	16.5	18.9	26.1	27.7
Other services (%)	19.6	15.7	12.2	10.2	10.6
Employment[b]					
Persons (000s)	471.9	650.9	1,021.0	1,576.2	1,748.1
Agriculture & quarrying (%)	7.3	3.8	1.6	0.3	0.2
Manufacturing (%)	15.7	22.0	28.9	27.5	23.3
Construction & utilities (%)	6.1	7.8	6.3	7.1	7.0
Commerce (%)	24.2	23.5	23.3	22.6	23.2
Transport & communications (%)	10.7	12.1	11.6	10.1	11.2
Financial & business services (%)	4.6	3.5	7.1	10.9	14.1
Other services (%)	31.4	27.3	21.2	21.5	21.0

[a] For GDP, the percentage shares may not add to 100%, since imputed bank service charges are deducted and import duties are added to arrive at total GDP, but account is not taken of these for individual industries.
[b] Employment figures for 1960 are from the 1957 Census and for 1969 from the 1970 Census.
Sources: Singapore (1964), Singapore, Department of Statistics (1981, 1983a, 1988, 1994, 1996, 1997).

One aspect of structural transformation in Singapore was the shift toward manufacturing (Table 3.2). Its share in total output grew from 16.6 percent in 1960 to 29.4 percent by 1979. In 1996, manufacturing contributed 27.4 percent of GDP and accounted for 23.3 percent of employment. The other structural change was the increasing importance of services, which in Singapore traditionally

include the three categories of transport and communications; financial and
business services; and public administration, community, social, and personal
services. After 1978, financial and business services, reflecting Singapore's
development as an international financial center, emerged as an engine of growth,
and were the economy's fastest-growing sector. In 1992, they provided 26.1
percent of GDP, or almost as much as manufacturing but, reflecting their often
capital-intensive nature, made up under 11 percent of employment, about a third
of that in manufacturing. By 1996, however, the employment share of financial and
business services had risen to 14.1 percent, three-fifths the size of manufacturing.

3.   Government Control and Export-Oriented Manufacturing

The basic distinction between a market system and economic planning is reliance
on the price mechanism or its replacement by government intervention involving
some combination of incentives, disincentives, commands, and controls aimed
at a consistent means-end hierarchy. This section shows how Singapore attained
international competitiveness and industrialized through government control and
directives, which replaced the price mechanism in three crucial areas. One
involved government direction of the labor market. Second, state-owned enterprises constituted a fundamental departure toward planning. Third, the government
instituted a program of forced saving. Each aspect will be discussed in turn and
then related to infrastructure provision and private-sector capital accumulation.

3.1 *Labor Market Direction and Multinationals as Entrepreneurial Substitutes*

Appropriate wage levels were fundamental to the internal supply response,
enabling Singapore to take advantage of export-oriented industrialization, which,
after 1965, was made possible by an international search for cheap labor in
developing countries. An interwar wage differential substantially above the rest
of Asia had persisted into the 1960s, leaving Singapore with wage costs "20–30
percent too high for world markets" (United Nations 1961: 115). Although
Singapore's wages might eventually have come down through market forces, the
government decisively effected adjustment to market-clearing levels. Two
measures, the Employment Act and the Industrial Relations (Amendment) Act
of 1968, "de-politicized the labor movement, established *de facto* government
control over unions [and] transferred bargaining power from workers to employers" (Lim and Pang 1986: 11). Few work stoppages occurred after 1967; by 1977
they were virtually eliminated. Singapore's total of two work stoppages involving
159 workers in the nineteen years 1978–96 cannot have reflected a free labor
market (Singapore, Department of Statistics 1991, 1997).

By 1969, for comparable job classifications in the key semiconductor and office machine assembly industries, hourly compensation costs in Singapore were less than one-eleventh of the United States' level, and below those in South Korea, Taiwan, and Hong Kong. Productivity in Singapore was equal to that of the latter three, and at least as high as in the United States (United States Tariff Commission 1970: 166–73; Leong 1971). Government direction of wages mobilized labor in Singapore by allowing it to realize a latent comparative advantage based on a relative abundance of unskilled workers. As was observed, "The electronic components we make in Singapore probably require less skill than that required by barbers or cooks, consisting mostly of repetitive manual operations" (Goh 1970: 27). Unemployment dropped from 8.9 percent in 1966 to 4.5 percent in 1973 — effectively, full employment (Singapore, Department of Statistics 1983a). Moreover, the proportion of own account (i.e. self-employed) and unpaid family workers in Singapore's labor force fell from 20.7 percent in 1970 to 7.8 percent by 1990 (Saw 1984: 40; Singapore, Department of Statistics 1993a).

Table 3.3: *Singapore Real Average Monthly Earnings for All Workers, 1978–96 (1993=100)*

1978	44.8	1988	76.1
1979	46.8	1989	81.7
1980	48.9	1990	86.4
1981	48.4	1991	91.0
1982	53.9	1992	96.2
1983	58.8	1993	100.0
1984	63.4	1994	105.5
1985	68.0	1995	110.3
1986	69.5	1996	115.0
1987	71.4		

Sources: Singapore, Ministry of Labour. Annual series 1988–96. Yearbook of Labour Statistics, Singapore; Singapore, Department of Statistics. Annual series 1988–96. Yearbook of Statistics, Singapore.

Full employment would almost certainly have set up strong inflationary wage pressure and internationally uncompetitive pay rises had not the government in 1972 inaugurated the National Wages Council, a tripartite body comprising government, employers, and trade unions, which published guidelines for pay increases. Although not mandatory, these were closely observed. The government controlled unions; more than this, a measure of its power was that, in the absence of any overt enforcement mechanism, foreign MNEs did not bid up wages, despite incentives to do so as a result of labor scarcity and Singapore's attractiveness as a production location due to its excellent infrastructure and cluster of complementary firms already there. Real wage rises averaged just 1.7 percent from 1973 to 1978 (Singapore, Ministry of Trade and Industry 1985: 20), but then, boosted

Table 3.4: *Singapore, United States, Japan and Asian Countries Hourly Compensation Costs for Production Workers in Manufacturing, 1975–96 (Current US$ and Index, United States=100)*

	1975		1980		1993		1996	
	$	Index	$	Index	$	Index	$	Index
United States	6.36	100	9.87	100	16.79	100	17.74	100
Japan	3.05	48	5.61	57	19.20	114	21.04	119
Singapore	.84	13	1.49	15	5.38	32	8.32	47
South Korea	.33	5	.97	10	5.37	32	8.23	46
Taiwan	.40	6	1.00	10	5.23	31	5.86	33
Hong Kong	.76	12	1.51	15	4.31	26	5.14	29
Asian NICs[a]	.50	8	1.15	12	5.15	31	6.89	39

[a] Asian NICs refers to a United States trade-weighted average level for Singapore, South Korea, Taiwan, and Hong Kong.

Sources: United States Department of Labor (1997).

Table 3.5: *Singapore Manufacturing Statistics by Capital Ownership, 1968–95*

	Output	Value added	Direct Exports
1968			
Total ($m)	**2,175.7**	**611.8**	
Wholly local (%)	41.1	40.8	
Majority local (%)	12.8	15.2	n.a
Wholly or majority foreign (%)	46.1	44.0	
1975			
Total ($m)	**12,610.1**	**3,411.1**	**7,200.7**
Wholly local (%)	18.0	24.3	8.9
Majority local (%)	10.7	13.0	7.0
Wholly or majority foreign (%)	71.3	62.7	84.1
1995			
Total ($m)	**113,358.0**	**34,882.4**	**69,012.6**
Wholly local (%)	15.5	17.0	8.1
Majority local (%)	8.1	11.5	6.0
Wholly or majority foreign (%)	76.4	71.5	85.9

Sources: Singapore, Department of Statistics or Economic Development Board. Annual Series, 1968-1995. Report on the Census of Industrial Production, Singapore.

initially by a three-year wage correction policy decreed by Singapore planners, doubled by 1990 (Table 3.3). Between 1975 and 1993, however, Singapore manufacturing labor costs grew more slowly than in the Asian NICs, and continuously moved toward the average in these countries (Table 3.4) — a yardstick used by the government to measure success in containing labor costs. The rapid rise in Singapore's relative labor costs from 1993 to 1996 (Table 3.5) may help to explain a slowdown by 1997 in Singapore's manufacturing economy as well as reflecting somewhat less government intervention in the labor market together with the pressures of full employment over a long period (Huff 1995: 1424–25).

Foreign multinationals were more dominant in Singapore than in any other less developed country export success story. The electronics industry quickly became, in terms of both job creation and output, the mainstay of this MNE presence and of Singapore's manufacturing industry. In 1975, wholly- and majority-foreign owned firms already dominated the manufacturing sector, and in 1995 accounted for over three-quarters of manufacturing output and 85.9 percent of direct exports (Table 3.5). Thus, within manufacturing, whatever linkages existed were largely to other foreign-owned firms (Lim and Pang 1986: 92).

The reliance on foreigners, together with Singapore's lack of an indigenous technological contribution to manufacturing, marks the Republic as not being a developed country. Singapore, even in 1986, was industrially "still predominantly a manufacturing production base. Products are designed overseas, and then only produced in Singapore factories on our production lines" (H. L. Lee 1986: 7; see also *Straits Times Weekly* 1990; Hu 1994). Although after 1981, as MNEs poured into Singapore to make computer components and peripherals, manufacturing took on an increasingly high-tech look, the Republic's chief attraction remained reliable and adaptable unskilled, especially female, labor at a fraction of the wages paid in developed countries. The speed of technical change emanating from developed country electronics industries meant that this labor could be retrained and redeployed more cheaply than a new machine could be designed, and afforded MNEs flexibility for short and varying production runs (Lim and Pang 1984). In 1990, 72 percent of those in electronics production were female, compared to 43 percent in the rest of manufacturing (Singapore, Economic Development Board 1992); wages in the electronics industry were below the manufacturing average, itself less than wages in most other industrial groupings (Singapore, Ministry of Labour 1993). The value-added share of gross output measures technical development in manufacturing. For the manufacturing sector other than electronics, this rose from 32.2 percent in 1978 to 35.5 percent by 1995, but over the same period in the electronics industry actually fell from 32.2 to 26.2 percent (Singapore, Department of Statistics 1978; Singapore, Economic Development Board 1997).

Growth accounting has failed to discover technical change in Singapore, measured as total factor productivity. It has been argued that total factor productivity growth was next to nil because the speed of technical change in Singapore did not give adequate time for "learning by doing" gains to be realized (Young 1992). This fails to understand the quickly exhausted nature of the learning curve, and so the limited gains available in the particular international division of labor on which Singapore's spectacular manufacturing growth depended. Singapore has in fact benefited from higher value-added activities (even in some parts of the electronics sector), and Singaporeans were increasingly employed as technicians and in supervisory positions. But for electronics, the bulk of technological progress and learning gains were found in developed countries where research and development and process and product design concentrated.

By the late 1980s it appeared doubtful that Singapore's legislation and policy instruments like the National Wages Council, which successfully regulated wage costs in a full-employment economy, would also be able to effect industrial restructuring toward higher value-added activities and the increased productivity that is the heart of the economic development process (Disney and Ho 1990; Lim and associates 1988: 35–36). That the Republic's leaders recognized the need for more indigenous development of technology as well as training programs and education to effect restructuring was indicated by a planning departure in the 1990s to achieve productivity gains through technical progress: the state was to spearhead research and development (Singapore, National Science and Technology Board 1991; *Straits Times Weekly* 1992a). This remains a problem in Singapore, which is the only country in the world with a target for annual total factor productivity growth (2 percent) and which launched a new government agency explicitly dedicated to its fulfillment (Wilson 1995: 242).

3.2 *State-Owned Enterprise*

After the PAP's early 1960s abandonment of a (colonial-inherited) ideology that confined government to the provision of infrastructure, the state moved aggressively into direct participation in industrial, commercial, and financial activities (Lee 1974). Thus, although private enterprise, strategically supported by the state, was regarded as the main force for growth, Singapore's government, like South Korea's (Song 1990: 118–19), recognized the potential for public enterprise as a lead factor in the development process and showed no hesitation in moving into any area of the economy essential to expanding technological and export capacity, notably iron and steel and ship-repair and ship-building. By 1974, public enterprises were thought to account for 14–16 percent of all manufacturing output (Lee 1974: 64). More important, many traded services came through public enterprises. These included Neptune Orient Lines (shipping), Intraco (trading), the Development Bank of Singapore, and Singapore Airlines — this last by the 1990s making Singapore as a country the world's fifth largest international air carrier behind the United States, United Kingdom, Japan, and Germany (*Straits Times Weekly* 1992b).

The Singapore development model carries the lesson that public enterprise organized through a sort of political entrepreneurship can be run efficiently and at a profit. In achieving this, Singapore's government had the advantage that public ownership began afresh rather than through the nationalization of already loss-making enterprises; subsequently, unsuccessful ventures were shaken up and, if unable to be turned around, eventually liquidated. By the mid-1980s, prior to privatization beginning in late 1985, the government wholly or partially owned some 490 companies, including 30 statutory boards through which the government organized infrastructure provision. However, these often had "substantial commercial operations" and their monopoly power, either legislated or natural, enabled the government to realize large profits, so long as reasonable commercial efficiency was maintained (Singapore, Ministry of Finance 1987). In 1984/85, seven statutory boards with commercial operations (i.e., excluding the Monetary Authority of Singapore, Central Provident Fund, and Board of Commissioners of Currency with large investment income earnings) made substantially higher profits than the ten most profitable companies listed on Singapore's stock exchange (Seah 1986).

Management of state-owned enterprise was highly centralized. Control was effected through three holding companies run by three government ministries. Interlocking companies and interlocking directorships gave a few top civil servants, each with more than ten directorships, considerable leverage over government holdings. Overall, the government "monopolised a fair share of entrepreneurial and business brains in its enterprise [and] tapped the private sector by seconding business elites into its enterprises" (Low 1984: 274).

The still-cautious course of privatization after over a decade (the government retains large stakes in major undertakings like Singapore Airlines) reflects the absence of any real argument in Singapore for the superior economic efficiency of private ownership, combined with the PAP's reluctance to surrender direction of strategic sectors of Singapore Inc. In part, however, privatization, which makes available on advantageous terms equity in enterprises built up with public funds, allays complaints that state-owned enterprise "crowds out" local private enterprises. More important for the government, partial privatization of state-owned enterprise, including statutory boards for telecommunications and post (like Singapore Telecom), introduces a depth otherwise lacking in the Stock Exchange of Singapore. Increased stock market capitalization is necessary to attract a critical mass of foreign fund managers and institutions to preempt competition from rapidly growing countries like Thailand and Malaysia and establish Singapore as the central stock market within the Association of South East Asian Nations, complementing its other international financial functions (Singapore, Ministry of Finance 1987: 43; *Financial Times* 1990, 1998c).

3.3 *Government-Forced Saving*

The driving force in Singapore's saving process was public-sector saving, which increased from less than a quarter of national savings in 1974 to three-fifths by 1984 and 66.8 percent in 1985, after which the government ceased to publish statistics (Huff 1994: 333). Public-sector saving consisted of the government's budget surplus and surpluses realized by statutory boards. Within the public sector, profits from natural monopolies in effect subsidized deficits in government priority areas like housing. Seven main boards — the Housing and Development Board, Jurong Town Corporation, Public Utilities Board, Port of Singapore Authority, Urban Redevelopment Authority, Telecommunication Authority of Singapore, and Sentosa Development Corporation — were central in determining public-sector saving.

The private sector's contribution to Singapore's high saving rate was substantially due to saving forced by the government through a social security scheme — the Central Provident Fund. In 1986 voluntary private saving, both household and corporate, constituted just 8.1 percent of total saving (ibid.: 330–32). One estimate was that between 1967 and 1989 the effect of the Central Provident Fund was to raise Singapore's overall saving rate by 3.8 percentage points (Monetary Authority of Singapore 1991b). The Central Provident Fund could increase the domestic saving rate because (unusually among developing countries) it operated on the provident fund principle: on retirement, individuals were paid benefits determined by total past contributions from themselves and their employers plus interest, rather than payments being made to retirees from the contributions of those still working. Contribution rates, divided about equally between employee and employer (including multinationals), rose from 10 percent in 1967 to 38.5 percent in 1980 and a peak of 50 percent in 1984 before declining somewhat.

In addition to the Central Provident Fund, the government had no hesitation in rigging the market to obtain control over remaining voluntary private saving. A large indirect transfer of savings from the private sector to the government resulted from voluntary deposits with the Post Office Savings Bank. The Bank was required to lend mainly to statutory boards or government corporations, or to lodge the deposits it took with the Monetary Authority of Singapore. Deposits with the Bank were tax exempt, and two years after becoming a statutory board in 1972, it began to offer a higher interest rate than commercial banks. By the mid-1980s, purely savings deposits with the Post Office Savings Bank exceeded those of all Singapore's commercial banks put together (Wong 1986; Lim and associates 1988; Monetary Authority of Singapore 1993).

3.4 Infrastructure and Housing Provision

Borrowing from the Central Provident Fund gave the Singapore government a cheap, typically below-market interest rates, noninflationary source of finance that could be used to provide infrastructure and public goods. At the same time, in its public-sector mobilization of finance by the extraction of saving through monopoly power to create large government surpluses, Singapore operated a state-directed capitalism that, in Gurley and Shaw's (1967) terminology, is a technology of finance resembling socialist central planning more than private free market capitalism. Domestic capital resources were mobilized for economic development when the government used its control over savings to invest in infrastructure and housing (Sandilands 1992).

Infrastructure provided under government auspices was the most modern and efficient possible, including port, airport, telecommunications, roads, and a mass rapid transit system. The effect was to provide a subsidy for business in Singapore, which reduced expenses both in operating within the Republic and in reaching world markets, so-called "distance costs" (Helleiner 1973). Ready-to-move-into factory sites were provided at Jurong and other industrial estates. Planning that emphasized technical education and industrial training further subsidized industry, while government promotion of education in English reduced distance costs by facilitating communication between expatriate MNE personnel and Singaporeans.

3.5 *Private-Sector Investment and Capital Accumulation*

The rapid accumulation of physical capital that characterized the Singapore model came principally from the private sector. Even from 1960 to 1966, when planning in Singapore stressed government provision of infrastructure, the public sector accounted for no more than 38 percent of all gross fixed capital formation in Singapore. From the 1970s onward, some three-quarters of this capital formation came from the private sector.

Singapore's high investment could increasingly have been domestically financed (Table 3.1), and beginning in the late 1980s gross national savings became greater than gross capital formation. However, well before this occurred, the government had begun to invest a high proportion of Singapore's public savings abroad in equities and bonds, real estate, and short-term assets, with a consequent accumulation of large foreign reserves, in 1997 conservatively estimated at US$84 billion, the world's highest on a per capita basis. In effect, through this government investment abroad, Singapore exchanged an outflow of national savings for an inflow into the domestic economy of private foreign capital, which brought with it technology and assured access to markets. The exchange explains a part of what might otherwise seem a paradox: that high saving largely relied on the public sector but high investment came chiefly from the private sector. Direct foreign investment made a growing contribution to Singapore's capital formation, and rose from perhaps a tenth of the total in 1967–69 to about a quarter by 1980–96.

Government injections in the form of infrastructure, investment incentives, and an increasingly educated work force were fundamental in explaining large private-sector investment. Every $1 increase over the preceding decade in public-sector capital formation was associated with an increase in private-sector capital formation of $3 during the 1970s and $2.5 for the 1980s (Huff 1994: 338–39). The relationship does not indicate causation, but is at least suggestive of the possibility of long-term "crowding in," rather than "crowding out," due to government expenditure. A crowding-in effect might also be expected because government injections were strongly complementary to the private sector and increased both the economy's absorptive capacity and investors' confidence (Aschauer 1989; Taylor 1991). Crowding in would help to explain the paradox of high public-sector saving and yet reliance on private-sector capital formation: public-sector saving that financed infrastructure brought even higher private-sector investment. But a possible drawback was that the private industry crowded in was largely foreign.

4.   Planning for Manufacturing Development

The leaders of independent Singapore began with a general belief in the effectiveness of planning, but no definite idea of the course it should follow. Singapore's leadership was, however, strong, largely independent of local interest groups, and dedicated to the goal of economic development — also characteristics of successful planning in South Korea and Taiwan. In Singapore, a coherent, clearly defined development strategy, essential to any shade of planning (Chakravarty 1991), emerged from the late 1960s as the political leadership/planners increasingly perceived the strength of the world economy's new flows of trade and foreign investment. As part of that strategy, Singapore's leaders found control over key domestic markets and institutions the most effective way to respond to these opportunities in the world economy in order to meet the main planning objectives of providing jobs, absorbing surplus labor, and rapid economic growth (K. S. Goh, interview with the author, 17 August, 1989). There was no ideological commitment to free enterprise as such: "The government has to be the planner and the mobilizer of the economic effort" but "the free enterprise system, correctly nurtured and adroitly handled, can serve as a powerful and versatile instrument of economic growth" (Goh 1972).

Interventionism in Singapore was organized around government directives, and so had considerably more force than indicative planning. Evaluation of development plans and planning objectives is complicated by the fact that, like most government matters in Singapore, described even now as a "corporate state that is mainly run by PAP technocrats" (Kim 1992: 119), principal documents were kept secret.[2] Only "highlights" of the *Economic Development Plan for the*

Eighties were published, although subsequent plans were discussed more fully, and plan review procedures have now been given a public facade (Singapore, SEP Working Group 1993). It is clear, however, that planning for manufacturing development in Singapore never involved detailed blueprints, because of the priority accorded to reaction to the international market, impossibility of predicting its course, and the need for flexibility to ensure a quick and competitive response. Instead, requirements common to all industries — good infrastructure and a cheap, disciplined, and trained labor force — were made prime objectives, and they were systematically met.

More than this, Singapore planners took a view of the future and, helped by intelligence from Economic Development Board overseas offices, closely monitored the world market. Initiatives were undertaken to attract industries regarded as desirable for long-term development. For example, the potential of electronics was spotted on a 1966 ministerial visit to Taiwan (Wee 1966; Goh 1992). The Economic Development Board targeted manufacturing activities, in that the Board looked for industries beneficial to Singapore — on criteria like value added, skill content, and capital intensity — which were likely to be attracted to the Republic, inquired as to the necessary incentives, and then provided them (Singapore, Economic Development Board 1993: 26–27). This incentive structure, including tax concessions associated with pioneer status for new industries and worker-training programs, was continually revised in light of planning objectives. The government also took significant equity shares in foreign, private-sector projects — petrochemicals, and in 1991 production of dynamic random access memory chips — to promote strategic industrial clusters (Low et al. 1993: 99; Hu 1994).

But in manufacturing, the aims remained general; Singapore planners' approach to the international economy contrasted with the targeted protectionism and idea of "picking winners" practiced in Japan, South Korea, and Taiwan, and perhaps possible for a large developing country. Rather, in keeping with a tiny domestic economy, Singapore adhered to free trade and tried to be attractive to a range of activities through supply-oriented policies, an approach later likened to backing all the horses in a race (Goh 1992; Singapore, Economic Planning Committee 1991: 68). In the public sector, largely responsible for infrastructural development, rolling five-year plans operated.

Singapore planning featured the concentration of decision-making in a few hands, also observed elsewhere in East Asia (Jones and SaKong 1980; Wade 1990). In Singapore's "top-down" approach, the planning system at the summit was described as "a high degree of good and eclectic steersmanship" (Low 1988: 259). Typically, the same men, for example, Goh Keng Swee, Hon Sui Sen, and Joseph Pillay, served as directors for a host of state-owned enterprises and PAP government development initiatives, which economized on entrepreneurial talent (*Singapore Trade and Industry* 1969a, 1969b; Lee 1984; Bryant 1985: 13).

Moreover, the policy helped to ensure loyalty to the government and to further its tight control. The PAP leadership achieved effective implementation of plans and policies through the lower levels of bureaucracy by a willingness to pay government officials as much as or more than the private sector and an emphasis on individual accountability (Chew 1988: 222–23).

Singapore planning was, as elsewhere in East Asia, strongly market oriented, but government-business cooperation, which in South Korea featured government as the senior partner controlling domestic entrepreneurs (Mason 1980: 294), found in Singapore government as a junior partner to the needs of foreign enterprise. The planning strategy of Singapore, like that of any country, is not directly applicable elsewhere, and the high foreign presence promoted may be its least transferable aspect.

5. Financial and Business Services: Natural Comparative Advantage and its Augmentation

In the development of financial and business services, a more precise planning strategy prevailed than for manufacturing. It was set out in a plan for the 1970s (Hon 1972), strengthened in the *Economic Development Plan for the Eighties* (Singapore, Ministry of Trade and Industry 1981), and further elaborated later that decade (Singapore, Ministry of Trade and Industry 1986a). Significantly, this more targeted approach to planning reflected Singapore's greater market power in attracting financial services based on "natural" comparative advantage — i.e., when a free, competitive market prevails. Location on the world's main east-west communications network and the existing presence in the Republic of a critical mass of international financial institutions, ancillary services, and infrastructure gave Singapore more freedom to "pick winners" in financial services than in manufacturing. Starting in the late 1960s, the rapid expansion of international financial intermediation emphasized and widened Singapore's locational advantages. The island linked the Atlantic, Middle East, and Pacific regions, which in the 1970s enabled Singapore to become a funding center, acting as an entrepôt between deposit centers like Bahrain in a region of surplus funds and arranging centers like Hong Kong near ultimate borrowers. Because Singapore bridged the time zone gap between the New York/London and Hong Kong/Tokyo markets, it could emerge as a leading foreign exchange dealing center with the initiation of twenty-four-hour international trading. By the 1990s, Singapore was the fourth-largest foreign exchange market after London, New York, and Tokyo (Singapore, Ministry of Trade and Industry 1993: 66).

Financial services would not have become an engine of growth in Singapore's economy in the absence of an activist government. In 1968, the Singapore government, in consultation with international banks, spotted the possibility of an Asian dollar market similar to that for Eurodollars. The government immediately reacted by abolishing for deposits made by Asian Currency Units (ACU) — any banking unit operating in the Singapore Asian Dollar Market — a withholding tax of 45 percent on interest paid to nonresidents, and quickly followed through with a variety of other measures aimed at establishing the market (Hodjera 1978). This activist government policy "stole the march on Hong Kong," where the authorities lacked a similar development commitment (Jao 1985: 44, 1979). Although Hong Kong subsequently moved to establish a dollar market, by then the advantage lay decisively with Singapore, and a successful challenge to the Republic proved impossible.

In the 1970s, the government moved aggressively to develop the economy's comparative advantage in financial and business services through the introduction of financial innovations. The Monetary Authority of Singapore, established in 1971 as a quasi-central bank, became a strong and responsive institution that, together with the Development Bank of Singapore, the government could use in its strategy to turn Singapore into the "Zurich of the East" (*Financial Times* 1973). When the market proved unresponsive, the government was willing to take the lead: the Development Bank of Singapore, and then the Singapore government itself, started the Asian Dollar Bond Market by floating U. S. dollar-denominated bonds. As the private sector, after initial hesitation, embarked on similar initiatives, the Asian Dollar and Bond Markets — with their respectively short- and longer-term maturities — introduced significant market specialization and complementarity in Singapore's offshore banking system (Singapore 1973; Lee, S. Y., 1986). The Asian Dollar Market remained the more important of the two, and after reaching US$54.4 billion by 1980, grew to US$478.9 billion in 1996, an annual average growth of 14.6 percent (Monetary Authority of Singapore 1994, 1996).

Government policy that aimed at attracting international financial institutions to Singapore was also demonstrably successful. From 1981 to 1996, the number of foreign banks rose from 86 to 131, and merchant banks from 39 to 79. There were 214 Asian Currency Units licensed to deal in Asian dollars, since virtually all banks and merchant banks dealt in Asian dollars (Monetary Authority of Singapore 1994, 1996).

Singapore's ever-growing cluster of financial institutions created opportunities for specialization and scale economies for these institutions, and so reinforced government efforts toward broadening and deepening financial services in the Republic. In association with the Monetary Authority of Singapore, the government targeted specific financial instruments and institutions and strongly encouraged them with fiscal incentives. The establishment of Singapore as a "'financial supermarket,' offering the widest range of financial services" (Singapore, Ministry of Trade and Industry 1981: 10–11), was central to the *Economic Development*

Plan for the Eighties; during that decade, every budget statement contained new measures aimed at financial innovation. By the late 1980s, as the government had planned, Singapore had a successful futures and options market, organized through the Singapore International Monetary Exchange (SIMEX) and linked to the Chicago Mercantile Exchange on a twenty-four-hour, mutual-offset basis; and merchant banking began to expand significantly (Singapore, Ministry of Trade and Industry 1991: 8, 69–70; Monetary Authority of Singapore 1991a: 29, 33, 1992: 40, 1993: 59–60). During the 1990s, however, fund management, after successful early growth, stagnated and is now the target for new government initiatives (*Financial Times* 1998c).

6. Macroeconomic Policy

Although macroeconomic policy is often regarded as only a short-term, even minor adjunct of structural and institutional planning, temporary macroeconomic instability can destroy attempts at longer-term planning. Macropolicy instruments evolved in Singapore were therefore essential to the overall planning effort and, like it, were made effective through a high degree of government control in selected areas.

Singapore's exceptionally low inflation was a principal achievement of macroeconomic policy, and became a cornerstone of it. Macroeconomic management was unconventional, in that a government's ability to secure international competitiveness through limiting wage rises to productivity gains is not typically among the range of policy instruments available. In Singapore, the substitution of an institution — the National Wages Council — for a conventional macropolicy instrument — the exchange rate — freed the latter to become a weapon targeted specifically on inflation. Because in a heavily reexport economy like Singapore's, with a large, internationally traded goods sector, import and export prices tended to rise about equally, domestic inflation was kept low by allowing the exchange rate to appreciate in line with foreign inflation. The expectation of a rise in value of the Singapore dollar consequent on increased world inflation would have led to a rush of foreign funds into the Singapore currency, unduly pushing up its value, and making impossible control by the Monetary Authority of Singapore, had not the Singapore authorities prevented the "internationalization" of the Singapore dollar. The Monetary Authority of Singapore achieved this by imposing a withholding tax on interest earned by nonresidents on Singapore dollar holdings, and issuing directives to the banking system not to make Singapore dollar loans to nonresidents or residents for use outside the Republic, except to finance Singapore's external trade. Banks had to submit in writing any proposals for such loans exceeding S$5 million (Corden 1984; Bryant 1985: 98–101; Lim and associates 1988; Peebles and Wilson 1996: 183–85).

To some extent, there was truth in the argument that Singapore's high, government-forced saving contributed to dampening inflationary pressures by mopping up private-sector purchasing power that would otherwise have gone into non-internationally traded goods — personal services, food distribution, and, above all, building and construction — and pushed up their prices. Changes in Central Provident Fund employee contributions were used to control private-sector purchasing power, and, in conjunction with National Wages Council "recommendations," to fine-tune Singapore's international wage competitiveness (Wong 1981; Hewson 1981; Lim 1982). High saving also helped to neutralize the expansionary effect of large inflows of foreign capital (Wong 1986; Sandilands 1992). However, the more important role of the high level of saving in macroeconomic management was to provide a noninflationary way to finance the three government-defined priorities of infrastructure, housing, and the accumulation of foreign reserves.

Insofar as the government "released" Central Provident Fund savings back into the domestic economy, purchasing power was directed toward the first two of these objectives. Workers' savings, and implicit taxation of them, enabled the government to avoid financing infrastructure development through high income taxes or, more important, through money creation. The refusal of the Singapore government to incur government deficits financed by borrowing from a central bank made possible continued adherence to a currency board system that itself promoted low inflation.

Government channeled part of forced saving into a program to increase home ownership. Beginning in 1968, individuals were allowed to make withdrawals at any time in their working life from compulsory Central Provident Fund savings to purchase homes, almost all of which the government built and sold at below-market prices. By 1990, 88 percent of households owned the houses they occupied compared to less than one-third in 1970 (Singapore, Department of Statistics 1983b, 1992). Home ownership was a government priority because of the social stability thereby promoted. The public housing program also allowed the PAP to manipulate electoral constituencies and disperse political opposition (Lim, Pang, and Findlay 1993: 125). In addition to housing, subsequent further liberalization of restrictions on the use of Central Provident Fund funds allowed withdrawals against spending on medical care, approved shares, and some educational expenses. Most of these expenditures are, in a broad sense, investment, not consumption.

The rapid gains in real wages (Table 3.3) and home ownership for Singaporeans induced acceptance of government wage control, which completed a "virtuous circle" of macroeconomic policy: low inflation, with consequent real exchange rate competitiveness, helped to ensure continued foreign capital inflows giving access to MNE technology and marketing, which made real wage gains possible. Furthermore, these gains were largely guaranteed, since Singapore citizens were almost assured of a job. The job security of Singapore nationals was, in part, underwritten through hosting up to 200,000 guest workers by the mid-1970s who could be sent home, and so bore much of the risk of unemployment in an economic downturn. In 1985, there was a net reduction of 96,000 jobs, but over three-fifths of those affected were foreign workers (Singapore, Ministry of Trade and Industry 1986b: 4).

7. Singapore and the East Asian Financial Crisis

The financial crisis in East Asia, which begin in mid-1997, unfolded as unexpectedly for Singapore as it did for everyone else. That its effects, by March 1998, were very much less severe for the Republic than for many East Asian countries may be traced in large part to the particular nature of Singapore's development. Even so, Singapore did not escape unaffected from the turmoil in East Asia.

The most important reason why Singapore differed from much of East Asia was the dominant role of foreign multinationals in its development model. In Thailand, Malaysia, South Korea, and Indonesia, local banks and firms, on the whole small and undiversified by international standards, had by 1997 contracted large amounts of short-term, U.S. dollar–denominated debt. The resources thus made available within these national economies, together with large foreign inflows of portfolio investment in rapidly expanding local stock markets, had the effect of dramatically bidding up real asset prices, a process further encouraged by historically high East Asian growth rates, and soon also taking on a dynamic of its own. But by August 1996 a slowing in Asian growth rates became apparent (*New York Times* 1996), and then, beginning with Thailand in July 1997, confidence in what had been seen as a remarkably successful East Asian growth model collapsed. International banks refused to renew loans and portfolio investment moved decisively out of East Asia, causing earlier asset price spirals to reverse catastrophically. At the same time, the withdrawal of international capital led to precipitate falls in the values of some East Asian currencies so that loan repayment in U.S. dollars became difficult if not impossible. By contrast, the foreign multinationals operating in Singapore either had not borrowed significantly to finance expansion there or insofar as they had borrowed were globally diversified and earned a substantial part of their profits in dollars so that the repayment of past borrowing posed no difficulties. Similarly, foreign banks had their base very largely outside Singapore and lent little to local Singaporean firms. An extreme reliance on foreign multinationals, which could be regarded as a weakness of the Singapore model, was also a considerable strength so long as the financial crisis remained confined to East Asia and did not spread to the West.

Nevertheless, Singapore's geographical location with Malaysia and Thailand immediately to the north and Indonesia to the south, its extremely open economy, and the international loss of confidence in East Asian development had a number of adverse effects, although it will not be possible to judge the full extent of these for some time. Certainly, Singapore's GDP growth rate, although 7.8 percent in 1997, will be reduced in 1998, perhaps by between three to as much as six percentage points (*Financial Times* 1998b, 1998c). Falling regional, and more important world, demand for the computer components that are the mainstay of Singapore's manufacturing sector seems likely to slow export growth and cause unemployment, although given the nature of the Singapore model many of those thrown out of work will be foreign workers.

The exposure of local Singapore banks to regional borrowers, and so to possible bad debt, is said to be 17.6 percent of total bank assets, and easily manageable. Singapore banks are likely to be further exposed, however, through loans to Singapore nationals who have invested in the region (*Financial Times* 1998a; *Straits Times Weekly* 1998a). It seems likely that some of Singapore's large foreign reserves, which together with its currency board system have helped to shield the Republic from regional financial contagion, would be used to support local banks should this become necessary. High reserves and the past refusal of the authorities to allow the Singapore dollar to become an internationally traded currency have served to limit a decline in its value in sympathy with falling currency values in much of East Asia. A prolonged fall in the Singapore dollar would threaten the low inflation rates basic to the Singapore model, but in the second half of 1997 inflation remained relatively modest (*Straits Times Weekly* 1998b).

The longer-term effects of events in East Asia necessarily remain speculative. Lee Kuan Yew's well-publicized assurance that the Asian model and in particular its accompanying "Asian values" are still sound indicates the importance that the Singapore government places on its credibility and reputation and on continued public confidence in the development model it has engineered (*Straits Times Weekly* 1997). The consequences for Singapore would be serious if low growth elsewhere in Asia continued dramatically to reduce growth in the Republic and, as a result, undermined confidence in government and its development model. Earlier analysis in this section suggests that this is unlikely.

A more real danger to the credibility of the Singapore model, although not one attributable to the East Asian financial crisis, would be a failure of Singapore's economy to move away from the factor-driven growth on which it has hitherto almost entirely depended and toward higher total factor productivity (TFP) growth (Young 1992, 1994, 1995; Krugman 1994). The latter would imply that growth was attributable to technical progress and allow the Republic to realize higher output from given quantities of capital and labor inputs. A failure to realize higher TFP growth than Singapore has hitherto recorded would bring a marked longer-term slowing in its growth rate, since labor force inputs are limited by population growth and levels of attainable education while capital inputs are constrained by the need to consume at least a proportion of national income. More important, investment of a much higher proportion of GDP than Singapore already invests probably means that diminishing returns drive the marginal product of capital to zero.

8.   Conclusion and Implications

The Singapore model is unlikely to be replicated elsewhere, including Caribbean countries (Griffith 1987), not only because the Republic is a city-state, but also because few others can develop services exports reliant on location, because of the unacceptability in many other polities of a heavy foreign economic presence, and because of difficulties in effecting the same degree of government control as in Singapore. When Milton Friedman looked at Singapore, he remarked that Lee Kuan Yew was a "benevolent dictator" and drew the lesson that "it is possible to combine a free private market economic system with a dictatorial political system" (1991: 12–13). But Singapore's experience was more subtle: its government used "dictatorial" means to make the "free market" work. There are, nevertheless, four main lessons to be adduced from Singapore's experience. If in a piecemeal fashion as opposed to an attempt to adopt a whole model, some of the lessons seem likely to prove useful to Caribbean policymakers.

One lesson is the positive role in economic development that extensive government intervention in selected sectors of the economy can play. Unable to influence the international economy, Singapore instead responded to international forces through manipulating the domestic economy. There, the PAP's control was total and, although replacing the price mechanism in fundamental respects, effective, because Singapore planners bore uppermost in mind international prices and costs. Wages were adjusted and kept to internationally competitive levels. As an institution, the National Wages Council compares with the national wage-fixing bodies championed for developed countries by J. Meade (1982). Likewise, the government replaced the market to force a high saving rate. Through taxation via the Central Provident Fund, the high MNE presence in Singapore was made to create an important fiscal linkage and conduce to continued economic development. Here, Singapore's experience is worthy of wider attention from all developing countries.

Second, Singapore illustrates the importance of investment in infrastructure and education. Both were paid for, in conjunction with government control of saving, by real resource transfers, not money creation, and so were not inflationary. Under these conditions, and due to concentration on sectors complementary to private investment, Singapore's public investment and infrastructural creation was consistent with "crowding in" not "crowding out." Singapore supports a case for planned capital accumulation and infrastructural investment to further the development process now being emphasized both by the new growth economists and those who attribute rapid East Asian growth chiefly to factor accumulation (Collins and Bosworth 1996).

Third, in an era of development theory whose practitioners are, even now, often wary, if not dismissive, of planning, Singapore is prominent as a country where economic planning, involving control over key macroeconomic variables and a systematic effort to coordinate public-sector investment decisions and attract private investment, succeeded. Singapore's planning, as Chakravarty (1991) noted of Japan and South Korea, accorded an important role to the market and to achieving growth through it. And, just as he observed that a discussion of "the market versus the Plan" offers too crude a dichotomy to explain what happened in Japan, South Korea, or Taiwan (Chakravarty 1987a: 137), so Singapore, within a continuum between these two extremes, had a distinct planning experience: it differed from the targeting and "governed markets" familiar in these other Asian countries (Boltho 1985; Amsden 1989; Wade 1990). Only internally could Singapore have features of a governed market since internationally Singapore, as a small country, is a price-taker. Singapore planners recognized the limitations of small size and extreme openness in departing from free trade to govern the market. Perhaps in this regard Singapore's brand of interventionism offers a more realistic pattern than the large East Asian NIC economies for developing countries in the Caribbean — tiny economically — which aim to become late industrializers.

Fourth, Singapore's experience suggests the weaknesses and limits of the kind of government control it exercised. Neither control over wages and subsidies to MNEs nor direction of savings delivered major technological gains in manufacturing, which, despite the importance of services in post-1979 growth and their likely future dominance, remains fundamental to the island's economy. A need to restructure the manufacturing sector, still low total factor productivity growth, and the danger that too-strong internal economic direction risks the loss of the substantial measure of consent from Singapore's population necessary for the long-term survival of any economic system are the three biggest problems faced by the Republic in the late 1990s. In comparison to these issues the Asian financial crisis dating from 1997 does not appear to pose difficulties of the same magnitude for Singapore and the continued success of its development model.

The chapter began by drawing attention to the need to examine more closely Singapore's development experience. Investigation of it consistent with such empiricism contradicts fundamentally neoclassical views and suggests a conclusion that might broadly be termed "neostructuralist." Principal themes in the Singapore model of economic development — government intervention and planning, industrialization, labor mobilization, and rapid capital accumulation — are what A. K. Sen (1983) identified as the core of development economics prior to a 1970s and 1980s neoclassical ascendance. In applying structuralist conclusions from the Singapore model to the Caribbean countries, however, specific country circumstances merit particular attention. The extreme smallness of many of these countries, both economically and in terms of population, often still low per capita incomes compared to Singapore in 1960, and the absence of its strong locational advantages offer less scope for development than Singapore had. Perhaps more important, wherever a lack of state capability exists, so too, in contrast to Singapore, the possibilities for effective state intervention in the domestic economy are similarly reduced.

Notes

1. Direct manufactured exports refer to goods not simply reexported, and exclude petroleum. Statistics for direct manufactured exports can be calculated from the sources for Table 3.2.

2. The main published planning documents in Singapore were Singapore, Ministry of Finance (1961), United Nations (1961), Singapore Economic Planning Unit (1964), Hon (1972), Singapore, Ministry of Trade and Industry (1981, 1986a), Singapore, Economic Planning Committee (1991), Singapore, National Science and Technology Board (1991), Singapore, SEP Working Group (1993).

References

Amsden, A. (1989). *Asia's Next Giant: South Korea and Late Industrialization*. New York: Oxford University Press.

Aschauer, D. A. (1989). "Does Public Capital Crowd Out Private Capital?" *Journal of Monetary Economics* 24: 171–88.

Benham, F. C. (1957). *Economic Survey Singapore 1957*. Singapore: Government Printing Office.

Benham, F. C. (1959). *The National Income of Singapore 1956*. London: Royal Institute of International Affairs.

Boltho, A. (1985). "Was Japan's Industrial Policy Successful?" *Cambridge Journal of Economics* 9(1): 187–201.

Bryant, R. C. (1985). "Financial Structure, and International Banking in Singapore." Brookings Discussion Papers, no. 29, Brookings Institution, Washington, D. C.

Chakravarty, S. (1987a). "The State of Development Economics." *Manchester School* 55(2): 125–43.

Chakravarty, S. (1987b). *Development Planning: The Indian Experience*. Oxford: Clarendon Press.

Chakravarty, S. (1991). "Development Planning: A Reappraisal." *Cambridge Journal of Economics* 15(1): 5–20.

Chew, S. B. (1988). *Small Firms in Singapore*. Singapore: Oxford University Press.

Chow, S. C. and G. F. Papanek (1981). "Laissez-Faire, Growth and Equity — Hong Kong." *Economic Journal* 91: 466–85.

Collins, S. M. and B. P. Bosworth (1996). "Economic Growth in East Asia: Accumulation versus Assimilation." *Brookings Papers on Economic Activity* (2): 135–203.

Corden, W. M. (1984). "Macroeconomic Targets and Instruments for a Small Open Economy." *Singapore Economic Review* 29(2): 27–37.

Disney, R. and S. K. Ho (1990). "Do Real Wages Matter in an Open Economy? The Case of Singapore, 1966–1987." *Oxford Economic Papers* 42: 635–57.

Financial Times (1973). "Growing Sophistication in the Financial Community (Singapore Survey)." 1 October.

Financial Times (1990). "Pressing Ahead with Privatisation (Singapore Survey)." 9 August.

Financial Times (1998a). "Singapore's Strengths Keep It From Turmoil." 6 February.

Financial Times (1998b). "Singapore Forecasts Slower Growth." 26 February.

Financial Times (1998c). "Backing for Singapore's Cautious Budget." 2 March.

Friedman, M. (1991). "A Welfare State Syllogism." Speech to the Commonwealth Club, San Francisco, June.

GATT (1993). *International Trade 1993 Statistics*. Geneva: author.

Giordano, R. and S. Kato (1993). "Singapore: The Most Successful 'Asian Dragon,'" *International Economics Analyst* (Goldman Sachs) 8(2): S.01–S.12.

Goh, K. S. (1970). "Decade of Achievement" (budget speech). Ministry of Culture, Singapore.

Goh, K. S. (1972). *The Asian*, 20 August.

Goh, K. S. (1992). "MNCs Brought Jobs and Sparked Change." *Straits Times Weekly*, August.

Griffith, Winston H. (1987). "Can CARICOM Countries Replicate the Singapore Experience?" *Journal of Development Studies* 24(1): 60–82.

Gurley, J. G. and E. S. Shaw (1967). "Financial Structure and Economic Development." *Economic Development and Culture Change* 15(3): 257–68.

Helleiner, G. K. (1973). "Manufactured Exports from Less-Developed Countries and Multinational Firms." *Economic Journal* 83: 21–47.

Hewson, J. C. (1981). "Monetary Policy and the Asian Dollar Market." Pp. 165–200 in *Monetary Authority of Singapore, Papers on Monetary Economics*. Singapore: Singapore University Press.

Hodjera, Z. (1978). "The Asian Currency Market: Singapore as a Regional Financial Centre." *IMF Staff Papers* 25(2): 221–53.

Hon, S. S. (1972). "Economic Pattern in the Seventies" (budget speech). Ministry of Culture, Singapore.

Hu, R. T. T. (1994). *Budget Statement 1994*. Singapore: Ministry of Information and the Arts.

Huff, W. G. (1994). *The Economic Growth of Singapore: Trade and Development in the Twentieth Century*. Cambridge: Cambridge University Press.

Huff, W. G. (1995). "The Developmental State, Government and Singapore's Economic Development Since 1960." *World Development* 23(8): 1421–38.

Islam, I. and C. Kirkpatrick (1986). "Export-Led Development, Labour Market Conditions and the Distribution of Income: The Case of Singapore." *Cambridge Journal of Economics* 10(2): 113–27.

Jao, Y. C. (1979). "The Rise of Hong Kong as a Financial Centre." *Asian Survey* 19(7): 674–94.

Jao, Y. C. (1985). "Hong Kong's Future as a Financial Centre." *Three Banks Review* 145 (March): 35–53.

Jones, L. P. and I. SaKong (1980). *Government, Business and Entrepreneurship in Economic Development: the Korean Case*. Cambridge, MA: Harvard University Press.

Keynes, J. M. (1980). *The Collected Writings of John Maynard Keynes*, D. Moggridge (ed.), volume 37: *Activities 1940–1946 Shaping the Post-War World: Employment and Commodities*. London: Macmillan.

Kim, S. P. (1992). "Singapore in 1991." *Asian Survey* 32(2): 119–25.

Krugman, P. (1994). The "Myth of Asia's Miracle." *Foreign Affairs* 73(6): 62–78.

Lee, H. L. (1986). "Singapore's Economic Policy: Vision for the 1990s." Speech at the Commonwealth Institute, London, January.

Lee, J. (1984). "How MAS Directs Singapore Inc.." *Euromoney* (September): 103–7.

Lee, S. Y. (1974). "Public Enterprise and Economic Development in Singapore." *Malayan Economic Review* 21(2): 49–73.

Lee, S. Y. (1986). "Developing Asian Financial Centres." Pp. 205–36 in *Pacific Growth and Financial Interdependence*, edited by A. H. H. Tan and B. Kapur. Sydney: Allen & Unwin.

Leong, M. K. (1971). *Wage Levels of Selected Countries*. Singapore: Ministry of Finance.

Lim, C. Y. (1982). "The N[ational] W[ages] C[ouncil] as I See It." In *Our Heritage and Beyond: A Collection of Essays on Singapore, its Past, Present and Future*, edited by S. Jayakumar. Singapore: National Trades Union Congress.

Lim, C. Y. and associates (1988). *Policy Options for the Singapore Economy*. Singapore: McGraw-Hill.

Lim, L. Y. C. and E. F. Pang (1984). "Labour Strategies and the High-Tech Challenge: the Case of Singapore." *Euro-Asia Business Review* 3(2): 27–31.

Lim, L. Y. C. and E. F. Pang (1986). *Trade Employment and Industrialisation in Singapore.* Geneva: ILO.

Lim, L. Y. C., E. F. Pang, and R. Findlay (1993). "Singapore." Pp. 93–139 in *Five Small Open Economies,* edited by R. Findlay and S. Wellisz. Oxford: Oxford University Press.

Low, L. (1984). "Public Enterprises in Singapore." Pp. 253–87 in *Singapore: Twenty-five Years of Development,* edited by P. S. You and C. Y. Lim. Singapore: Nan Yang Xing Zhou Lianhe Zaobao.

Low, L. (1988). "The Singapore Economy in 1987." *Southeast Asian Affairs* 15: 253–65.

Low, L., et al. (1993). *Challenge and Response: Thirty Years of the Economic Development Board.* Singapore: Times Academic Press.

Mason, E. S., et al. (1980). *The Economic and Social Modernization of the Republic of Korea.* Cambridge, MA: Harvard University Press.

Meade, J. E. (1982). *Stagflation.* Volume I: *Wage Fixing.* London: George Allen & Unwin.

Monetary Authority of Singapore (1991a). *Annual Report 1990/91.* Singapore: author.

Monetary Authority of Singapore (1991b). *Savings-Investment Balances in Singapore: Determinants and Medium-Term Outlook.* Singapore: Economics Department, Monetary Authority of Singapore.

Monetary Authority of Singapore (1992). *Annual Report 1991/92.* Singapore: author.

Monetary Authority of Singapore (1993). *Annual Report 1992/93.* Singapore: author.

Monetary Authority of Singapore (1994). *Annual Report 1993/94.* Singapore: author.

Monetary Authority of Singapore (1996). *Annual Report 1995/96.* Singapore: author.

New York Times (1996). "Export Growth Slows for Asia's Tiger Economies." 3 August.

Nolan, P. (1990). "Assessing Economic Growth in the Asian NICs." *Journal of Contemporary Asia* 20(1): 41–63.

O'Connor, M. (1966). "E[conomic] D[evelopment] B[oard] Plays a Vital Role in Industrial Finance." *Singapore Trade* (July): 37–38, 40, 48, 62–63.

Peebles, G. and P. Wilson (1996). *The Singapore Economy.* Cheltenham: Edward Elgar.

Rodrik, D. (1997). "The 'Paradoxes' of the Successful State." *European Economic Review* 41: 411–42.

Sandilands, R. J. (1992). "Savings, Investment and Housing in Singapore's Growth, 1965–90." *Savings and Development* 16(2): 119–43.

Saw, S.-H. (1984). *The Labour Force of Singapore (census monograph no. 3).* Singapore: Singapore National Printers.

Seah, R. (1986). "Statutory Boards: Tight Grip on a Hoard of Treasure." *Singapore Business* (February): 43–47.

Sen, A. K. (1983). "Development Economics: Which Way Now?" *Economic Journal* 93: 745–62.

Silcock, T. H. (1959). *The Commonwealth Economy in Southeast Asia.* Durham, NC: Duke University Press.

Singapore (1961). *Legislative Assembly Debates,* part 2 of second session, first Legislative Assembly, 24 May, cols. 1516–45.

Singapore (1963). *Legislative Assembly Debates,* vol. 22, no. 2, 28 November, col. 103.

Singapore (1964). *Census of Population 1957.* Singapore: Government Printer.

Singapore (1973). *Parliamentary Debates,* vol. 32, no. 10, February, col. 460.

Singapore, Department of Statistics (1978). *Report on the Census of Industrial Production 1978.* Singapore: Singapore National Printers.

Singapore, Department of Statistics (1981). *Yearbook of Statistics Singapore 1979/80*. Singapore: Singapore National Printers.

Singapore, Department of Statistics (1983a). *Economic and Social Statistics. 1960–1982*. Singapore: Singapore National Printers.

Singapore, Department of Statistics (1983b). *Census of Population 1980: Administrative Report*. Singapore: Singapore National Printers.

Singapore, Department of Statistics (1988). *Singapore National Accounts 1987*. Singapore: Singapore National Printers.

Singapore, Department of Statistics (1991). *Yearbook of Statistics 1990*. Singapore: Singapore National Printers.

Singapore, Department of Statistics (1992). *Singapore Census of Population 1990: Release 2. Households and Housing*. Singapore: Singapore National Printers.

Singapore, Department of Statistics (1993a). *Singapore Census of Population 1990: Release 4. Economic Characteristics*. Singapore: Singapore National Printers.

Singapore, Department of Statistics (1993b). *Yearbook of Statistics 1992*. Singapore: Singapore National Printers.

Singapore, Department of Statistics (1994). *Yearbook of Statistics 1993*. Singapore: Singapore National Printers.

Singapore, Department of Statistics (1996). *Singapore System of National Accounts 1995*. Singapore: Singapore National Printers.

Singapore, Department of Statistics (1997). *Yearbook of Statistics 1996*. Singapore: Singapore National Publishers.

Singapore, Economic Development Board (1992). *Report on the Census of Industrial Production 1990*. Singapore: Singapore National Printers.

Singapore, Economic Development Board (1993). *Yearbook 1992/93*. Singapore: Economic Development Board.

Singapore, Economic Development Board (1997). *Report on the Census of Industrial Production 1995*. Singapore: Singapore National Publishers.

Singapore, Economic Planning Committee (1991). *Strategic Economic Plan*. Singapore: Singapore National Printers.

Singapore, Economic Planning Unit (1964). *First Development Plan. 1961–1964: Review of Progress*. Singapore: Government Printing Office.

Singapore, Ministry of Finance (1961). *Development Plan 1961–1964*. Singapore: Government Printing Office.

Singapore, Ministry of Finance (1987). *Report of the Public Sector Divestment Committee*. Singapore: Singapore National Printers.

Singapore, Ministry of Finance, Trade Division (1970). *Annual Report 1969*. Singapore: Government Printing Office.

Singapore, Ministry of Labour (1993). *Report on Wages in Singapore 1992*. Singapore: Singapore National Printers.

Singapore, Ministry of Trade and Industry (1981). *Highlights of Singapore's Economic Development Plan for the Eighties*. Singapore: Curriculum Development Institute and Ministry of Trade and Industry.

Singapore, Ministry of Trade and Industry (1985). *Economic Survey of Singapore 1985 (second quarter)*. Singapore: Singapore National Printers.

Singapore, Ministry of Trade and Industry (1986a). *The Singapore Economy: New Directions (Report of the Economic Committee).* Singapore: Singapore National Printers.

Singapore, Ministry of Trade and Industry (1986b). *Economic Survey of Singapore 1985.* Singapore: Singapore National Printers.

Singapore, Ministry of Trade and Industry (1991). *Economic Survey of Singapore 1990.* Singapore: Singapore National Printers.

Singapore, Ministry of Trade and Industry (1993). *Economic Survey of Singapore 1992.* Singapore: Singapore National Printers.

Singapore, Ministry of Trade and Industry (1994). *Economic Survey of Singapore 1993.* Singapore: Singapore National Printers.

Singapore, Ministry of Trade and Industry (1997). *Economic Survey of Singapore 1996.* Singapore: Singapore National Publishers.

Singapore, National Science and Technology Board (1991). *Window of Opportunities: National Technology Plan 1991.* Singapore: Singapore National Printers.

Singapore, SEP Working Group (Ministry of Trade and Industry) (1993). *Implementation of the Strategic Economic Plan.* Singapore: Ministry of Trade and Industry.

Singapore Trade and Industry (1969a). "Hon Sui Sen: Key Man for New Era of Industrial Development." January: 44.

Singapore Trade and Industry (1969b). "Public Servant With a Talent For the Bold Plan, Wide Sweep." April: 8–14.

Song, B. N. (1990). *The Rise of the Korean Economy.* Hong Kong: Oxford University Press.

Straits Times Weekly (1990). "Singapore Needs 10 More Years to Become a More Mature Society" (interview with Lee Kuan Yew), 5 May.

Straits Times Weekly (1992a). "PM: Get Ready For the Super League Contest," 22 August.

Straits Times Weekly (1992b). "SIA Makes It To Ranks of World's Top Five Airlines," 24 October.

Straits Times Weekly (1997). "Asian Economic Model Still Sound," 20 December.

Straits Times Weekly (1998a). "No Danger of Banking Crisis, House Told," 17 January.

Straits Times Weekly (1998b). "Crisis Has Little Impact on Living Costs," 21 February.

Szezepanik, E. (1958). *The Economic Growth of Hong Kong.* London: Oxford University Press.

Taylor, L. (1991). *Income Distribution, Inflation and Growth: Lectures on Structuralist Macroeconomic Theory,* Cambridge, MA: MIT Press.

United Nations (1961). *A Proposed Industrialization Programme for the State of Singapore.* New York: UN Commission for Technical Assistance.

United Nations (1992). *World Investment Report 1992.* New York: United Nations Centre on Transnational Corporations.

United States, Department of Labor (1997). *International Comparisons of Hourly Compensation Costs for Production Workers in Manufacturing 1996* (USDL: 97-213). Washington DC: U. S. Department of Labor, Bureau of Labor Statistics.

United States Tariff Commission (1970). *Economic Factors Affecting the Use of Items 807.00 and 806.30 of the Tariff Schedule of the United States.* Washington D.C.: U.S. Tariff Commission.

Wade, R. (1990). *Governing the Market.* Princeton, NJ: Princeton University Press.

Wee, C. C. (1966). "Export — Singapore's New Road to Prosperity." *Singapore Trade and Industry* (August): 47, 50–54.

Wilson, Peter. (1995). "Sources of Economic Growth and Development in ASEAN." *Singapore Economic Review* 40(2): 237–53.

Wong, K. P. (1981). "The Financing of Trade and Development in the ADCs: The Experience of Singapore." Pp. 129–49 in *Trade and Growth of the Advanced Developing Countries,* edited by W. Hong and L. B. Krause. Seoul: Korea Development Institute.

Wong, K. P. (1986). "Saving, Capital Inflow and Capital Formation." Pp. 45–78 in *Singapore: Resources and Growth,* edited by C. Y. Lim and P. J. Lloyd. Singapore, Oxford University Press.

World Bank (1984). *World Development Report 1983.* Washington DC: author.

World Bank (1993). *The East Asian Miracle: Economic Growth and Public Policy (World Bank Policy Research Reports).* Oxford: Oxford University Press.

World Bank. (1997). *World Development Report 1997.* Oxford: Oxford University Press.

Young, A. (1992). "A Tale of Two Cities: Factor Accumulation and Technical Change in Hong Kong and Singapore." *NBER Macroeconomics Annual* 7.

Young, A. (1994). "Lessons From the East Asian NICs: a Contrarian View." *European Economic Review* 38(3/4): 964–73.

Young, A. (1995). "The Tyranny of Numbers: Confronting the Statistical Realities of the East Asian Growth Experience." *Quarterly Journal of Economics* 110(3): 641–80.

CHAPTER 4

Transition into Poverty

The Mongolian Experience, 1989–95[*]

Joe Remenyi

You must see that justice is done,
and must show kindness and mercy to one another.
Do not oppress widows, orphans...or anyone else in need.
And do not plan ways of harming one another.
Zechariah 7:9–10

1. Introduction

Transition in Mongolia began with the birth of perestroika in the former Soviet Union and the democracy movement in Eastern Europe in late 1989. The change wrought was peaceful and swift, despite the dramatic nature of the reforms ushered in. Mongolia's first multiparty elections to the Peoples' Great Hural were held on July 29, 1990, and a new constitution was enacted in February 1992. The new constitution restructured the legislative branch of government, creating a unicameral legislature, the State Great Hural (SGH; *hurals* are the elected representatives of the seventy-six-member national parliament). The SGH members, the first of whom was elected on June 28, 1992, are popularly elected by district for four-year terms. Local *hurals* are elected by the eighteen *aimags* (the twenty-one provinces outside the capital) plus the capital, Ulaanbaatar, and the cities of Darhan and Erdenet.[1]

These political reforms were brought into effect in a period of remarkable economic decline and widespread deprivation of the most basic needs, with the result that the terms "poverty" and "transition" are synonymous in Mongolia. Ever since the collapse of the central planning system and cut in the flow of funds from

---

* I acknowledge the debt I owe to my hosts in Ulaanbaatar, without whose generous advice and openness I would not have been able to write this chapter. In particular I would like to thank Mrs. Sodovyn Onon, Director, Poverty Alleviation Program Office, Ministry of Population, Policy & Labor, Ulaanbaatar, and Mr Mike Reynolds, Consultant to PAPO, World Bank, Ulaanbaatar.

the old Soviet bloc in 1989–90, Mongolia has been struggling to adjust to a regime of basic needs prices set by global markets instead of bureaucrats in the Kremlin or in Ulaanbaatar. As the exchange rate collapsed from less than 5 to more than 400 tugrik (the Mongolian monetary unit) to the U. S. dollar between 1989 and 1992, price trends saw the terms of trade shift radically against Mongolia, putting once affordable consumer imports of every conceivable type, including food and fuel, plus producer goods beyond the reach of all but the wealthiest or privileged Mongolian.

The history of Mongolia left the people in every part of the country vulnerable to the pain that has been associated with transition from a planned to a market economy. Mongolia became independent from China in 1921, and in 1924 followed the Soviet Union as only the second sovereign state to freely choose to become a communist People's Republic. In so doing Mongolia aligned itself with Soviet Russia, on which it was to become economically and politically dependent. Until early in 1990 the closest of economic and political ties between Mongolia and the Soviet Union delivered Mongolians a lifestyle and level of living that ran heavily in favor of Mongolia. However, over the two generations that this relationship existed, Mongolia evolved an economic structure based on import and export prices that were underwritten by nonsustainable implicit subsidies. Relative to world prices for what Mongolia exports, the Soviet bloc exchanged imports at prices that were politically but not economically justified. Hence, when the political power to deliver these subsidies disappeared, the transition to world prices was all the more shocking. Overnight, Mongolians found themselves thrown back to the horse and buggy days, with factories unable to operate for want of fuel oil for power, transport paralyzed for want of diesel, petrol, or gas, and yields in agriculture drastically reduced for want of imported fertilizer, chemical inputs, or spare parts for farm machinery. (Some indicators of the decline commonly shared are given by the official statistics in Table 4.1.)[2]

Table 4.1: *Indicators of Economic Decline, 1989–96*

	1989–91 (Average)	1992	1993–95 (Average)	1996
Cattle head (millions of head)	25.4	13.1	26.8	29.3
Wheat harvest (000s of tons)	607.1	25.7	209.6	215.3
Transported goods (millions of tons)	50.8	11.4	9.4	n.a.
Passengers transported (millions)	236.3	15.2	149.4	109.1

Source: Government of Mongolia (personal communication 1996).

2. Economic Priorities in Mongolia Before Transition

The glorious era of central planning in Mongolia was the fifty years from 1940 to 1990. The keystone to this strategy of economic management was the Treaty of Friendship and Mutual Assistance signed with the Soviet Union in 1946, which formed the basis for integrating the Mongolian economy into the Soviet planning system. This relationship delivered to Mongolia exceptionally favorable terms of trade, but it also severely undervalued capital, overvalued labor, and transferred technology at well below market rates. As a result Mongolia developed a "modern" sector that was exceptionally capital intensive for a capital-scarce economy. In order to support these new industries, Mongolia grew dependent on technical assistance and the location of large numbers of technical advisers from the Soviet bloc in Mongolia to guide and direct growth in the major supervising ministries responsible for industrial development. Hence, very little of Mongolia's modern sector was home-grown or founded on domestic human resource availability or know-how, but was acquired as imported turnkey projects from one or other Soviet bloc member. It is little wonder that on the eve of the collapse of the Soviet bloc and the cessation of the flow of subsidized capital, technology, and skilled personnel, more than 90 percent of Mongolia's trade was with Russia or the other economies in the Soviet bloc of centrally planned countries.[3]

Development priorities in Mongolia in the fifty years prior to 1990 had little to do with the creation of a modern work force of technically able workers or the delivery of domestically produced basic needs at falling real prices. In many respects, development in Mongolia had left the rural economy behind, influencing it in only the most ephemeral ways. The cheapness of imported fuel encouraged the nomadic herding folk, who account for the majority of the people in rural Mongolia, to use Soviet-built trucks instead of horses and camels to transport their gers (Mongolian felt tents) and possessions from site to site. But when fuel became unaffordable, they just as quickly abandoned their vehicles and returned to traditional modes of travel. Where development had a more profound effect was in the urban centers, especially in the three cities of Ulaanbaatar, Darkhan, and Erdenet. These centers became the focus of Stalinist-style high-rise apartment complexes that are the residences for Mongolians employed in the public sector administrations and production ministries, including mining. Priority in development investment was given to urban-based intermediate and capital goods industries and mining, much of the product of which was the core of Mongolia's modern sector exports. The viability of these industries was closely tied to continuing demand from traditional trading partners in the Soviet bloc, global trends in demand notwithstanding. Very little attention was given to the development of consumer goods industries or to the creation of value-adding capacity to process local agricultural production.

Because the pattern of development was very capital-intensive, very little of the investment in increased industrial capacity also resulted in significant industrial employment generation. What industrial employment was created was concentrated in the urban centers with little backward spill-over effects into the rural economy. In fact, prices received by rural producers for crop or livestock products barely altered in nominal terms for almost the whole of the three decades to 1990 and state rules dictated that all new industries should be government-owned "monopolies of significant size." Employment for those ready and able to work was guaranteed in these monopolies, on the state farms, or in the civil service. As a result, development priorities were not pressured by the need to create jobs because all who could work and wanted to work were provided with the opportunity to undertake paid employment, the resources for which came from the transfers of direct and indirect aid received through Mongolia's ties to the Soviet bloc. Hence, in contrast to many planned economies, in the years before 1990 Mongolia did not experience the evolution of a parallel "informal" economy or "floating population," as the Chinese terms it, to soak up the hidden or officially nonexistent unemployed. This also meant that nowhere in the Mongolian system was there a reservoir of experience with private sector activity or an understanding of the way in which the trade cycle or labor markets depend on the derived demand for commodities produced.

It is impossible to appreciate the unique structure of the Mongolian economy unless one realizes the extent of the isolation that separates markets and economic sectors across that huge country. Mongolia has less than 1,500 kilometers of paved road, only one north-south rail link, and the primary means by which trade and commerce between the capital city, Ulaanbaatar, and the provincial centers were connected was by airplane. After 1989, a goodly part of internal commerce ceased as subsidies to air transport were stopped or cut, or was transferred to the vagaries of draught power. Shortages of basic needs appeared in many populated areas across Mongolia, even on the largest state farms or urban-based factory communes. For the first time in more than two generations Mongolians came face to face with hunger, increasing rates of maternal death in childbirth, and families were forced to withdraw children from school.[4]

Overall, the development experience in Mongolia 1939–89 is a record of achievement that proved to be unsustainable. The Achilles heel of the strategy of development adopted was its dependence on an ongoing and increasing flow of subsidies that rendered the cost of capital unrealistically low. The industries established and the technologies transferred into Mongolia on the basis of these artificially low factor price ratios resulted in returns to capital that were similarly low and clearly not competitive with those relevant in the open markets of Europe, North America, or Asia. In time the total value of Mongolia's imports plus exports came to exceed its GDP, which was fine as long as someone else was there to finance the resource gap. With the collapse of the Soviet Union and the cessation of aid flows into Mongolia, the strategy was permanently undone. Unfortunately, for average Mongolian citizens this undoing also meant a loss of the resource flows that had enabled them to enjoy levels of health care (life expectancy had improved from less than fifty years in 1960 to more than sixty years in 1990, attributable in large part to the successful extension of primary health care to virtually the entire population, almost all babies are immunized, and the abolition of malnutrition), education (literacy is virtually universal in Mongolia and average years of schooling is around seven years for both males and females), good nutrition levels (based in part on cheap imported foods), and access to other basic needs (two-thirds of the population have access to potable water, clothing was cheap because import prices were artificially low, etc.), well above those that could be supported by domestic productivity alone.[5]

3.   Poverty Trends in Mongolia

Socialism, extensively subsidized by transfers from trading partners within the Soviet bloc, had delivered to Mongolians a level of living that had banished poverty and unemployment from the land. Everyone, from the highest official to the least among the orphans and the disabled, had ready access to the basic needs of food, clothing, shelter, and health for daily living. The differences between rich and poor were slight, but the rewards for initiative and success were no more present than the penalties for laziness and the lack of these virtues. The result was an economy set in a comfortable but low-level equilibrium trap, seriously out of step with global trends in technology, energy prices, the commercial parameters of international trade, and political trends in competition between East and West. It is not surprising, therefore, that the transition that has been forced on Mongolia since 1989 has been painful and colored by nostalgia for the comfort zones of the past.

Prior to 1990, frictional unemployment excepted, there was no unemployment in Mongolia, nor were there "street kids," rampant petty crime, or a rising tide of homeless and hungry people, children included, for whom malnutrition and begging is now a fact of daily life. Since 1989 these have become more commonplace than Mongolians find acceptable. The government of Mongolia has instituted a National Poverty Alleviation Program in response to increased poverty, with the express intention to establish a new regime in which the causes of these same symptoms of poverty can again be banished from the land, but this time in a sustainable manner. In large measure, therefore, the national poverty alleviation program is one and the same as structural adjustment to the dislocations of transition from the former subsidized central planning priorities to the current globalized parameters in which prices and priorities are largely determined by world market pressures. It is appropriate, therefore, that we should spend some time examining the course of poverty trends in Mongolia in recent years.[6]

Some of the main macroeconomic trends and key indicators of poverty for Mongolia are summarized in the tables that follow. However, prior to examining these more closely, a word of warning. Data on the Mongolian economy or social trends are not only scarce but must be regarded as, at best, rubbery "guesstimates." The figures for the years prior to 1990 suffer from conversions at exchange rates that history has proven to bear little relationship to the underlying productive capacity of the economy. Moreover, Mongolia retains a significant subsistence sector and a large public sector. It is not clear that the data available are a true reflection of output or employment levels in these sectors. It is almost inevitable that the reactions of decision-makers within these sectors have included steps to cushion the impact of transition in ways that have created a degree of hidden unemployment, significant increases in underemployment, and the transfer of assets into the private sector at prices that have been described in conversations with officials as "favorable" to the beneficiaries. Nonetheless, the basic trends in major macroeconomic indicators are discernible, significant gaps in the data shown in the following tables notwithstanding.

The collapse in macroeconomic growth 1990–93 is shown in the data in Table 4.2. Although there has been some recovery since 1993, national income and income per person remain at not more than a quarter of what they were in the years immediately prior to 1990. Population increase has declined as income per head has fallen, though the shift to urban living has not abated. Depreciation in the exchange rate has continued, but at a decreasing rate as inflation has come down, investment has recovered, and the balance of trade has improved. For many Mongolians, however, life remains difficult and especially so for those who now find themselves unemployed in an economy where expenditures on social services by the government are minimal, at around 10 percent of GDP in the five years 1989–94.

Trends in the structure of the Mongolian economy are explored in Table 4.3. Because of the continuing importance of subsistence production, especially in the nomadic sector of Mongolian society, agriculture contributed only around one-fifth to GDP in 1994. Nonetheless, this represented a small increase in productivity as the share of the work force active in agriculture fell from 40 percent in 1980 to 32 percent in 1994. However, virtually the whole of the shift in employment was absorbed by the tertiary sector, with employment in industry remaining at less than a quarter of the work force. The contraction in economic activity in the early 1990s saw exports halved in nominal terms, but the fall in domestic production fell even faster, with the result that exports as a share of GDP increased from an average of 25 percent in 1989–90 to 50 percent in 1993–94. The resource gap between savings and investment also moved in a similar

Table 4.2: Trends in Population and Income, and Economic Activity, Mongolia, 1980–98

	1980	1989	1990	1991	1992	1993	1994	1995	1996	1997	1998
Population (millions)	2.00	2.10	2.15	2.19	2.22	2.25	2.28	2.32	2.35	2.4	2.5
Aged 15–64 years	1.00	n.a.	n.a.	n.a.	n.a.	n.a.	1.00	n.a.	n.a.	n.a.	0.8
Urbanization (%)	52.1	n.a.	58.0	n.a.	n.a.	n.a.	60.3	n.a.	n.a.	62.0	n.a.
Unemployment (000s of persons)	0.0	0.0	n.a.	55.4	54	71	74.9	45.1	55.4	n.a.	150.0
GDP											
$US, billions	2.33	3.59	2.24	1.76	1.08	0.62	0.74	0.78	0.80	.86	n.a.
$US, per capita	1686.3	1712.0	1042.0	803.0	487.0	430.9	320.0	335.0	338.4	330.3	n.a.
Annual increase (%)											
GDP	5.7[a]	4.2	−2.5	−9.2	−9.5	−3.0	2.3	6.3	2.6	3.3	3.5
GDP per capita	n.a.	1.5	−5.2	−11.5	−11.5	−4.9	0.6	4.7	1.0	1.2	1.4
Investment (Tg billion)	n.a.	4.8	3.4	4.0	5.3	45.2	62.2	91.5	102.4	n.a.	n.a.
Inflation rate (%)	0.0	0.0	52.7	208.6	321.0	183.0	145.0	75.0	53.2	23.8	6.5
Exchange rate (Tg/$US)	n.a.	3.0	4.3	8.0	35.8	294.4	465.0	n.a.	830.0	1240.0	n.a.
Exports ($US millions)	442.7	721.5	660.7	348.0	388.4	382.6	356.1	473.3	422.9	461.0	n.a.
Imports ($US millions)	n.a.	963	924	360	418.3	379	258.4	415.3	438.3	503.0	n.a.

[a] 1981–89.

Sources: National Poverty Alleviation Program Office, Ulaanbaatar; UNDP (1996); World Bank (1996); World Bank (1999).

Table 4.3: *Trends in Structure of the Economy, Mongolia, 1980–1998*

	1980	1989	1990	1991	1992	1993	1994	1997	1998
Distribution of GDP (%)									
Agriculture	14.0	16.8	17.0	17.4	31.9	28.0	21.0	n.a.	32.9
Industry	28.0	31.9	33.1	27.2	35.0	35.1	45.0	n.a.	27.5
Services	57.0	51.3	49.9	55.4	33.1	36.9	34.0	n.a.	39.6
Exports	19.0	20.1	29.5	19.8	35.9	61.7	48.1	54.6	n.a.
GD Investment	46.2		42.3				20.9	22.4	n.a.
GD Savings	27.0						15.0	21.9	n.a.
Government consumption	>50[a]						14	n.a.	n.a.
Government expenditure	>50[a]						17.4	n.a.	n.a.
Labor force (%) in									
Agriculture	40.0		32.0				32	n.a.	n.a.
Industry	21.0		22.0				23	n.a.	12.0
Services	39.0		46.0				46	n.a	n.a.

[a] Personal estimate.
Sources: National Poverty Alleviation Program Office, Ulaanbaatar; World Bank (1996; 1995; 1994); Wu (1994); World Bank (1999).

direction, despite a massive fall in investment activity. The period 1990–93 was one of dis-saving, in which the private, public, and social capital of the nation was not only not maintained but declined in absolute and relative terms, no matter how measured. In an attempt to arrest the decline, external debt was increased from negligible levels to near 10 percent of GDP in 1994, and bank interest rates were allowed to climb into three-digit levels, as reflected in Table 4.4.

Table 4.4: Trends in Structure of the Economy, Mongolia, 1980–97

	1980	1990	1992	1994	1997
Nominal bank deposit rate (% annual)	< 6.0	18.0	> 70.0	92.3	n.a.
Nominal bank lending rate (% annual)	<12.0	<60.0[a]	<240.0[a]	233.6	n.a.
External debt ($US millions)	0.0			443.0	718.0
Debt Service Ratio (%)	0.0			9.6	9.7

[a] Personal estimate.
Sources: National Poverty Alleviation Program Office, Ulaanbaatar; World Bank (1994, 1995, 1996, 1999).

The data in Tables 4.2–4.4 plus those in Table 4.5 present a picture of economic and social deterioration, especially in the years 1989 through 1993. It is a picture of an economy that is small by international standards, complicated by the geographic spread that the economy must service. Even in the three principal cities of Mongolia, which account for almost one-half of the whole population, the size of the market and the capacity to buy are severely limited by demographic structure and the pervasiveness of poverty. Agriculture, much of which remains subsistence in focus, is still an important source of income and employment. However, the services sector includes significant remnants of the government

Table 4.5: *Poverty Trends in Mongolia, 1980–97*

	1989	1990	1992	1993	1994	1997
Total population below poverty line (%; head count index)	<1	n.a.	16.0	018.0	26.5	36.3
Poverty line (Tg/head/month)						
Urban	n.a.	n.a.	345.0	3200.0	3200.0	n.a.
Rural	n.a.	n.a.	216.0	2900.0	2900.0	n.a.
Mortality ratios (per 1000 live births)						
Maternal	1.7	1.2		2.4		
Infant	61.0			72.0	53	52
Life expectancy at birth (years)	60	60	n.a.	n.a.	64	66
Population with access to potable water (%)	n.a.	n.a.	n.a.	66	n.a.	n.a.

Sources: PAPO; World Bank (1995, 1996, 1999).

parastatal structure from pre-1990, so there is little hope that the tertiary sector can be a key source of job creation in the immediate future. New employment and productivity gains in agriculture, industrial production, processing of rural produce, and mining output are where the serious gains in value added must be made before the services sector can be expected to deliver rates of return that can bear the cost of capital.

Table 4.6: *Change in Sources of Household Income, 1989 and 1993*

Sources of Household Income (%)	1989	1993
Urban		
Cash	100.0	97.0
Subsistence/barter	–	3.0
Wife's salary	< 5	20.0
Rural		
Cash	>70	65
Subsistence/barter	<30	35.0
Wife's salary	<10	12.0

Source: PAPO.

The costs of transition are reflected in the deterioration that Mongolia has experienced in the exchange rate, its soaring rate of inflation, expanding gross margins between deposit and lending rates at the banks, rising head count index, and deteriorating social indicators, including mortality rates, alcoholism, petty crime, and school truancy.[7] These trends have had two contrary effects. First, a significant proportion of the economically active population has reverted to subsistence activity and barter trade, especially in the rural areas and among the unemployed in the urban centers (see Table 4.6).[8] Second, Mongolians who are forced to live in the monetized world for employment and access to basic needs have had to learn to adjust to circumstances of inflation and rising interest rates of which they have had no prior experience or knowledge. This is especially so of the nascent and newly privatized banking system, which is concentrating its activities in ways that protect its assets but disenfranchise the poorer households and smaller enterprises. Mongolia has become an economy in which the excess demand for working capital is so great that the margin between deposit and lending rates has exploded to match the inflation rate.

The collapse in income per head from more than US$1,700 to not much more than US$300 in only five years is dramatic in anyone's terms. The fall cannot be divorced from the cessation of aid flows into Mongolia that aid from the Development Assistance Council of the OECD (DAC) members has not replaced. The level of aid flowing into Mongolia prior to the collapse in 1990–91 has been officially estimated at around one-third of Mongolia's GDP. If one took that same level of aid as a proportion of Mongolia's GDP in 1994, it would amount to about three-quarters of current GDP. This is consistent with Boone's (1993) estimate that the withdrawal of Soviet and COMECON assistance resulted in a decline in national purchasing power in Mongolia, 1989–91, of almost 62 percent. Tied to the Soviet economy, Mongolia had become one of the most aid-dependent economies in the world. Its present transition and struggle with poverty is not, therefore, only a process of transition from a socialist planned economy to a market economy, but also from an aid-dependent economy to one that is self-reliant and finds its future in the productive use of its substantial natural and human resources.

The cessation of the flow of resources from abroad left Mongolia in a very difficult economic position. The degree of difficulty was exacerbated by the fact that the aid from Russia stopped in a year when the world prices for wool, a major export commodity for Mongolia, and wool products were at historical lows. Massive global stockpiles of wool, dramatic declines in traditional markets for wool (such as the demand from the former Soviet bloc), and increased competition in the market for knitted products (especially from cotton producers and manufacturers) meant that Mongolia could find little relief in nontraditional world markets for its wool. Similarly, the market for meat, livestock, and livestock products was not especially buoyant, but the prices for essential imports, especially oil- and petroleum-based products, had to increase severely in order to equalize with the prices that had become internationally "normal" in the wake of OPEC-led energy price rises inherited from the 1970s but not reflected in the barter terms of trade applied to Mongolia within COMECON. Transition in Mongolia is about coming to terms with these new price relatives at terms of trade that are very mush less favorable than existed prior to perestroika.

Mongolia is showing signs of adjustment and economic recovery, evident in the macroeconomic statistics for 1994 and beyond, shown in Tables 4.2–4.5.

These signs of recovery are yet to be reflected in the unemployment statistics, and the increase in foreign indebtedness appears to be controlled and appropriate to an economy of the size and export potential (in the mining sector) of Mongolia. Nonetheless, it is a worry that capital outflow from Mongolia continues to exceed capital inflow on an annual basis, despite a significant increase in the inflow of official development assistance into Mongolia from bilateral donors, the multilateral banks, and private development agencies. This inflow reached almost one-quarter of GDP in 1995, but at this level it is still well below what had been incoming at the height of the assistance flows from the Soviet bloc.[9]

The progress of poverty in Mongolia had achieved crisis proportions by the end of 1992. In 1990 Mongolia was ranked 88th out of 100 countries by the United Nations Development Program (UNDP) Human Development Index. In 1993 Mongolia's ranking had declined to 100th out of 173 countries, and in the 1995 Human Development Report it had slipped to 110th out of 174 countries. By 1994 the head count index, as measured by the percentage of the population with incomes below the poverty line, has exceeded one-quarter of the population. Households were increasingly dependent on the income earning capacity of all members of the family, but especially the female spouse. As the purchasing power of government pensions deteriorated with the progress of inflation into triple-digit territory, those on pensions found themselves forced back into the work force or in need of assistance from family and friends.

The seriousness of the economic deterioration was reflected in the increase in maternal and infant mortality rates between 1989 and 1994. Mongolians had come to expect mortality rates of children and mothers in childbirth to continue to fall and they were proud that these indicators of well-being were already below those for other countries at a similar stage of development. To see them rise was a shock to many inside and outside public sector employment.

If economic transition is to really begin in Mongolia and if the symptoms of worsening poverty are to be reversed, it is essential that the signs of economic recovery evident in the macroeconomic data for 1994 should materialize into significant further improvements in the rate of economic growth, a lower pace of inflation, less punitive interest rates, greater competitiveness of Mongolian industries, and increases in the rate at which job opportunities are created. However if this is to happen, then government interventions, and especially those intended to directly target poverty, should be founded on a clear understanding of the causes of poverty and the survival strategies of the poor.

What follows is an attempt to contribute to our understanding of the structure of poverty in Mongolia and the nature of the survival activities of households that find themselves below the poverty line. Consider the conceptual framework of poverty in Mongolia presented in Figure 4.1.

The structure of poverty in a country like Mongolia can be conceived as

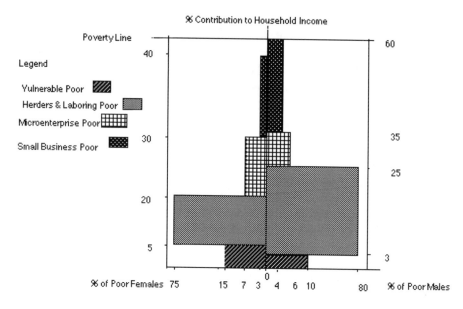

Figure 4.1: *An indicative gender-specific poverty pyramid for Mongolia. A conceptual framework for an audit of constraints to escape from poverty.*

forming a pyramid, the shape and structure of which is a useful framework to use for an economic activity–focused "audit" of poverty. The poverty pyramid framework is described in Remenyi (1991, 1993, 1994a, 1994b, 1995). The pyramid presented here is purposefully gender sensitive, to indicate awareness of the differential impact of poverty on females and their separate role in household survival strategies.

The poverty pyramid shows the least productive and most vulnerable of the poor at the bottom, with successively more productive strata of survival activities above them, reaching up to and then beyond the poverty line. The gender-specific poverty pyramid for Mongolia presented in Figure 4.1 is impressionistic and based on a limited amount of "rapid appraisal" data collection in the course of discussions and interviews in Mongolia in September 1995. The numbers assigned to each stratum are "informed guesstimates," based on responses made by persons who are knowledgeable and have lived through the transition from socialism to a limited free-market economy, 1989–95. Hence, while I have confidence that the figures shown in Figure 4.1 are likely to be in the right ballpark, they are intended to be indicative as opposed to conclusive. At this time I am not aware of any data that would allow one to be more statistically authoritative. However, feedback derived from consultations with development workers in Mongolia, civil servants responsible for various aspects of the Mongolian National Poverty Alleviation Program, and academic colleagues suggests that the characterization and the percentages shown in Figure 4.1 do not do such violence to their perceptions of the state of poverty in Mongolia as to render this picture wholly inaccurate or useless for the appreciation of the poverty problem in Mongolia.

Let us consider the structure of Figure 4.1 in closer detail. The poverty line marks the upper boundary of the poverty pyramid. The vertical axis shows the estimated contribution of each stratum to total household income, and the horizontal axis indicates the estimated proportion of males and females who are involved in the survival activities at each stratum.

The vulnerable poor make up the lowest stratum and include those poor people whose primary source of daily survival is not the earnings of their own efforts, but the earnings of others. Hence they are the true "vulnerable" poor, because they are so dependent. This stratum includes children, the old, and the disabled. In Mongolia we can take it that the vulnerable poor are largely synonymous with those persons who are defined in the statistics as the "very poor," i.e., those who belong to households that have an average income per person that is only 40 percent of the income defined as the poverty line. Their vulnerability derives not only from their low income, but also from the lack of income-generating opportunities of this group, their susceptibility to illness because of the circumstances in which they live, and their desperate lack of assets that might be liquidated to create a base on which to build a new and better life. It is also the vulnerable poor who are often the most deprived of even rudimentary standards of basic needs. Their malnutrition, their lack of access to potable water, their vulnerability to sickness because of poor sanitation, and their divorce from social networks of assistance because they are homeless, otherwise displaced, or separated from traditional sources of social security make their escape from poverty without assistance extremely difficult. The assistance the vulnerable poor require to remove the constraints that keep them poor includes immediate income and asset transfers to lessen the desperation of their plight, plus longer-term investments in the social overhead capital available to them and their human resource development that will make them more able to maintain good health, increase their income earning opportunities, reestablish their links to the institutional foundations of income and wealth creation in their communities, and facilitate their ability to accumulate productive assets. Strategic public works expenditures in potable water facilities, schools, basic health centers, leisure centers, or public facilities for emergency storage or shelter and communications can be the key to open a new world of opportunities and prosperity for the vulnerable poor.

The largest stratum of the poverty pyramid in terms of persons and households is that covering subsistence production by herders and rural or urban persons whose principal source of economic survival is the sale of their labor for cash or in-kind wages. The number of people in this stratum cannot be reduced unless the productivity of the survival activities of its members is increased. The challenge is to identify those factors that prevent the economic activities of people in the herder and laboring poor stratum from being more valuable. If the constraint to increased productivity in herding and laboring is technological, as it might be in the case of cropping, livestock raising, horticulture, or the processing of rural output, then the solution is clear. The root cause of why these people stay poor will not be overcome until they are:

- assisted to find a better and more profitable set of technologies;
- encouraged to adopt new and possibly unfamiliar economic activities, in order to diversify the base of household production;
- given the opportunity to increase their stock of marketable skills; or
- guided in the identification of ways to improve the effectiveness with which existing household assets, including cash savings and surplus labor power available in the winter months, are used to generate an improved standard of living.

It is a mistake to believe that the solution to the poverty of the herders and laboring poor is essentially technological, though it may be for a significant proportion. For many of the people in this stratum their escape from poverty is dependent upon finding a way to migrate out of this stratum and into the micro-enterprise and small business stratum, eventually to climb beyond the poverty line altogether. Self-employment in a microenterprise that can sustain a higher own-wage may well be an option, if only the constraints that have thus far prevented those who might take this route out of poverty can be identified and overcome. Where this constraint is access to credit for productive investment purposes, it is essential to examine why the existing agencies of lending have not filled the void. Often the result will be a finding that the private commercial banks (PCBs) are not suited to the task and are unable to respond as required because of the structure of their transactions costs and their inability to manage the risk associated with a credit and savings program for the poor. It is my impression that in Mongolia it is indeed the case that the PCBs are inappropriate agencies for undertaking "banking with the poor," but there is also a dearth of experienced NGOs in Mongolia willing and able to fill this gap. PAPO may wish to explore the options available to address this apparent failure in the market for financial services to operate efficiently. A domestic solution could be to encourage the creation of a nonbank financial intermediary sector targeted at the poor that can nurture links to the PCBs, or to find ways to encourage the PCBs to adapt their banking practices to accommodate the financial servicing of poor households for income generation and wealth creation.

The top two strata of the poverty pyramid for Mongolia describe what can be characterized as "the flavors of the month" in international development circles. Nonetheless, despite their high rankings in the popularity stakes, it remains the case that both microenterprise development and small business development are still poorly understood strategies for sustainable poverty alleviation among most practitioners and NGOs. This is no less true in Mongolia, a fact that is reflected in what appears to be an uniformly poor record of the ten or so credit-based microenterprise and small business expansion projects that have been launched here since 1989. This is to be regretted because programs that assist with microenterprise development, small business development, and microfinance can form the crux of pivotal strategies of sustainable poverty reduction and transition to market based self-reliance.[10]

As with the lower strata, the critical questions are always similar: What prevents those already in the microenterprise or small business stratum from being more productive so as to tip them above the poverty line? What prevents more people from lower strata migrating up into these strata and then on to higher levels of household income? For the government of Mongolia the questions must be: Are the provisions of the National Poverty Alleviation Program (NPAP) targeted at these constraints? Can the provisions of the NPAP be sharpened so as achieve more effective targeting? It is important for successful poverty reduction and a smooth transition to greater market-based self reliance that the ongoing monitoring and evaluation program associated with the various components of the NPAP should result in a flow of information that will enable those responsible for the implementation and management of NPAP to answer these questions in a constructive and a pragmatic manner. But ultimately, poverty reduction cannot succeed unless the causes of poverty are addressed effectively.

4. Summary

Mongolia is a land of contrasts. Its vast open plains and mountains are home to an internationally famous nomadic culture that now embraces less than half the population. Mongolia is becoming ever more an urban society — not a traditional nomadic one. The Mongolian countryside is both beautiful and rugged, the sort of place that has apparent potential as the basis of a highly profitable and unique foreign tourism industry, but the harsh and unforgiving quality of the isolation and the changeable weather make it difficult to exploit this potential by opening up the land to the volume market of innocent and unwary travelers.

Macroeconomic statistics indicate that Mongolia is economically poor, but it has a rich culture that less than a millennium ago conquered almost all of the known world. Despite the very disturbing increase since 1990 in the number of people below the poverty line, Mongolia is rich in natural resources (current levels of minerals exports amount to more than US$100 per person per year) and the people boast one of the highest literacy rates in the Third World. Why, then, has the blight of poverty come to scourge Mongolia? Is there a way out?

In order to answer these questions one must acknowledge the importance of history. For almost the whole of this century, Mongolia has been closely aligned with the old Soviet bloc of socialist economies. Long-term economic transfers from Russia and the other members of COMECON, as direct aid but especially as a result of exceedingly favorable terms of trade for the commodities that Mongolia exported relative to those it imported caused the Mongolian economy to take on a structure that was not sustainable after the break-up of the USSR and the collapse of COMECON.

The economic restructuring that has followed the abandonment of the socialist way and the opening up of the Mongolian economy to global markets and the discipline of the forces of supply and demand in the selection of development priorities has not been easy. Mongolia could no longer afford the old ways. Mongolian socialism had relied heavily on government paternalism and leadership, fostering a reluctance on the part of individuals to take initiatives and follow the paths of self-help and self-reliance. Hence, a significant part of the "transition" that has to be nurtured by the NPAP and other government structural adjustment assistance programs in Mongolia must be about giving people "permission" to be innovative and to take risks, where this is essential. Mongolians have to learn a new way of responding to a new set of signals, a process that requires government to encourage its citizens to confidently pursue their own self-interest in areas where the discipline of market forces is intended to replace government and its agencies of central planning.

Notes

1. The modern history of Mongolia is yet to be written, but in the course of research for this chapter I have garnered details of recent political and economic history from various articles on the Internet plus a number of unpublished reports in the files of the World Bank, United Nations Development Program, and the Mongolian Poverty Alleviation Program Office in Ulaanbaatar, including Boone (1993), Story (1993), Goldstein and Beall (1994), Griffin et al. (1994), Harper (1994), World Bank (1994, 1995a, 1995b), Wu (1994), Ebdon et al. (1995), and Swift (1995).

2. In addition to the statistics in Table 4.1, Boone (1993) and Wu (1995) concur in my estimate that the cessation of aid flows from the Soviet bloc reduced national income in Mongolia by at least 50 percent in 1990–91.

3. The unsustainable structure of Mongolia's "modern" industry sector prior to 1990 is described in Goldstein and Beall (1994) and World Bank (1994, 1995b).

4. It was the deterioration in these social indicators of declining quality of life that prompted the adoption of a national poverty alleviation program and the establishment of a national poverty alleviation program office, commonly referred to in Ulaanbaatar by its acronym, PAPO. See GoM (1994), Harper (1994), and PAPO (1994, 1995) plus note 2.

5. See GoM (1994), PAPO (1994), UNDP (1996), and World Bank (1995a, 1995b, 1996).

6. See GoM (1994); and PAPO (1994, 1995).

7. While there are no statistics available to document trends in truancy, alcoholism, and petty crime, the perception of local officials and a broad cross section of people the author met while in Ulaanbaatar in September 1995 was that these are the areas of social life that have suffered most as poverty spread across the land and deepened in intensity. The gross primary school enrollment rate deteriorated from an average of 92 percent of the eligible age group in 1980–85 to 82 percent in 1989–94. See World Bank (1996).

8. Data collected by the National PAPO in Ulaanbaatar for 1989 and 1993 showed barter increasing in both urban and rural households. In addition, reliance on earnings of the wife also increased, especially among urban households. Statistics for the years since 1993 are not available, but those for 1989 and 1993 are summarized in Table 4.6.

9. See Boone (1994) and World Bank (1994, 1995a, 1995b, 1996).

10. The time is ripe for an in-depth, discrete research program that examines the record of these experiences and shares the results with cooperators and the community of agencies that may wish to enter this field in the future. It would not be inappropriate for PAPO to sponsor such a research program, though the results are likely to be better received if the task can be contracted out by the interested parties (Asian Development Bank, International Fund for Agricultural Development, PAPO, Save the Children's Fund, UNDP, United Nations International Program for Women, United States Agency for International Development, World Bank, etc.), to independent researchers external to the agencies currently involved in such programs. Funding could be taken from the technical assistance budget that most agencies include in their projects and that is intended to facilitate quality control, monitoring, and evaluation. A related question would be the replicability of a Grameen Bank style program in Mongolia, which I venture to suggest would need to begin with savings mobilization rather than credit disbursement. There is an increasing stream of relevant literature on these matters, among which I would suggest that interested readers should consult, e.g., Gibbons and Kasim (1990), Hulme (1990), Colter and Suharto (1993), Getubig (1993), Marx (1994), Rutherford (1995), Todd (1996), and Getubig, Remenyi, and Quinones (1997).

References

Boone, P. (1993). *Grassroots Macroeconomic Reform in Mongolia.* Mimeo. Boston: Harvard Institute for International Development.

Colter, J. M. and P. Suharto (1993). "Grameen Bank in Indonesia: Impact on Karya Usaha Mandiri." Report prepared for the Indonesian Banking Development Institution, Jakarta. Seremban, Malaysia: Cashpor Inc. (reprint).

Ebdon, R., et al. (1995). "Draft Report of PRA Workshop on Poverty Alleviation." Mimeo, Chuluut Sum, Arkhangai, 28–30 September, Centre for Social Development, IAMD, Ulaanbaatar.

Getubig, I., ed. (1993). *Overcoming Poverty Through Credit: The Asian Experience in Replicating the Grameen Bank Approach.* Kuala Lumpur: APDC.

Getubig, I., J. Remenyi, and B. Quinones, eds. (1997). *Creating the Vision: Microfinancing the Poor in Asia-Pacific: Issues Constraints and Capacity Building.* Kuala Lumpur: Asia Pacific Development Centre.

Gibbons, D. S. and S. Kasim (1990). "Banking on the Rural Poor in Peninsular Malaysia." Final report of Project Amanah Ikhtiar Malaysia.

Kuala Lumpur: APDC and University Sains Malaysia Goldstein, M. C. and C. M. Beall (1994). *The Changing World of Mongolia's Nomads.* Hong Kong: Odyssey.

Government of Mongolia (GoM) (1994). "Poverty Alleviation Program." Mimeo, June, Ulaanbaatar.

Griffin, K., et al. (1994). "Poverty and the Transition to a Market Economy in Mongolia." Report of a UNDP Mission to the Government of Mongolia (mimeo of final draft). April, Ulaanbaatar.

Harper, C. (1994). "An Assessment of Vulnerable Groups In Mongolia." World Bank Discussion Paper #229: Strategies for Social Policy Planning. Washington DC: World Bank.

Hulme, D. (1990). "Can the Grameen Bank Be Replicated? Recent Experiments in Malaysia, Malawi and Sri Lanka." *Development Policy Review* 8(3): 287–300.

Marx, M. T. (1994). "Grameen Bank in Philippines: DUNGGANON and CARD." Report prepared for Deutsche Gesellschaft für Technische (GTZ), Germany. Seremban, Malaysia: Cashpor Inc. (reprint).

PAPO (1994). "Poverty Program Document." Mimeo, June. Ulaanbaatar: PAPO.

PAPO (1995). "Project Implementation Manual: Local Development Fund." Draft, mimeo. National Poverty Alleviation program, MPPL, September, Ulaanbaatar: Government of Mongolia.

Remenyi, J. (1991). *Where Credit Is Due: Income Generating Programs for the Poor in Developing Countries.* London: ITP.

Remenyi, J. (1993). "The Role of Credit in a Holistic Strategy for Sustainable Poverty Alleviation in Southwest China." World Bank consulting report prepared for the 2nd Southwest China Poverty Mission, July–August. Washington, DC, and Geelong: Centre for Applied Social Research at Deakin University.

Remenyi, J. (1994a). "Poverty Targeting." Pp. 261–93 in *Anthropology and Third World Development,* edited by B. Geddes, J. Hughes and J. Remenyi. Geelong: Deakin University Press.

Remenyi, J. (1994b). "The Role of Credit in the Qinghai Community Development Project, Pingan, Haidong County, Qinghai, PRC." Consulting report prepared for CARE Australia, Hassall and Associates and the Australian International Development Assistance Bureau, Canberra.

Remenyi, J. (1995). "Monitoring and Evaluation in the Mongolian National Poverty Alleviation Program." World Bank consulting report prepared for the East Asia Office, Vulnerable Groups in Mongolia Project, by Remedy Research (Torquay). Washington, DC: World Bank.

Rutherford, S. (1995). *ASA: The Biography of an NGO.* Dhaka: Association of Social Advancement.

Story, R. (1993). *Mongolia: A Travel Survival Kit.* Melbourne: Lonely Planet.

Swift, J. (1995). "Draft Interim Report on Fieldwork, Arkhangay Aimag, Mongolia." Report prepared for IFAD (mimeo), Ulaanbaatar.

Todd, H., ed. (1996). *Cloning Grameen Bank: Replicating a Poverty Reduction Model in India, Nepal and Vietnam.* London: ITP.

UNDP (1996). *Human Development Report, 1996.* New York: Oxford University Press.

World Bank (1994). "Mongolia Country Economic Memorandum: Priorities in Macroeconomic Management." Report No. 13612-MOG, Country Operations Division, China and Mongolia Department, East Asia and Pacific Regional Office, Oct. 31., Washington, D.C.

World Bank (1995a). "Mongolia: Poverty Alleviation for Vulnerable Groups Project." Staff Appraisal Report # 13963-MOG, Poverty, Population and Human Resources Division, China and Mongolia Department, East Asia and Pacific Regional Office, May 22. Washington, D.C.

World Bank (1995b). "Briefing Notes on Poverty in Mongolia." Mimeo, Ulaanbaatar.

World Bank (1996). *World Development Report, 1996.* New York: Oxford University Press.

World Bank (1999). Mongolia Country Brief, available at http://www.worldbank.org/html/extdr/offrep/eap/mn2.htm; and at http://www.worldbank.org/data/countrydata/aag/mng_aag.pdf.

Wu, K.B. (1994). "Technical Notes on Poverty, an Attachment to the World Bank-UNDP Aide-Memoir." Mimeo (April), Ulaanbaatar.

CHAPTER 5

Public Policy Interventions, Market Economics, and Income Distribution

The Impact on Sri Lanka and Other Asian Countries

Patrick Mendis

1. Introduction

Over the years, economists and policymakers have long been convinced that economic growth fosters greater social equity. Theoretically, it is logical to assume the existence of such a positive relationship between the two. With higher income, people have better access to education and the health delivery system; therefore, the trickle-down of economic growth is said to reach to many people through education and the health care mechanism. Thus, education and health would serve as the wealth and income equalizing forces (Mendis 1995). Furthermore, the World Bank, a perennial advocate of economic growth strategies, has recently taken the position that social development is economic development. Speaking on behalf of the World Bank at the United Nation's Economic and Social Council (ECOSOC), Nancy Birdsall (1993) has highlighted the Bretton Woods position.

It is generally viewed that Japan and the Newly Industrialized Countries (NICs) of Hong Kong, Singapore, South Korea, and Taiwan have such a pattern of relatively more equitable income and wealth distribution as their income has risen. In fact, according the World Bank's The *East Asian Miracle* report, the experience in the NICs has overall shown that there exists a pattern of general direction as they moved toward a more industrialized stage (World Bank 1993). In this process, social inequality is expected to increase in the early stages of economic growth but later on a more egalitarian socioeconomic equilibrium is anticipated and can eventually be achieved. But this pattern is not commonly demonstrated in all Asian countries; each has its own unique experiences, which are influenced by a multiple of economic, social, political, and cultural factors.

This essay surveys the income distribution and economic growth in Sri Lanka and East Asian NICs. There is no universal agreement on problems and issues related to theoretical debate, sources of comparable data, and the methodologies used in countries under discussion. The existence of obvious variations in cross-national experiences should be acknowledged in economic growth strategies, indicators of income distribution and Gini coefficient, level of poverty alleviation, and other indicators of quality of human development. With such caution, this chapter reviews selected studies in theoretical and empirical aspects of income distribution, economic growth, and development strategy in Section 2. The experience of the NICs is discussed in Section 3. Section 4 presents a range of public policy interventions and their impact on income distribution and poverty in Sri Lanka over the past four decades. Section V concludes the chapter with two observations of the analysis as lessons to be learned.

2. Theoretical and Empirical Underpinnings

In an analysis of the general notion of the growth and equity relationship, Simon Kuznets in his 1955 study observed a general pattern of income distribution as economies develop. This well-known Kuznets inverted-U curve pattern demonstrates that inequality exists to a point before more equality appears as countries increase their GNP per capita (Kuznets 1955; see also Bacha 1979). The reason noted for this inverted-U curve is that productivity and income begin to rise more rapidly in the modern industrialized sector than in rural agriculture at the beginning of the industrialization and modernization process. When the agricultural labor surplus is absorbed by the other industrialized and service sectors of the economy, wages and salaries are expected to rise. In practice, the Kuznets theory in the NICs is consistent with the conventional notion of the linkages between economic growth and social equity.[1]

Many researchers in the past, however, have raised questions on the conventional and theoretical understanding of the industrialization and modernization process and its impact on income distribution and poverty alleviation.[2] The theoretically expected transfer of surplus agricultural labor to the industrialized sector did not produce a more satisfying result in income distribution of all these countries, as expected by some economists and policymakers. With direct foreign investment, for example, it is anticipated that Western investors would substitute domestic labor for imported financial and physical capital while the local work force would be fully utilized to produce materials for the export market. The incentive to use surplus labor with lower wages at entry-level manufacturing jobs as opposed to capital investment was seen favorably by both foreign investors and local policymakers.

In the initial transition period, the labor force is transferred largely from rural agriculture to the industrial sector, and foreign companies are expected to manufacture goods and services at relatively low costs. Many countries, like Sri Lanka, have established free trade zones and relaxed strict legislation to encourage foreign investors to resuscitate their stagnated economies, which have experienced high inflation, growing unemployment, rising interest rates, and a shortage of foreign exchange. In the process, when the demand for labor has been fully absorbed by the industrial and service sectors, the excessive labor force has remained unemployed or underemployed. This has created a growing frustration, especially among the educated cohorts on two fronts: there is an increasing income gap between those who are employed and those who are not fully employed. Consequently, some of the unemployed, with their idle time and energy, often express their frustration in destruction, while others find creative forms of adapting to new and different kinds of opportunities in the informal sector. The evidence of such violent expressions in South Korea, China, and even in Sri Lanka has been widely reported in the mass media. Alternative forms of adapting to changes by unemployed youth have also been reflected in illegal activities. The anticipated economic or social equilibrium does not, therefore, appear to take place in these societies, and the continued disequilibrium has created an imbalance in their economic and social systems. This, however, does not suggest that the conditions of those countries have necessarily become worse; it rather seems to indicate that high expectations of the industrialization and modernization process have not been fully satisfied and the negative externalities (such as corruption, prostitution, baby selling, Mafia, and drug problems) have not been completely addressed or resolved.

In countries where income distribution patterns tend to follow the Kuznets curve, those patterns do not essentially result from the introduction of industrialization and modernization processes alone. Some countries had relatively more equitable income distribution before their export-led industrial growth took effect. Prior socioeconomic and cultural conditions have seemingly laid the foundation needed for a comparatively rapid pattern of income distribution. Some researchers have noted that land reform in South Korea and Japan had a major impact on a more equitable income distribution (Mason et al. 1980; Mizoguchi 1985). In the Sri Lankan experience, two World Bank economists have indicated that the already existing conditions of physical distribution of properties (like the ownership of land) and other assets are viewed as more important than the export-led industrialization strategy (Bhalla and Glewwe 1986; Bhalla 1988). This suggests that industrialization strategy alone does not bring about equity in income distribution but a set of public policy interventions does have a significant impact on social welfare. Economic growth strategies do increase per capita income, but the distribution of that accumulated income is a different matter. The experience demonstrates that the level and the pattern of income distribution resulting from both growth strategies and policy interventions are unique for each country.

3.   The Equity and Growth Experience of Nics

The East Asian NICs and Japan have demonstrated rapid economic growth with relatively equal income distribution (Rao 1988). Japan's Gini coefficient of .372 in 1968 improved to .316 in 1979 as her per capita income grew (Table 5.1). South Korea has achieved more equality as reflected by the Gini coefficient, which changed from .414 in 1976 to .363 in 1988. This seems to be attributable to the introduction of their export-led development strategy. Prior to the 1970s, South Korea did in fact have a relatively more equitable income distribution. Many observers attributed this to the result of land reform initiatives. In Table 5.1, the Gini coefficient ratio indicates the relative distribution of income in several selected Asian countries as well as Sweden and the United States for the purpose of comparison.

In theory, if all incomes are equal, the Gini coefficient should be zero; if one person or household has all the income, the Gini coefficient should be one. In practice, if the Gini coefficient is .3 or below, it reflects a low level of inequality; if it is above .5, it should be considered high inequality. Table 5.1 indicates that Malaysia's Gini coefficient was over .5 in the early 1970s and continues to remain relatively high in Asia. The higher income earners in Malaysia are largely concentrated in the highest 20 percentile (over 50 percent), higher than any other East Asian nation. Japan, with its .32 coefficient, like Sweden, demonstrates a more equitable income distribution in the Asian region. The share of income distribution in Table 5.1 also illustrates that Sweden with its social welfare policies has achieved a relatively more egalitarian society.[3] India, with its heavy government intervention in the economy, also had a more egalitarian income distribution in 1980s. India's socialistic economy tends to follow a distribution of income similar to that of other South Asian countries.

The experience of income distribution among the NICs of Asia is mixed. Figure 5.1 shows an interesting path of income disparity in Japan and South Korea as well as in Sweden and the Philippines. All these countries have reached a comparatively equitable income distribution after a period of widening income gap (consistent with the Kuznets curve). Prior to 1970, for example, Japan, South Korea, and the Philippines had a pattern of rising income disparity. Stephan Haggard writes of South Korea that "land reform is the most plausible explanation, though no doubt the destruction of the Korean War also had a powerful leveling effect" (1992: 225). This is also prior to the effective period of export-led economic growth under military rule. For other countries, land reform policies, particularly in Japan and the Philippines, may have been associated with the demonstrated pattern. Figure 5.1 further illustrates that other countries, including the United States and Malaysia, have a collection of mixed experiences. The exact reason for the existing pattern in the United States is difficult to discern, but a

Table 5.1: *Share of Income Distribution and Gini Coefficient in Selected Countries*

| Country | Year(s) | Share of Income Received by | | Gini Coefficient |
		Lowest 20%	Highest 20%	
Hong Kong	1970–85	–	–	.450
	1980	5.4	47.0	.428
India	1954–64[a]	–	–	.400
	1963–64[b]	–	–	.418
	1964–65	6.7	35.2	.414
	1970–85	–	–	.420
	1975–76	7.0	49.4	.422
	1983	8.1	41.4	.349
	1989	8.8	41.3	.334
	1992	8.5	42.6	.338
Indonesia	1976	6.6	49.4	.446
	1987	8.8	41.3	.335
	1990	8.7	42.3	.342
	1993	8.7	40.7	.317
Japan	1968[b]	–	–	.372
	1969	7.9	41.0	.389
	1979	8.7	37.5	.316
Malaysia	1970	3.3	56.6	.529
	1973	3.5	56.1	.521
	1987	4.6	51.2	.469
	1989	4.6	53.7	.484
Philippines	1965b	–	–	.465
	1970–71	5.2	54.0	.472
	1985	5.5	48.0	.439
	1988	6.5	47.8	.321
South Korea	1964–70[b]	–	–	.340
	1965[b]	–	–	.344
	1970[b]	–	–	.362
	1976	5.7	45.3	.414
	1988	7.4	42.2	.363
Sweden	1972	6.6	32.0	.351
	1979	7.2	37.2	.346
	1981	8.0	36.9	.328
Thailand	1970–85	–	–	.470
	1975–76	5.6	49.8	.446
	1988	6.1	50.7	.442
	1992	5.6	52.7	.462
United States	1970[b]	–	–	.315
	1972	4.5	42.8	.428
	1978	4.6	50.3	.470
	1980	5.3	52.0	.394
	1985	4.7	41.9	.419

Sources: (a) Chenery (1974); (b) Ahluwalia (1976); other Gini coefficients are calculated by data presented in the UN Development Programme (1991) and World Bank (1986, 1989, 1990, 1994). The latest available data are according to the World Bank (1996: 196–97).

host of factors may be associated with changing public policies, such as direct government interventions in agriculture and industry as well as in social welfare programs. Some economists have argued that the loss of manufacturing jobs to lower-priced imports has been a cause of more inequality in the United States.

4.   *Dirigisme* Policies and Analysis of Poverty in Sri Lanka

Surprisingly, a variety of social welfare programs and land reform legislation in Sri Lanka did not yield an anticipated greater income distribution as they did in

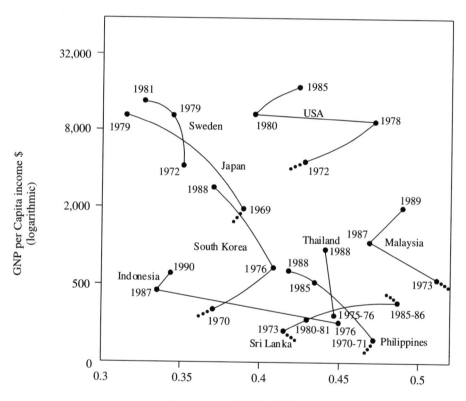

Figure 5.1: *Relationship between GNP per capita income and Gini coefficient in selected countries.*
Sources: *Gini coefficients are calculated from income distribution data presented in UN Development Programme (1991) and World Bank (1986, 1989, 1990, 1994).*
Numbers indicate the survey year(s) of income distribution. Dotted line indicates the direction of previous survey's Gini coefficient.

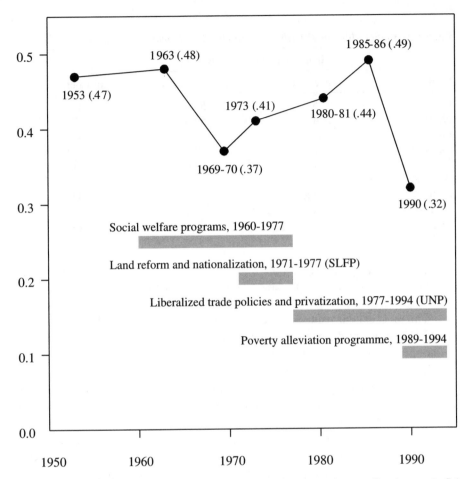

Figure 5.2: *Direction of income inequality and periods of significant policy impact in Sri Lanka.* Sources: *Gini coefficients for 1953, 1963, and 1973 are from Fields (1980); others are from income distribution data presented in UN Development Program (1991) and World Bank (1986, 1989, 1990, 1994).*

some other countries. In fact, the experience in Sri Lanka illustrates that the gap between the rich and poor has increased despite the nationalization and land reform policies of 1972 and 1976. The general direction of Gini coefficient in Sri Lanka suggests that income distribution has widened from the early 1970s to the mid-1980s (Figure 5.2). This period includes both the prosocialist Sri Lanka Freedom Party (SLFP), which implemented the nationalization and land reform, and the procapitalist United National Party (UNP), which introduced open-market policies and trade liberalization. As expected, income inequality accelerated after the introduction of trade liberalization by the UNP administration in 1977.

Table 5.2: *Share of Income Distribution and Gini Coefficient in Sri Lanka*

| Year(s) | Share of Income Received by | | Gini Coefficient |
	Lowest 20%	Highest 20%	
1953[a]	5.2	53.8	.468
1963[a]	4.5	52.3	.476
1963–70[b]	–	–	.450
1969–70	7.5	54.4	.371
1973[a]	7.2	42.9	.412
1970–85[c]	–	–	.450
1980–81	5.8	49.8	.436
1985–86	4.8	56.1	.491
1990	8.9	39.3	.320

[a] Fields (1980: 197).
[b] Chenery (1974: 42).
[c] UN Development Programme (1991).
Note: The remaining Gini coefficients are calculated from data in World Bank (1984, 1989, 1990, 1994).

The most salient feature of income equity demonstrated in Table 5.2 is that the Gini coefficient dropped to .32 in 1990, the lowest recorded in Sri Lankan economic history. The Gini coefficient in Sri Lanka is as low as that of Japan (.316) in 1979 and Sweden (.328) in 1981 (cf. Tables 5.1 and 5.2). One of the most likely reasons for this phenomenon is the massive income transfer through the Poverty Alleviation Programme (known as Janasaviya, which means "people's strength" in Sinhalese) that was implemented in the late 1980s by the UNP government. With the Janasaviya Programme, a target group of people below the poverty line (estimated as one-half of the population) was eligible to receive income in the form of cash and food items (Mendis 1992). Other reasons may include the benefit of the Accelerated Multi-Purpose Mahaveli River Development Programme, which benefited the rural population through irrigation, government-initiated welfare programs (e.g., free school textbooks, midday school meals, and school uniforms), and the Million Housing Programme for the poor (Mendis 1994). The disaggregate impact of these programs on poverty and income distribution is difficult to identify and to verify. It does, however, demonstrate that direct public policy intervention can abruptly change the direction of income inequality. The newly elected coalition government led by the SLFP in 1994 assured the country that they would continue to pursue, even on an aggressive scale, a similar program for the welfare of the poor while advocating free market economic policies, including the privatization of state-owned enterprises. The massive islandwide Janasaviya Programme was somewhat modified and changed to the Samurdhi Programme (which means "prosperity" in Sinhalese). As long as such monetary transfer in the form of public intervention continues, a more egalitarian income distribution can continue in Sri Lanka.[4]

In fact, the share of income distribution from the lowest quintile of income earners increased from 5.2 percent in 1953 to 8.9 percent in 1990 (Table 5.2). A drastic reversal trend is shown for the richest quintile of income earners: 53.8 percent in 1953 reduced to 42.9 percent in 1973, and then to 39.3 percent in 1990. This seems to imply that the poorest 20 percent accrued more income during these years. A series of land reforms, nationalization of estate plantations (tea, rubber, and coconut), and food stamps and food subsidy schemes may have been associated with such changes in the early 1970s but there is still some question that the gap between rich and poor has gradually begun to increase throughout the 1970s, especially after 1973. By 1980–81, for example, the share of income accruing to the poorest 20 percent had declined to 5.8 percent from 7.5 percent in 1969–70. The share further dropped to 4.8 percent by 1985–86.

Furthermore, Table 5.2 indicates that the Gini coefficient of .371 in 1969–70, the lowest since independence from Great Britain in 1948, reached .412 in 1973. The average Gini coefficient during the 1970–85 period was .45. The available data on the share of income distribution also shows that the share of national income for the lowest 20 percent of the population increased up to 7 percent during the 1969–73 period. Simultaneously, the share of the highest 20 percent income earners declined from 54.4 percent in 1969–70 to 42.9 percent in 1973. This is a significant departure from the past, when the share of income accruing to the richest 20 percent remained higher than 50 percent of the total. As the share of income among the poorest quintile accounted for only a little over 7 percent of income, the equity of income distribution improved during this period. This may be associated with the initial land reform legislation in 1972; however, the Gini coefficient of .41 in 1973 remained relatively higher than .37 in 1969–70. A possible reason for this contrasting situation is that the benefits of the fifty-acre ceiling on land ownership did not trickle down to the lowest 20 percent although it adversely impacted the richest 20 percent, whose share of income changed with respect to the lowest income group. The increase of share of income distribution at the lowest quintile does not suggest that the poverty rate changed. The change in the income gap is not a clear indication of relative poverty. The Gini coefficient increased from .41 in 1973 to .44 in 1980–81, and to .49 in 1985–86. The share of income in the richest quintile also grew from 43 to 50 and to 56 percent, respectively, in those years. Two Sri Lankan researchers who also identified a similar trend write that "during the period 1969–70, the inequality in income distribution increased sharply for both the urban and rural sectors. The worsening in income distribution has, however, not led to an increase in poverty. In both sectors, the real incomes of the lowest income groups appear to have increased marginally while those of higher income groups grew rapidly" (Gunatilleke and Perera 1994: 155).

The foregoing analysis attests that the level of poverty as represented by the comparative Gini coefficient ratios has been reduced from 1969–70 to 1990. In terms of the incidence of poverty, Gunatilleke and Perera assert that "while absolute poverty in the rural sector appear to have remained at the same level during 1969–1985, there was a significant reduction of poverty in the urban sector based on available data" (ibid.: 160). This may suggest that the introduction of trade liberalization and export-led development strategies after 1977 may have caused the transfer of agricultural labor to the industrial sector, especially through the newly-created free trade zones.

5. Concluding Remarks

The post-1977 economic strategies in Sri Lanka appear to have increased income inequality. This is in contrast to both the Kuznets curve and the paths of other NICs. But Sri Lanka and some NICs have essentially followed similar economic and trade policies. Some may argue that Sri Lanka, afflicted by entrenched ethnic conflict and guerrilla warfare, may have potentially blocked the path to NIC status. But similar experiences in South Korea, in the form of repression and authoritarian governance, caused some setbacks even after Park Chung Hee (military strongman from 1961 to 1979). The negative impact on economic growth appears to have been milder in South Korea than in Sri Lanka. The nature of the political leadership may be associated with this, since relatively more democratic Sri Lankan leaders must accommodate the will of the people in elections.

The Asian experience suggests that the "best way" would not always result in a more equitable income distribution. Some countries, particularly Sri Lanka, Malaysia, and even the United States, have not necessarily followed the path prescribed by mainstream economists and policymakers, who advocate that greater equity follows with economic growth. Other factors may have influenced the direction of change. A host of public policy interventions could well be associated with such a change as demonstrated in Sri Lanka and other countries.

In general, this analysis provides two lessons for development thinkers and practitioners: First, the socialist experiment in Sri Lanka did not result in a more equitable distribution of income as envisioned. The equality of income distribution tends to follow the direction of economic growth positively if the necessary conditions prevail in the economy during the initial take-off period, as other East Asian countries have demonstrated. The NICs of East Asia, with their efficient and broad-based employment-intensive strategies, have promoted economic growth and social infrastructure in education and health care systems. These education and health care systems in return have reinforced the economic development process, especially in resource development. This has been a "virtuous circle" for them. The best way then for NICs as well as others to achieve a more equitable income distribution is by investing in human capital as a long-term investment for higher rates of return. Second, government intervention in the form of public policies or a set of programs of monetary or nonmonetary transfers to poor people could change the income distribution more effectively and rapidly than the trickle-down of economic growth (see e.g., Bhagwati 1988; Sen 1981). The question of funding such income transfer programs without economic growth would be challenging for some countries, especially Sri Lanka and other South Asian countries, where the foreign debt service rate and the volume of external financial assistance are already relatively high in their national budget portfolios. The best way to achieve a higher human development is then by promoting economic growth while ensuring that growth is closely linked with human well-being, as opposed to jobless economic growth.

Notes

1. There exist numerous studies of evidence of the Kuznets hypothesis, see e.g., Ahluwalia (1976).

2. For some empirical studies on policy effect on income distribution, poverty alleviation, and economic growth, see Adelman and Taft Morris (1973), Adelman and Robinson (1978), and Chenery (1974).

3. Sweden is considered here because of its well-known social welfare programs and relatively less income disparity compared to those of Asian countries.

4. It is too early for a comprehensive analysis of the Samurdhi Programme or other economic strategies of the SLFP alliance because the implications of such policies have not yet been evaluated nor have programs been fully developed and implemented. In late 1995, the government formed the National Development Council to coordinate economic and social welfare strategies.

References

Adelman, I. and C. Taft Morris (1973). *Economic Growth and Social Equity in Developing Countries*. Stanford, CA: Stanford University Press.

Adelman, I. and S. Robinson (1978). *Income Distribution Policy in Developing Countries: A Case Study of Korea*. New York: Oxford University Press.

Ahluwalia, M. (1976). "Inequality, Poverty, and Development." *Journal of Development Economics* 3: 307–42.

Bacha, E. L. (1979). "The Kuznets Curve and Beyond: Growth and Changes in Inequalities." Pp. 52–73 in *Economic Growth and Resources,* Volume 1, edited by E. Malinvaud. New York: St. Martin's.

Bhagwati, J. (1988). "Poverty and Public Policy." *World Development* 16(5): 539–55.

Bhalla, S. S. (1988). "Is Sri Lanka an Exception: A Comparative Study of Living Stan-dards." Pp. 89–117 in *Rural Poverty in South Asia,* edited by T. N. Srinivasan and P. K. Bardhan. New York: Columbia University Press.

Bhalla, S. S. and Paul Glewwe (1986). "Growth and Equity in Developing Countries: A Reinterpretation of the Sri Lankan Experience." *World Bank Economic Observer* 1(September): 35–64.

Birdsall, N. (1993). *Social Development Is Economic Development.* Washington, DC: World Bank.

Chenery, H. (1974). *Redistribution with Growth.* New York: Oxford University Press.

Fields, G. S. (1980). Poverty, Inequality, and Development. Cambridge: Cambridge University Press.

Gunatilleke, G. and Myrtle Perera (1994). "Urban Poverty in Sri Lanka: Critical Issues and Policy Measures." *Asian Development Review* 12(1).

Haggard, S. (1992). *Pathways from the Periphery: The Politics of Growth in the Newly Industrialized Countries.* Ithaca, NY: Cornell University Press.

Kuznets, S. (1955). "Economic Growth and Income Inequality." *American Economic Review* 45(March): 1–28.

Mason, E. S., et al. (1980). *The Economic and Social Modernization of the Republic of Korea.* Cambridge, MA: Harvard University Press.

Mendis, P. (1992). "The Economics of Poverty Alleviation: The Janasaviya Programme in Sri Lanka." *South Asia Journal* 5(3): 289–98.

Mendis, P. (1994). "The Role of Indigenous Culture and Evolving Development Strategies: Is There a Right Policy Mix for Sri Lanka?" *Marga Quarterly Journal* 13(1): 1–32.

Mendis, P. (1995). *Capitalism in Human Scale.* Department of Applied Economics Staff Paper P95-9, University of Minnesota, St. Paul.

Mizoguchi, T. (1985). "Economic Development Policy and Income Distribution: The Experience of East and Southeast Asia." *Developing Economies* 23(December): 312–18.

Rao, V. V. B. (1988). "Income Distribution in East Asian Developing Countries." *Asian Pacific Economic Literature* 2(March): 29–39.

Sen, A. (1981). "Public Action and the Quality of Life in Developing Countries." *Oxford Bulletin of Economic and Statistics* 43: 287–319.

UN Development Programme (various years). *Human Development Report.* New York: Oxford University Press.

World Bank (1993). *The East Asian Miracle: Economic Growth and Public Policy,* Policy Research Report. Washington, DC: World Bank. World Bank (various years). *World Development Report.* New York: Oxford University Press.

CHAPTER 6

See Through a Glass, Darkly

Models of the Asian Currency Crisis of 1997–98[*]

Kanishka Jayasuriya

The noble silver drachma, that of old
We were so proud of, and the recent gold,
Coins that rang true, clean-stamped and worth their weight
Throughout the world, have ceased to circulate.
Instead, the purses of Athenian shoppers
Are full of shoddy silver plated coppers
Just so when men are needed by the nation,
The best have been withdrawn from circulation.
Aristophanes, *The Frogs* (translation by David Barrett)

1. Models of the Currency Crisis

The recent Asian currency crisis has led to a proliferation of explanations about its origins, which makes it difficult to answer one of the central issues of this crisis: did the crisis originate in some problem inherent in the East Asian developmental model or was it due to circumstances and conditions that were beyond the control of East Asian governments? Indeed, a skeptical philosopher of social science would elaborate by observing that various models of the crisis are themselves dependent on broader research programs or paradigms where assumptions and normative principles are beyond simple falsification; in fact, the crisis seems like a textbook example of how competing research programs can use the same evidence to support diametrically different conclusions about the origins of the crisis.

The purpose of this chapter is twofold: first to provide a heuristic classification of various models that we have identified to explain the origins of the current crisis: the neoclassical, institutional, and globalization models; the second is to

---

* I wish to gratefully acknowledge the expert assistance given by Robert Roche, who provided me with up-to-date on-line and other published documents on the Asian currency crisis.

provide a brief critique of these models. Analysis of competing perspectives on the currency crisis allows us to more fully evaluate the strengths and weakness of each of these models, and more importantly, explore the potential of these models to generate solutions and provocative research questions. Our objectives in this essay are modest: it is hoped that the classification can be used by the reader as a guide through the thicket of studies on the origins of the currency crisis. It should be noted that this chapter is written as the complications inherent in this crisis are still unfolding, and for this reason this essay is very much a first "cut."

The explanatory models are determined by the permutation of two distinct variables: one relates to the identification of the internal or external source of the economic crisis, and the other relates to assumptions made about the nature of markets. As the crisis has unfolded, it is clear that important debates about the crisis have tended to focus on the extent to which the source of the crisis can be located in the mainsprings of the distinctive structures of East Asian capitalism or "the developmental state" (Wade 1990; Weiss and Hobson 1995) rather than in the operation of the unregulated dynamics of the global market economy.[1] Hence this debate is about the whether the pathogenesis of the crisis is internal and specific to East Asia or whether the causes are to be found in the international economy beyond the domain of national control. It follows that debate over the internal or external source of the crisis has significant ramifications for the future viability of the East Asian economic model. If the causes are found to be external in origin, it can be safely assumed that the model itself is not the source of the economic woes that currently beset the region; then, the solution to the crisis lies not in changes to the distinctive pattern of East Asian economic governance but in the modification of those aspects of the international economy held responsible for the current economic crisis.

In conjunction with this debate over the origin of the crisis, there are deeper ontological disagreements over the nature of markets: one perspective takes a static and abstract view of markets and recognizes economic behavior as independent of historical experience, institutional context, and informational or knowledge deficits; another perspective takes a view of markets as a structure that is determined by a complex historical past and one in which economic outcomes are strongly colored by the texture of the institutional environment. Zysman neatly encapsulates this institutionalist logic when he notes that each "market economy is defined by the institutions and rules that permit it to function, or to put differently, each national system can be defined by the 'institutional structure' of the economy, that which shapes how buying, selling and the very organisation of production takes place" (1996: 177). These ontological debates over the proper constitution of markets and of "economic time" have important ramifications for the way we comprehend the East Asian model. By adopting a dynamic conception of "economic time" it is simply not possible to talk about the East Asian model.

Rather, we need to understand the way the model has unfolded over time. The resort to a dynamic conception of markets demands a recognition that markets cannot be disconnected from the wider ensemble of political and economic power. A comprehensive understanding of economic behavior is possible only within the context of the wider set of political and institutional structures.

		Source of crisis	
		Internal	**External**
Markets	**Static**	Neoclassical	Static globalization
	Dynamic	Institutionalist	Embedded globalization

Figure 6.1: *Models of the currency crisis.*

These two major clusters of disagreement over the endogenous nature of the crisis and the degree to which markets are embedded in a wider context of political and social power (static or dynamic nature of markets) produce a number of different perspectives on the currency crisis. Hence these debates in turn reflect deep-seated differences over the analysis of the East Asian pattern of economic governance. Figure 6.1 outlines the different models of the currency crisis.

On the basis of this diagram we can identify three main perspectives, which may be characterized as follows. The globalization models are subdivided into two categories:

1. Neoclassical. A neoclassical perspective that locates the crisis in fundamental structural flaws in the East Asian model but employs a conception of the economy that is essentially static.
2. Institutional. A historically based institutional perspective, not to be confused with rational choice institutionalism, which, like the neoclassical model, places great emphasis on the source of the crisis as endogenously driven but differs from the neoclassical model in locating these dynamics in the changing power relationships and institutional context of East Asian political economy.
3. Globalization. Static globalization: A static globalization perspective, which locates the crisis in the external dynamics of global short-term capital markets. Embedded globalization: A variant of the globalization perspective, which locates the crisis in the power relationships in the external economy. Unlike the static globalization perspective, which has a static conception of the market, this perspective draws pointed attention to the way international financial flows reflect deeper underlying power relationships.

2. "The Economist Sings the Blues" (The Neoclassical Model)

This is without doubt the most influential perspective on the crisis: the boardroom of the IMF, the op-ed columns of the *Asian Wall Street Journal* (AWSJ), and the influential journal *The Economist* bear testimony to the dominance of this model in contemporary theorizing. In essence, this perspective places great emphasis on the role of misguided government policies, distorted corporate governance, and corrupt state business links in triggering the crisis. Michel Camdessus, the managing director of the IMF, has consistently argued that the Asian crisis is due to flawed government policies and has rejected external accounts of the crisis by noting that "it would be a mistake to blame the hedge funds as the central agent of turmoil in Asia" adding that speculators do not "act when a macro-economy is strong and government policies are sound" (quoted in *Asian Wall Street Journal* 1997). While the model itself has come in for serious criticism from a number of academic commentators and international and domestic policymakers, this model remains the only policy game in town.

The key assumption of this model is that the currency crisis is due to significant market distortion caused by collusion between the private financial and investment community and the government. In framing the explanation in these terms, the neoclassical model implicitly accepts that one of the chief features of the East Asian model has been the close and collaborative relationship between government and business, a surprising concession because when the "Asian" miracle was in full swing the tenor of neoclassical rationale — neatly captured in the East Asian miracle report of the World Bank — argued that the East Asian high-performance economies (HPAE)[2] largely "achieved high growth by getting the basics right. Private domestic investment and rapidly growing human capital were the principal engines of growth"[3] (1993: 5). Be that as it may, the neoclassical model gives pride of place to rent-seeking behavior by firms and banks as decisive contributory factors in the crisis.

From a neoclassical perspective, rent-seeking is defined as any market income above and beyond what individual economic agents would have received in a competitive economic environment (Krueger 1974). Rent-seeking systematically distorts market structure, giving wrong signals to economic actors. These signaling problems, in turn, cause errors in both governmental and corporate policy, eventually cascading to a full-blown crisis. It should be evident that within this perspective the concept of rent-seeking entails both a normative and analytical burden in that it not only tells us why the crisis occurred but also hints at a cure for the crisis as well.

In this vein, Frankel argues that the main causes of the East Asian crisis must be seen in terms of its structural character rather than in macroeconomic terms. He notes that deep flaws afflicted the financial system. They include excessive leverage, and a banking system based excessively on directed banking, connected lending and other collusive relationships. Ten years ago, finance experts called it relationship banking, and thought it might help to minimize "problems of asymmetric information and incentive incompatibility"; today we call it "crony capitalism." (1998: 2)

One of the central facets of this neoclassical explanation is that it highlights the important differences between the U. S. system, where firms rely heavily on the capital market for lending, and the Japanese and Asian systems, which rely on credit-based systems where banks are the key providers of investment capital; moreover, these credit systems are often strongly influenced (in countries like Japan and Taiwan) and even controlled by the government or ruling political elites (in countries like Indonesia, Malaysia, and — until recently — Korea).[4]

One important ramification of these forms of close and collaborative relationship between firms, banks and the state is to create the problem of what is regarded as a "moral hazard." Moral hazard exists when domestic banks and other financial intermediaries consider that they have an implicit insurance of governmental help if they encounter any financial difficulty (Roubini, Corsetti, and Pesenti 1998). The net effect of the moral hazard problem was to establish a climate where overborrowing and overlending became the norm. In short, the credit-based financial system of East Asia entrenched collusive links between firms, banks, and the state and the main effects of these links were, first, to induce overlending and overborrowing by both firms and banks because of implicit state guarantees; second, to reduce the kind of credit safety nets that banks and firms would have been expected to provide in a capital market–based system (Frankel 1998); and finally, on account of the lack of credit safety nets, to make the banks exceedingly vulnerable in a period of severe economic downturn. It is precisely this high degree of vulnerability that is evident in the current economic crisis.

This credit-based system is manifested in highly leveraged economic systems. Indeed, Ramos (1998) dramatically illustrates the magnitude of these problems when he notes:

Japan, Thailand, Malaysia, Korea, Hong Kong and Singapore all have domestic banking systems with total loans from 115% to 200% of their economies' annual output, as compared to only 10% to 70% of GDP for Latin America before the 1980s crises. Plus foreign-bank lending to the private sector accounts for another 17% to 35% of GDP for Korea, Indonesia, Malaysia, Thailand and the Philippines, totalling at least 274 billion.

In brief, collusive state business practices along with implicit state guarantees of bailout produced debt-laden economies that were highly vulnerable in times of economic crisis.

A related feature of this structure is the tendency toward overinvestment. Given that the World Bank's miracle report identifies East Asia's high rate of investment as one of the prime causes of high economic growth, the discovery of the problems of overinvestment by neoclassical economists is another one of those engaging ironies thrown up by the current crisis. However, this is the currently chastened neoclassical reasoning, which argues that there has been a constant dynamic of overinvestment in the economy, which has been deftly woven into complex structures of industrial policy. In fact, in his analysis of the political economy of communism, Kornai (1992) argues that overinvestment is a consequence of what he identifies as soft budget constraint faced by both firms and bank and this is equally applicable to East Asia. Nevertheless the process of overinvestment, while being capable of generating high economic rates of growth in the short term, was not sustainable in the long run; the East Asian debt chickens have come home to roost.

Clearly, in this explanation of Asia's financial crisis there are a number of important parallels with the putative causes of the collapse of the Soviet Union. In particular, Kornai's analysis of "soft budget" constraints of state socialism seems to have much in common with neoclassical models of the Asian crisis. In state socialism, because

> the budget constraint is soft, decision makers are not afraid investments may lead to financial failure. Any such fear is even less justified because responsibility is shared with the superior organizations, which have endorsed the investment project and may even have forced the firm to implement it. (ibid.: 270)

While this seems like a fairly accurate description of the dynamics of overinvestment in East Asia it needs to be noted that Kornai's work on state socialism was distinguished by its attempt to place the dynamics of overinvestment in a political context. This is what seems to be singularly lacking in neoclassical accounts.

Moral hazard as a crisis trigger is complemented in most neoclassical accounts by a model of the crisis as caused by persistence of fundamental weakness in governmental policy, which contributed to serious and significant real appreciation of currencies and large and growing trade current account deficits (Roubini et al. 1998). Of course, most of the usual suspects to be rounded up in a time of crisis seem to be absent in this East Asian crisis! In previous "Latin American type debt" crises, suspect indicators were low growth, high budget deficits, high inflation, low savings rates, and low investment. In contrast East Asian governments have done admirably in some of these areas; therefore the evidence for an indictment of East Asian states on the grounds of "bad policy" fundamentals remains rather circumstantial (Radelet and Sachs 1998). Nevertheless, East Asian governments have been found guilty of a policy-induced crisis by many orthodox economists as well as by the International Monetary Fund. The moral hazard and policy-induced models are not necessarily inconsistent though most analysts such as Roubini et al. (1998) are not very explicit about the relationship between the two models (see Figure 6.2). However, it is clear that bad policy fundamentals served to "tip" East Asia into a crisis, the depth and significance of which was then determined by moral hazard type issues discussed above. The neoclassical model of the crisis can be illustrated as follows:

BAD POLICY FUNDAMENTALS

$\Leftarrow$

Collusive State-Business Relations

$\Leftarrow$

Collusive Lending

$\Leftarrow$

Overinvestment

$\Leftarrow$

CRISIS

Figure 6.2: *Policy-induced and moral hazard models.*

There are clearly a number of strengths in this analysis: the role of moral hazard and the identification of the problem of overinvestment. Nevertheless, the static nature of the model renders it incapable of providing an analysis of the manner in which East Asian political economies have changed over time, such that elements that were once seen as pillars of the "Asian model" are now seen to be the crumbling foundations of a flawed developmental model.

For example, the emphasis on overinvestment is useful and important but in order to fully understand the dynamics of overinvestment, attention needs to be paid to the kinds of industries and sectors that are characterized by surplus capacity. There is no doubt that in many East Asian countries such as Thailand, over the last few years overinvestment has been in the nontradable sector of the economy. Much of this investment has been driven by a changing political environment that has given greater political influence to the nontradable sector. Moreover, it is apparent that these changes have had significant implications for the sustainability of the Asian model.

From a neoclassical perspective, the most useful research question to arise is the relationship between the dynamic of overinvestment and rent-seeking. One important line of inquiry is to probe the relationship between models of political capitalism, particularly the close relationship between business and government and the resultant tendency toward overinvestment. This inquiry may well point to historical parallels between East Asia and other systems of authoritarian capitalism such as imperial Germany in the latter part of the nineteenth century. A further useful strategy of inquiry is to explore similarities between the collapse of the system of state socialism and the crisis of the East Asian developmental model. Kornai's (1992) work on these issues is invaluable; for example, one point Kornai makes is the role of price and nonprice signals in various systems of economic coordination. He makes the important observation in relation to the analysis of state socialism that it is not merely a question of the failure of price signals in state socialism but rather the fact that the relative weight attached to price and nonprice signals is different from that of capitalism. As he notes, "[T]he distinction is not that price signals alone operate under capitalism and non-price signals alone under classical socialism, but rather that the systems differ in the relative weights they attach to them" (Kornai 1992: 159). It is clear that the stability of East Asian capitalism, dependent on its own distinctive combination of price and nonprice signals, has now broken down. Therefore an important research question within the neoclassical tradition is to explore the nature of price and nonprice signaling in East Asian capitalism.

One of the major problems with the neoclassical model is its static understanding of economic behavior, which creates difficulties in delineating the circumstance or conditions that triggered collapse of a system of economic coordination that has been remarkably stable over a long period of time. Similarly, the analysis of governance structure between firms, banks, and the state demonstrates a high degree of historical naivete (even for economists) because forms of governance are not voluntarily chosen but are determined by complex historical factors (Zysman 1983). The more interesting question is to determine the conditions that led to the disruption of a fairly stable and successful set of economic governance structures. In short, any proper analysis of the currency crisis needs to move beyond the froth and bubble of "bad fundamentals" and "moral hazard" to consider the political economy of the crisis.

3.   "It All Depends" (Institutional Model)

The developmental state model has been central to the conceptualization of East Asia by political scientists such as Chalmers Johnson (1982) and Robert Wade (1990). These writers have been prominent in suggesting rather heretically that strategic and targeted government intervention has been a vital ingredient in producing the East Asian economic miracle. The developmental state is a generic label originally applied to capture the distinctive configuration of economic and political governance of East Asia, but it may with some justification be employed to portray the nature of state organization and structure in Southeast Asia. The developmental state has to be understood in terms of three main features: first, an insulated and autonomous set of economic agencies with a strong capacity to implement economic policies and programs; second, an activist industry policy that develops competitive export-oriented global industries; and third, an understanding of governance that places strong emphasis on the role of the state in securing economic development and security (Wade 1990).

Wade, in a recent article coauthored with Veneroso, a prominent exponent of the "government intervention does matter" school, has vigorously counterpunched on behalf of institutionalist models (Wade and Veneroso 1998). This exposition, which if not winning any points from the IMF, at least manages to keep the developmental state theorists in the bout after what appeared to be a knockout blow from neoclassical economics. In essence, the Wade and Veneroso argument is that the crony capitalism explanation of the crisis misses the fact that there is a "financial rationale for cooperative, long-term, reciprocal relations between firms, banks and government in a system which intermediates high savings into high corporate debt/equity ratios" (ibid.: 10).

Pivotal to the argument of Wade and Veneroso is that East Asian capitalism has been characterized by high debt to equity ratios. No doubt this is also central to the moral hazard type of argument, but Wade and Veneroso argue that this structure is the outcome of two key institutional features of East Asian political economy. First, savings are much higher than in other regions. In most East Asian nations domestic savings are about one-third of GDP (World Bank 1993) and as most of savings are held in bank deposits, it follows that bank lending is geared toward borrowing by firms. Second, in order to compete in large export markets, local firms need to expand considerable resources, which can only be facilitated by extensive borrowing. Put simply, the only means of financing the export industrialization of the kind experienced by Japan, Korea, and Taiwan over the last three decades is through the mobilization of the large reserves of domestic savings by local corporations.

However, such a system requires a high degree of collaboration between firms, banks, and the state; in other words, the high debt-to-equity ratios of East Asian capitalism need to be underpinned by a complex institutional infrastructure of regulations. Admittedly, the system is highly vulnerable to systemic shocks that depress the flow of capital, and for this reason the system must be safeguarded against such systemic shocks as well as to having a system of constant monitoring of private firms and banks by the state. Indeed, the whole system depends on the effective monitoring of the corporate debt by the state. Furthermore, restrictions "on the freedom of firms and banks to borrow abroad, and coordination of foreign borrowing by government, are a necessary part of this system" (Wade and Veneroso 1998: 7).

Contrary to the neoclassical explanation of crisis, Wade and Veneroso suggest that there is a virtuous cycle between high savings, high levels of debt to equity ratios, close and collaborative links between state, banks, and firms that in turn lead to high investment, high levels of export performance and growth rates. But this virtuous cycle is dependent upon a high level of restrictions of financial regulation of external borrowing because, among other things, this will lead to lower levels of monitoring by the state; in essence, given an absence of credit safety nets to stabilize the system, the high wire act of East Asian capitalism required high levels of governmental capacity and monitoring. To put this in Kornai's (1992) terms, the means that the governmental monitoring of private firm and bank behavior is a system of nonprice signaling vital for the stability of the distinctive system of economic coordination in East Asia. Nevertheless, the ability of the state to keep financial restrictions in place proved to be the chink in the armor of the developmental state. The crisis is explained by the fact that financial deregulation undertaken by East Asian governments:

> removed or loosened controls on companies' foreign borrowing, abandoned coordina-
> tion of borrowings and investments, and failed to strengthen bank supervision. By
> doing so, they violated one of the stability conditions of the Asian high debt model,
> helping to set the crisis in train. (Wade and Veneroso 1998: 9)

In short, the virtuous cycle of the East Asian political economy became in fairly short order a particularly vicious cycle, plunging these economies into deep crisis. For Wade and Veneroso (1998), opening up financial markets is akin to allowing, indeed encouraging, unlimited access to the cookie jar.

It is worthwhile underlining significant differences between this historically inclined institutional model and the neoclassical moral hazard model. First, it places the structure of the financial system in a broader framework, which locates determinants of economic governance in systemic features of East Asian political economy. Economic governance needs to be embedded in a wider institutional framework. Second, the model highlights the importance of understanding the crisis in dynamic terms, which raises critical research questions about the conditions or circumstances that may have led to the disruption of the high-debt model of East Asian capitalism. Institutional models unlike neoclassical models are premised on a historical notion of economic time, which leads to a fundamentally different set of research questions

Much of what may be termed the "decline of monitoring capacity" argument is persuasive and takes us beyond the static neoclassical models outlined above. However, this analysis is flawed in one major respect: it fails to account adequately for the removal of financial restrictions by East Asian governments. Why did East Asian governments liberalize financial markets when the results were obviously so deleterious? For Wade and Veneroso, these policy actions were irrational and the policymakers were misled by international financial organizations.

However, the difficulty with this argument is that policy mistakes were made not just in one country but across the entire region. These facts would seem to suggest that there are deeper structural forces at work in reducing the capacity of East Asian governments to monitor the credit behavior of firms and banks. From a social science perspective, a structural explanation, rather than the simple attribution of mistake to policymakers, is more satisfying in explaining the disruption and instability of the East Asian model of economic governance.

Robison and Rosser (1998) argue that any discussion of the crisis needs to locate patterns of economic governance within the ensemble of class interests that sustain the "East Asian developmental model." Their argument is predicated on the fact that

> processes of change in economic systems are more usefully explained if markets are understood as political constructions embedded in systems of social power and interest. Because they cannot be understood in abstraction from the rules which govern them and they are forged in the process of bitter social and political struggle, capitalist economies will always operate in a variety of institutional and policy frameworks. (Robison and Rosser 1998: 4)

In the light of this framework, they argue that the crisis can be explained in terms of the shifts in social and political power in the last decade, which led — for example in the Indonesian case — to coalitions of powerful business interests and bureaucratic officials. Deregulation of product and capital markets only served to entrench powerful conglomerates within the Indonesian political economy. They note, for example, that

> deregulation created the opportunity for a sudden and extensive growth in the private sector and for the economic dominance of large, predominantly Chinese-owned conglomerates as well as business groups owned by powerful political families notably the Suharto family. (ibid.: 10)

Deregulation and liberalization provided — in sharp counterpoint to the neoclassical perspective — an opportunity for the big conglomerates to entrench and consolidate private economic power; the changing ensemble of class relations facilitates, in the Robison and Rosser variant of the embedded-market argument, the path from the virtuous cycle of high-debt capitalism to the vicious whirlpools of moral hazard.

The crucial point here is that there are deeper social and structural forces that push East Asian capitalism away from the stability provided by the high-debt model of capitalism. In short, the Indonesian crisis is in part due to the fact that there has been a leakage of power from technocratic agencies to private economic interests. As such, it is a much more satisfying explanation than attribution of policy stupidity or mistakes to senior technocrats, as is done by Wade and Veneroso (1998),[5] even though one of the more diverting aspects of the current crisis has been the almost religious zeal to lay blame, be it on banks, policy-makers, or financial market players.

Indeed, the "leakage argument"[6] as a prime disruptive catalyst for the model of East Asian capitalism can be plausibly seen in a number of other East Asian countries. For example, in Thailand, for long the "teacher's pet" of the World Bank for its conservative macroeconomic and monetary policy, there has been a continual shift in political power to business groups and politicians and away from central state agencies (see Laothamatas 1992). Similarly, in Malaysia, there has been a shift away form state managers to business groups associated with the dominant political party, the United Malay National Organization (UMNO). Indeed, Bowie notes that in Malaysia there has been an

> erection of a corporate empire blessed with unrestricted access to state-issued
> licenses and Malay preferences that is under the direct control of the governing
> party, UMNO, and is used to raise for constituent and electoral purposes (1994: 182)

The hub of the argument is that the accentuation of business is at the cost of the attenuation of the power of key state economic managers, which in turn has reduced their monitoring capacity. While the "leakage argument" is persuasive, it needs to be recognized that this was not a leaking of power from state to civil society, but a relocation of power within the state. Previously Jayasuriya (1995) has noted that the illiberal character of democratization in East Asia is reflected in the increasing fragmentation and polycentric distribution of power within the state. The rise of "electoralism" and the growth of legislative institutions enable business to increasingly penetrate the state, thereby fundamentally altering the asymmetric relationship between capital and state elites. It is important to realize that this is not a leakage of power from state elites to groups outside the state but a reconstitution of the state. As evidence of this process, Jayasuriya (1995) notes the important role of electoral politics ("money politics" in Thailand and Malaysia) and legislative institutions (Korea). In brief, the increasingly important role played by electoralism and legislative institutions reflects the increasing role of business within the state. This inclines one to the view that what has occurred has been a reorientation within the state, rather than between state and civil society, which has shown up as a polycentric distribution of power in the state. It was evident in the increasingly important role played by certain kinds of coalitions between business and politicians often at the expense of technocrats in key economic agencies. [For a further elaboration of this argument see Jayasuriya (1995).]

The link between democratization (or the increasing fragmentation of the state) and the currency crisis deserves greater elaboration, particularly in the cases of Thailand and Korea. Mo and Moon (1998) highlight some of these issues in a study of the relationship between democratizaton and the Korean economic crisis. They argue that even though Korean society has made much progress in procedural democracy since 1987, the government–big business coalition has not changed, and may even become stronger under democracy. According to this view, it is the unwillingness of the government and business elite to sacrifice their private interests or give up some of their privileges that has defeated most reform initiatives (Mo and Moon 1998: 9).

In Thailand the close relationship between politicians and business groups has been at the expense of central economic agencies such as the Ministry for Finance. In this context, although Laothamatas places undue weight on the role of corruption, he maintains that

> with electoral politics in full gear in the later 1980s and early 1990s corrupt dealings between government and business have again picked up. In a country where vote-buying is often needed to win an election and funding for party activities and election campaigning comes mostly from covert donations (rather than legitimate government sources or publicly acknowledged donations), corruption becomes a crucial means for politicians to draw money from businesses. (Laothamatas 1994: 209)

While Mo and Moon's (1998) argument places a great deal of emphasis on the policy gridlock in the relationship between democratization and economic crisis, their evidence is equally consistent with the argument that this policy gridlock is reflective of a fundamental reconstitution of the state.[7] The point is that this polycentric distribution of power makes the stability of the developmental state deeply problematic.

While it is beyond the brief analysis of this chapter to explore in detail the nature of these linkages between democracy and the developmentalist state, it is important to highlight how this explanation differs from the neoclassical model: Economic policy and governance are not taps that can be turned off and on at the whim of technocratic policymakers, but are embedded in a broader array of class and political institutions. This is a much more persuasive line of reasoning than that of either the neoclassical or a static globalization perspective. Central to this embedded-market analysis is the need to understand the nature of the forces and institutions that are prone to disrupt the high-debt model of East Asian capitalism, and also to acknowledge that these forces have an endogenous origin, which of course can vary from policy mistakes of technocrats (Wade and Veneroso 1998), to changes in class power (e.g., Robison and Rosser 1998), or to changes in political process or systems (e.g., Mo and Moon 1998).

However, one of the major flaws in institutional models of the crisis lies in their failure to properly recognize the role of the international economic and political system in contributing to the disruption of the institutional stability of the East Asian economic coordination system. Take, for example, financial deregulation. Most institutional theorists of whatever hue concur that financial deregulation has been a major factor in the declining capacity of governments

to monitor private economic behavior. However, financial deregulation in East
Asia can only be understood in terms of the political pressure applied by international organizations and the U. S. government to liberalize financial markets. More
generally we need to acknowledge that the increasing globalization of the
international economy has placed a range of obstacles in the path of governments
wishing to maintain strategic forms of industry policy.

4.   "It's the International Economy, Stupid!" (Globalization Models)

Whereas the neoclassical as well as the institutional embedded-market models
focus on the endogenous origins of the crisis, the globalization models locate the
source of the crisis in the operation of international markets, in particular, in the
role of financial markets. A number of serious analytical models have attributed
to global markets a key causative role in triggering the crisis. As is the case with
internalist-type models, globalization models are of two kinds: those that are static
in nature and those that emphasize the embeddedness of global markets in
international power relations. But both lay equal emphasis on the role of global
financial markets as a catalyst for the crisis. In fact, both utilize the same evidence
of global capital flows in their models.

   These globalization models have been popular with East Asian politicians
for two reasons: first, they absolve policymakers and state officials from any
blame for the crisis, and of course this is always a handy excuse; second, they
allow East Asian governments to combat the IMF adjustment programs, which
would strike at the vested interests of key political and economic elites. Indeed,
Prime Minister Mahathir of Malaysia has been prominent in spreading conspiracy
theories about the crisis with a view to sheltering his political leadership during
a turbulent political and economic period.

4.1 Static Model of Globalization

Static models of globalization have a theoretical counterpart in internal neoclassical models, but instead of recognizing the crisis as essentially a rational response
by investors, they place emphasis on the "herding" behavior of international
investors. Hence the crisis, at least in part, is due to a form of market failure
brought on by the rapid withdrawal of capital from East Asia. Whereas neoclassical arguments stress the need to introduce market reforms as a solution to the
crisis, models premised on financial panic would suggest the need to constrain
or regulate the flow of capital. Therefore, there are major differences between
economists on the appropriateness of IMF-type solutions to the present crisis.

   By any measure, the outflow of capital from East Asia has been remarkable and dramatic. Consider these figures: In 1997 five of the most affected Asian economies (South Korea, Indonesia, Malaysia, Thailand, and the Philippines) had an outflow of US$12.1 billion compared to a net inflow in 1997 of US$93 billion — a change that accounts for about 10 percent of GDP. As Rodrik notes "three of these economies (Indonesia, Thailand and South Korea) are mired in a severe crisis the magnitude of which would have seemed inconceivable even to the most knowledgeable and insightful observers of the region" (1998:2). From this perspective, a key element in understanding financial panic lies in the rapid decline of capital inflow, which had a number of macro- and microeconomic effects, the most important of which is the fact that exchange rates dramatically depreciated and domestic interest rates increased after the withdrawal of foreign credit. In combination, exchange rate depreciation and higher interest rates led to "a rapid rise in nonperforming loans (NPLs) in the banking sector of the Asian economies especially as the real estate projects went into bankruptcy" (Radelet and Sachs 1998:7). Radelet and Sachs argue that policy mistakes, particularly the policy error of attempting to defend an exchange rate peg, were important contributory factors to the crisis; moreover, they argue that IMF policies, particularly with regard to bank closures in Indonesia, were especially shortsighted, as they only serve to restrict liquidity in the midst of a financial panic.

More generally, it has been argued that short-term capital flows create specific vulnerability to financial panic because of problems of asymmetric information, and "a mismatch between short-term liabilities and long-term assets leaves financial intermediaries vulnerable to bank runs and financial panic" (Rodrik 1998:4). Kindleberger, whose historical analysis of financial panic bears close reading, sums up the vulnerability of financial markets when he points out:

> [C]redit is a dangerous thing. Expectations can be quickly altered. Something, sometimes almost nothing, causes a shadow to fall on credit, reverses expectations, and the rush for liquidity is on. (quoted in Radelet and Sachs 1998:26)

Models of financial panic, while providing a reasonably sound account of the course of the crisis, find themselves on shakier ground when assessed in terms of their capacity to explain the causes of the crisis. The problem is that at critical junctures in their argument Radelet and Sachs (1998), among the most prominent of the proponents of the financial panic model, rely heavily on the attribution of mistakes to policymakers as a contributory factor in the crisis. To cite one example, Radelet and Sachs contend rightly that the defense of pegged exchange rates was a crucial policy error in countries such as Thailand and Korea. However, what they fail to note is the political support for an overvalued exchange rate by key sectors in dominant political coalitions in East Asia. In particular, one of the dominant characteristics of East Asian political economy in the last decade has been the shift of power from the tradable to the nontradable sector (this again is associated with electoral politics), and it is the nontradable sector that has a clear interest in maintaining an appreciating exchange rate.

Further support for this proposition is found in the fact that a considerable proportion of capital inflows into East Asia went into the nontradable sector, e.g., real estate (Radelet and Sachs 1998). The point here is that a simplistic analysis of financial panic in terms of short-term capital movements and policy errors fails to recognize the underlying political forces (the shift of power from tradable to nontradable sectors) that determined not only the kinds of sectors and industries that capital flowed into (because these investments have political guarantees), but also constrained the kind of choices available to policymakers. An analysis of this kind would require a dynamic and political account of economic policy.

4.2   Embedded Models of Globalization

In contrast to static models of globalization, embedded notions of globalization emphasize the power relationships inherent in the increasing influence of financial capital. No doubt this point of view shares much common ground with financial panic arguments, but this is combined with an analysis of the way liberalization of capital and financial markets has been driven by specific coalitions of international political and economic actors who stand to benefit from the emergence of a new global economy dominated by financial capital.

Central to the emergence of these new political and economic structures is the role of the United States. This for instance suggests that the United States by retaining "a position of dominance in the global financial order...has allowed it to not only pursue its own national interest, but to impose a particular sort of order internationally. Promoting an open financial order allowed the U.S. to maintain policy autonomy and shift the burden of adjustment that its own general declining economic position implied onto other countries" (Beeson 1998: 10). The nature of IMF programs in Korea, Thailand, and Indonesia certainly adds credence to the view that the crisis was seen as a window of opportunity that could be used to implement a U.S.-type market economy in East Asia.

Bello (1998) has recently resurrected a version of dependency theory to explain the crisis. For Bello, the crisis is due to financial liberalization and privatization pursued by successive East Asian governments, which only fueled the swift flow of portfolio capital into unproductive areas. He clearly regards the rapid development of highly mobile capital as the main engine of the financial crisis in East Asia. Of course, shorn of the rather old-fashioned dependency language, this account has much in common with the more empirically based analysis of Radelet and Sachs (1998). However, where it differs from the latter is in Bello's argument that financial capital represents a particular constellation of U.S.-dominated political and economic interests. In fact, these arguments lead him to suggest that one of the major consequences of the crisis is that

> radical free-market reform may lead not to the transformation of Asian capitalism but to its unravelling, since policies that re-create the international economy in the image of the U.S. economy do nothing to build on the strengths of the existing economies but simply establish an arena in which the economic actors that followed one particular historical road to advanced capitalism — free market/minimal-state road — will have an unparalleled competitive edge. (Bello 1998: 9)

The problem with Bello's type of dependency argument is that it fails to note that the IMF programs in both Thailand and Korea have significant support with sections of the domestic business and state constituencies. Indeed, what can be observed in Korea and Thailand is the emergence of significant reform coalitions. In the case of Korea, neoliberal economic policies were being implemented throughout the 1990s; to be sure, the crisis has accelerated the process, but it is broadly driven by domestic pressures.

It follows that these embedded globalization models need to be supplemented by an account of the way domestic states have responded to globalization pressures. For example, measures to deregulate financial markets were not just imposed by global forces but were driven by domestic imperatives. Calder, commenting upon the Japanese financial liberalization process of the last decade, notes that politicians,

> whose strengths in the policy processes grew slowly but steadily during the late 1980s, helped to produce a financial system in which the security industry held unusual and rapidly rising influence. Politics in this sense played a major role in producing the gradual divergence of the Japanese financial system from the French model during the post-1975 decade, calling into question John Zysman's argument for Japanese-French similarity. (1997: 53)

Calder's comment underlines the importance of understanding the manner in which globalization is refracted through the domestic political process, but it also underscores the importance of the role played by fragmentation within the state and also of the role of the nontradable sector in diminishing the monitoring role played by central economic agencies.

An understanding of the relationship between globalization and the state cannot be effective without focusing on the transformation of state structures in East Asia. The argument (see Jayasuriya 1998) is that there has been a significant shift in East Asia from the developmental to the regulatory state, which parallels the transformation from an embedded liberal mode of governance to a form of authoritarian liberalism. It is suggested that embedded liberal forms of governance permitted the emergence and expansion of both welfare and developmental state forms; however, the advent of authoritarian liberalism and the burgeoning juridical cast of international trade increasingly encompass large areas of domestic economic policy and make problematic key components of the development state such as the pursuit of industry policy.

5. Conclusion

An advantage of this typology — the models approach — to an understanding of the Asian currency crisis is that the kind of model used to explain the onset of the East Asian financial crisis can, in large part, determine the solutions and responses to the crisis as well as delimit the possible postcrisis scenarios for East Asia. From a neoclassical perspective, the solution to the crisis lies in three key areas: first, the transition to a capital market–based financial system; second, greater transparency in public and corporate decision-making as well as more effective regulation of banks and the financial system; finally, greater deregulation of product and capital markets, as demanded by organizations like the IMF as a means of reducing state interference in the economy. Institutionalists would seem to be divided on responses to the crisis. For example, Wade and Veneroso (1998) advocate some winding back of the extensive financial deregulation that has taken place over the last decade. In contrast, more structurally based analyses would argue that the key research question in postcrisis East Asia is the extent to which reform coalitions (Robison and Rosser (1998) — of both societal and state actors or forms of state organization (Jayasuriya 1998) — can be consolidated behind neoliberal reconstruction projects. From a globalization perspective, the solution to the crisis would require a national — or more effectively, a global — response to restrict the flow of short-term capital. It also means postponing the liberalization of the capital account in countries such as China, which still have a great many restrictions in place. Another strategy, much debated in East Asia, is to develop a regional response to problems of currency instability. It is beyond the scope of this chapter to consider the appropriateness or plausibility of these responses to the crisis, but the point that needs to be underscored is that the solution or response to the crisis depends on the perspective adopted to explain its origin.

One important lesson that emerges from a consideration of this heuristic classification of the various explanations of the currency crisis is the extent to which static models — whether they focus on internal or external origins of the crisis — fail to recognize the nature of the underlying political changes that have made the East Asian model of capitalism unsustainable. Admittedly, moral hazard and financial panic models provide useful insights into the unfolding of the crisis, but they fail to explain the kind of structural changes in East Asian capitalism that make them highly vulnerable at this time to the kind of crisis that engulfed East Asia. In short, a fuller understanding of the crisis needs a dynamic analysis that locates the economy in the context of broader political structures. Undoubtedly Wade and Veneroso (1998) are correct to identify the transition from the stability of high-debt capitalism to the crisis-ridden economic model of 1997 as the critical issue in any analysis of the currency crisis.

However, given these parameters, each of the different perspectives generates interesting and different research questions about the crisis. From a neoclassical perspective, the key research question is the analysis of the breakdown of the configuration of price and nonprice signals (to use Kornai's terms) that constituted the East Asian system of economic coordination. From an institutionalist perspective, the key research question is to examine the complex relationship between political institutions, shifting coalitions, and the decline of the infrastructure of institutional regulation needed to keep the developmental state afloat. From a globalization perspective, the key research question is to explore how changes in the global economy have been refracted domestically through changes in state organizations or through the reconstitution of dominant social and political coalitions. Whatever the outcome of these inquiries, one thing remains certain: the debates engendered by the Asian crisis are likely to keep the social scientists who are working on East Asia busy for quite some time.

Notes

1. The term "developmental state" originated in the Japanese context (see Johnson 1982) but it has been applied in the East Asian context by Wade (1990). See also Weiss and Hobson (1995) for an excellent survey of the literature. A number of studies have attempted to apply it to Southeast Asia and the transitional economies of Vietnam and China.

2. In the light of economic crisis, international policymakers are well advised to come up with a new set of acronyms to identify Asian economies. In a somewhat light vein I propose calling them "MIME" (Miracle into Mirage Economies).

3. In essence, for the neoclassical version of the crisis to work, it requires the analyst to adopt something like the developmental state model. This is ironic because of the acrimonious debate surrounding the World Bank miracle report, particularly over the contentious issue of the role of the state in economic development.

4. Krueger (1974) provides the best introduction to the use of a rent-seeking framework within the neoclassical framework. However, there has been no work that has applied these concepts to the East Asian economic model; perhaps because it was hard, at least within a neoclassical model, to reconcile the existence of both high rates of economic growth and rent-seeking.

5. Curiously enough, the Korean prosecutor is investigating charges of negligence by the former minister of the economy. Perhaps the cause of the crisis is not moral but criminal hazard!

6. In fact, Robison and Rosser (1998) suggest that the argument has much wider relevance for much of East Asia.

7. Indeed, I would argue that the crisis has only served to accelerate this process of fragmentation and polycentricity within the state.

References

Asian Wall Street Journal (1997). "IMF Chief Blames Crisis on Polices." 3 December, p. 1.

Beeson, M. (1998). "Globalisation, the East Asian Crisis and Indonesia." Paper presented to the ICSSR-IIAS Conference on Identity, Locality and Globalisation. February. New Delhi-Sariska.

Bello, W. (1998). "The End of the Asian Miracle, Inside Indonesia." *Bulletin of the Indonesia Resources and Information Programme (IRIP)* 54(April–June): 7–10.

Bowie, A. (1994). "The Dynamics of Business-Government Relations in Industrialising Malaysia." Pp. 167–94 in *Business and Government in Industrialising Asia,* edited by A. Macintyre. Sydney: Allen & Unwin.

Calder, K. E. (1997). "Assault on the Bakers' Kingdom: Politics, Markets and the Liberalization of Japanese Finance." Pp. 17–56 in *Capital Ungoverned: Liberalizing Finance in Interventionist States,* edited by M. Loriaux et al. Ithaca, NY: Cornell University Press.

Frankel, J. A. (1998). "The Asian Model, The Miracle, The Crisis and the Fund." Paper delivered at U. S. International Trade Commission, April. Available at http: //www.stern.nyu.edu/~nroubini/asia/AsiaHomepage.html.

Jayasuriya, K. (1995). "Political Economy of Democratisation in East Asia." *Asian Perspective* 18(2, Fall–Winter): 141–80.

Jayasuriya, K. (1998). "Globalisation, Authoritarian Liberalism and the Developmental State." Keynote paper presented at International Workshop on Globalization and Social Welfare in East Asia. Research Centre on Development and International Relations, Aalborg University, Denmark.

Johnson, C. (1982). "MITI and the Japanese Miracle: The Growth of Industry Policy." Stanford, CA: Stanford University Press.

Kornai, J. (1992). *The Socialist System: The Political Economy of Communism.* Princeton, NJ: Princeton University Press.

Krueger, A. O. (1974). "The Political Economy of the Rent Seeking Society." *American Economic Review* 64(3): 291–303.

Laothamatas, A. (1992). *Business Associations and the New Political Economy of Thailand.* Boulder, CO: Westview.

Laothamatas, A. (1994). "From Clientelism to Partnership: Business-Government Relations in Thailand." Pp. 195–215 in *Business and Government in Industrialising Asia,* edited by A. Macintyre. Sydney: Allen & Unwin.

Mo, J. and C. Moon (1998). "Democracy and the Origins of the 1997 Korean Economic Crisis." Paper available at http: //www.nautilus.org/napsnet/fora/15_AMo&Moon.html, 1-13. [Also forthcoming in *Democracy and the Korean Economy,* edited by C. Moon and J. Mo. Stanford, CA: Hoover Institution Press.

] Radelet S., and J. Sachs (1998). "The Onset of the East Asian Financial Crisis." Harvard Institute for International Development. Paper available at http: //www.stern.nyu.edu/~nroubini/asia/AsiaHomepage.html.

Ramos, R. (1998). "A Double Burden on Asia's Economies." *Asian Wall Street Journal* 12 February, p. 10.

Robison R., and A. Rosser (1998). *Resisting Reform: Indonesia's New Order,the IMF and the Contest for Change.* Perth: Murdoch University, Asia Research Centre.[Forthcoming in *World Development.*]

Rodrik, D. (1998). "Who Needs Capital Convertibility?" Contribution to a symposium edited by P. Kenen. Available at http: //www.stern.nyu.edu/~nroubini/asia/AsiaHomepage.html. [Forthcoming as part of *Princeton Essays in International Finance,* Harvard University.]

Roubini, N., G. Corsetti, and P. Pesenti (1998). "What Caused the Asian Currency and Financial Crisis?" Unpublished paper, available at http: //www.stern.nyu.edu/~nroubini/asia/AsiaHomepage.html.

Wade, R. (1990). *Governing the Market: Economic Theory and Role of Government in East Asian Industrialization.* Princeton, NJ: Princeton University Press.

Wade R., and F. Veneroso (1998). "The Asian Crisis: The High Debt Model Versus the Wall Street-Treasury-IMF Complex." *New Left Review* (March/April): 1–24.

Weiss, L. and J. Hobson (1995). *States and Economic Development: A Comparative Historical Analysis.* Oxford: Polity.

World Bank (1993). The East Asian Miracle. Washington, DC: Author.

Zysman, J. (1983). *Governments, Markets and Growth: Finance and the Politics of Industrial Change.* Ithaca, NY: Cornell University Press.

Zysman, J. (1996). "The Myth of 'Global Economy': Enduring National Foundations and Emerging Regional Realities." *New Political Economy* 1(2): 67–184.

)

CHAPTER 7

South Korea in 1997–98

A Critical View of the Financial Crisis and the IMF Remedies

Pablo Bustelo

1. Introduction

The Republic of Korea (Korea hereafter) has the eleventh largest economy in the world, as measured by its gross domestic product (GDP) in current dollars. Its importance in world affairs was fully acknowledged in December 1996 when Korea became the second Asian member of the Organization for Economic Cooperation and Development (OECD), the exclusive club of the leading economies of the planet.

Korea's foreign trade amounts to more than US$280 billion, which makes it the sixth largest trading powerhouse in the world. Its outward direct investment, by its huge conglomerates (*chaebol*), such as Samsung, Hyundai, Daewoo, or LG, has reached a sizable amount (more than US$4 billion a year in 1996–97). South Korea is also the world's largest producer of ships and DRAM (dynamic random access memories)-type semiconductors, the fourth largest of consumer electronic goods, the fifth largest of automobiles and petrochemicals, the sixth largest of steel, and the seventh largest of textile products.

The importance of Korea in the world economy calls for an analysis of its evolution in the 1990s, an assessment of its financial crisis in late 1997, and a critical review of the ensuing IMF-sponsored program. The chapter is organized as follows: Section II briefly summarizes the extraordinary economic development of Korea in the last three decades; Section III elaborates on the changing environment of the 1990s and deals particularly with the difficulties of 1996; Section IV explains the onset of the 1997 crisis, explores its nature, and lists its differences with respect to the crises in Southeast Asia; Section V reviews, from a critical perspective, the IMF program; Section VI lists some conclusions about the vulnerability of newly industrializing economies in a globalized world and the adequacy of the IMF's approach in dealing with their financial crises; finally, Section VII offers general conclusions about the IMF bailout and the dangers of globalization.

2. The Economic Background

The development of this newly industrializing economy in the last decades has been impressive by all standards, but especially with respect to growth, structural change, and social conditions (see, e.g., Asian Development Bank 1997a). In fact, Korea has transformed itself, in less than a generation, from an agrarian economy afflicted with mass poverty to an industrial powerhouse with a high per capita income and with social indicators similar to those of a developed economy.

2.1 Sustained Growth

In the mid-1950s, Korea's per capita GDP was lower than those of Angola and Mozambique and was equivalent to only two-thirds of that of Brazil. Between 1960 and 1994, it grew, in 1987 dollars, from US$520 to US$5,210, while Brazil's increased only from US$823 to US$1,993. In purchasing power parity, its per capita GDP reached US$12,390 in 1997, a figure that doubled that of Brazil. The annual average growth of Korea's GDP was 8 percent between 1963 and 1995, a period during which total production increased twelvefold. Per capita GDP increased seven-fold, with an annual average growth rate of 7 percent.

The growth record was even more impressive in the 1970s and 1980s, despite the external energy, trade, and financial shocks of these two decades. Korea's developmental model, overdependent on oil imports, on the export of manufactures to the OECD markets, and (at the beginning of the 1980s) on a sizable external debt, was prone to suffer badly from the two oil shocks of 1973 and 1979, from the slow growth of international trade after the 1960s' boom, and from the increase in the value of the dollar and the rising interest rates in the early 1980s. However, Korea managed to adjust to these shocks rather well, as shown in Table 7.1. Furthermore, Korea overcame the debt problem that has been so common in the Third World in recent decades: in 1980, the ratio of total external debt to GDP was higher in Korea (47.9 percent) than in Brazil (31.8 percent), but from 1980 to 1994 the debt-service ratio (with respect to exports of goods and services) was reduced from 20.3 to only 7.0 percent, a much lower figure than those recorded in Brazil (35.8 percent), Indonesia (32.4 percent), or the Philippines (21.9 percent) in 1994.

Table 7.1: *Average Annual Growth Rates of GDP, 1960–70, 1970–80, 1980–90, and 1990–1995*

	1960–70	1970–80	1980–90	1990–95
South Korea	8.5	9.6	9.4	7.2
HIEs[a]	5.1	3.2	3.2	2.0
LMIEs[b]	5.0	5.3	3.1	2.1
World	5.0	4.2	3.1	2.0

[a] High-income economies.
[b] Low- and middle-income economies.
Source: World Bank (various issues).

2.2 Structural Change

The relative weight of the industrial sector grew markedly from the 1960s to the 1980s, as depicted in Table 7.2. Moreover, the structural transformation in the manufacturing sector was also impressive. In the mid-1990s, Korea was producing a large range of capital-intensive goods, such as steel, petrochemicals, passenger cars, and semiconductors.

Table 7.2: *Sectoral Distribution of GDP (Percentages)*

	1962	1970	1980	1995
Agriculture	40.0	29.8	14.2	6.7
Industry	19.0	23.8	37.8	30.5
Services	41.0	46.4	48.1	62.8

Source: World Bank, (1997, Table 12), Asian Development Bank (1997b: Table A6).

2.3 Social Improvements

Life expectancy at birth increased from 53.9 years in 1960 to 71.5 years in 1994. The adult literacy rate, already high by Third World standards in 1970 (88 percent), reached 98 percent in 1994. The percentage of total population with access to safe water grew from 66 percent in 1975–80 to 93 percent in 1990–96. The infant mortality rate (per 1,000 live births) was reduced from 85 in 1960 to 10 in 1994. The education enrollment rate at all levels (as a percentage of total population between 6 and 23 years of age) increased from 66 percent in 1980 to 82 percent in 1994. According to the United Nations Development Program (UNDP), the human development index (HDI) increased from 0.398 in 1960 (the current level of Nigeria) to 0.890 (the same as Portugal) in 1994 (UNDP 1997: Table 5). Moreover, the distribution of total income was fairly equitable by developing countries' standards during the period. For instance, the ratio 20/20 (the percentage share of total income of the highest income quintile divided by the percentage share of the lowest income quintile) was 7.9 in 1976 (in Brazil it had reached 33.3 in 1972) and 5.7 in 1988 (the figure for Brazil was 32.1 in 1989).

2.4 *A Nonorthodox Developmental Path*

Korea has not followed the prescriptions of the *Washington consensus*, as its developmental strategy differed markedly from the liberal path suggested by economic orthodoxy (cf. Amsden 1989; Chang 1994). Contrary to many conventional neoclassical assumptions, and also to the recent *market-friendly approach* put forward by the World Bank [see World Bank 1993; and a critique in Bustelo (1994) and Singh (1995)], Korea's development has not followed a liberal path, that is, one with competitive internal and external environments for private firms. State intervention has been pervasive through state-owned enterprises and banks, active industrial policy, and state-guided technological learning. Moreover, with respect to its integration with the world economy, Korea was able to achieve a high growth with significant import controls and extensive guidance of foreign direct investment.

3. The Challenges of the 1990s

During the last decade, the Korean economy has been subjected to mounting challenges. Despite the fact that the average growth rate of its GDP reached 7.2 percent in 1990–95 (one of the highest rates in the world, which compared favorably with the 9.4 percent figure of the 1980s), especially since the mid-nineties growth momentum has somewhat decelerated, with the exception of 1994–95, as shown in Figure 7.1.

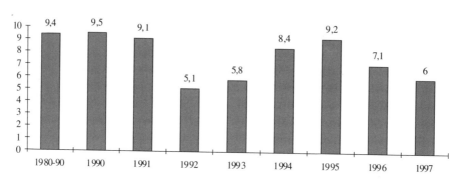

Figure 7.1: *Annual growth rate of GDP, 1980–97.*
Source: *International Monetary Fund (various issues: statistical appendices).*

3.1 The New Economic Environment

Several reasons explaining this slowdown may be outlined as follows: the simultaneous competition in third markets from China and Southeast Asia in labor-intensive products on the one hand and from Japan in capital- and technology-intensive goods on the other; the overextension and overindebtedness of the *chaebol*; a rapid and uncontrolled financial liberalization, which created a domestic financial sector lacking prudential regulation; a massive outward investment by huge companies as a response to the pressures of globalization; an increased trade and financial openness, due to the agreements with the GATT-WTO and the OECD; the bottlenecks in infrastructures in transport and communications; and the crisis in the traditional model of industrial relations, based, until the late eighties, upon stable employment but also on limited union rights and relatively low wages.

3.2 The Deceleration in 1996

In 1996 Korea suffered what was interpreted there as a *recession,* as the growth rate of GDP declined more than two percentage points (9.2 percent in 1995 and 7.1 percent in 1996). The main reasons for this deceleration may be divided into short-term and structural factors.

Among the former, the main were the low increase in import demand from the OECD area (which grew 17 percent in 1995 and only 2 percent in 1996); Japan's higher level of competitiveness, due to the depreciation of the yen with respect to the U.S. dollar since mid-1995; and the large drop in prices in the international market for electronic components, which represent more than a fifth of Korea's total exports (for instance, the price of a DRAM device slumped from US$80 in late 1995 to only US$10 a year later).

The structural factors were much more far-reaching: the increase in unit labor costs, as total labor costs increased at an average annual rate of 8.2 percent between 1985 and 1995, a period in which labor productivity grew substantially less, at 6.5 percent; the stricter monetary policy to fight against the inflationary pressures of the early 1990s and against the worsening current account since 1994; the saturation of transport and communications infrastructures; the trade opening due to the agreements with the WTO (the average tariff rate decreased from 25 percent in 1982 to 10 percent in 1996, and the nontariff barriers were virtually eliminated); the growing protectionism in Western markets; and the increased competitive pressure from the newly exporting economies of East Asia, such as China, Thailand, Malaysia, and Vietnam.

Besides, the year 1996 witnessed a large increase in the trade and current account deficits, as shown in Table 7.3. The appreciation of the Korean *won* with respect to the Japanese yen and the Chinese *renminbi*, the drop in the price of semiconductors, the weakness in Western import demand, and the trade liberalization explain such deterioration.

Table 7.3: *The External Sector, 1993–96*

	1993	1994	1995	1996
Exports (US$ billion)	80.9	93.7	123.2	128.3
Growth rate (%)	7.3	15.7	31.5	4.1
Imports (US$ billion)	79.1	96.8	127.9	143.6
Growth rate (%)	2.5	22.4	32.1	12.2
Trade balance (US$ billion)	1.8	−3.1	−4.7	−15.3
Curr. acc. bal. (US$ billion)	0.3	−3.9	−8.3	−23.7
As % of GNP	0.3	−1.0	−1.8	−4.9

Source: Asian Development Bank (1997b: Table 2.2).

4. The Financial Crisis of 1997–98

The first half of 1997 witnessed the bankruptcies of several *chaebol,* such as Hanbo, Sammi, and Jinro. However, this was then interpreted by analysts merely as a result of a much-needed rationalization in the overexpanded industrial sector. The economy was growing at an annualized rate of 6 percent, inflationary pressures were easing, and the trade and current account deficits were decreasing.

Even after the beginning of the financial crisis of several Southeast Asian economies in July, nothing suggested that Korea was going to follow the path of its southern neighbors. Korea did not suffer a high current account deficit (it had an average of 3.3 percent of GDP in 1995–96, much less, for instance, than the 8.2 percent recorded by Thailand). Moreover, the Korean government did not establish a pegged exchange rate with the U.S. dollar in the 1990s, also in stark contrast with Southeast Asia, and therefore was able to avoid a similarly sharp appreciation of the currency in real terms after the rise of the U.S. dollar from mid-1995 onward. Furthermore, the financial liberalization undertaken since the mideighties, although relevant, had been more gradual than in Southeast Asia: for instance, several controls still remained in place, such as ceilings in foreign investment in Korean manufacturing and financial companies (Cho and Koh 1996).

Despite all these differences, after September the situation deteriorated sharply. The stock exchange index dropped from 800 points in June to 500 points in November, and the currency depreciated quickly, as the exchange rate increased from 914 *won* per dollar in mid-October to 1,550 *won* per dollar at the end of December. The speculative attacks on the *won* were enormous. The exhaustion of the foreign exchange reserves, which diminished from US$30.5 billion in September to US$7.5 billion in December, was the result of the initial willingness to defend the currency, but all the efforts were in vain. Rumors that the foreign debt was in fact much larger than disclosed prompted several rushes away from the *won*. In fact, external pressures obliged the government to make public in November a revised estimation of the total private and public foreign debt, which according to the new figures amounted to an impressive US$156.9 billion, of which at least US$92 billion was in short-term liabilities. This very short maturity in the structure of debt aggravated the liquidity crisis. Moreover, international bank lending to Korea decreased from a monthly average of US$1.3 billion in July–September to only US$300 million in October. Together with the attack on the currency, the withdrawal of foreign credits led to soaring interest rates.

4.1 A Multifaceted Crisis

The speculative selling of *won*, combined with the sudden withdrawal of lending from international private financial institutions, created almost immediately a risk of default, that is, a *solvency crisis*. These two phenomena made apparent the Korean economy's main domestic problem, rampant since the early 1990s, namely, the overindebtedness of manufacturing companies and financial institutions, that is, a *liquidity crisis*. The currency depreciation increased the domestic resource cost of foreign lending, the supply of which was moreover contracting quickly. Meanwhile, the automatic rise in interest rates, as a result of the decline in foreign capital inflows, led to growing financial difficulties in the manufacturing sector and to a substantial increase in the proportion of nonperforming loans in the banking sector.

The *liquidity crisis* of Korean companies was the result of a debt-driven overexpansion of manufacturing activity and bank lending. Already in 1996, thirteen of the thirty largest conglomerates (and four of the ten largest) were operating at a loss. In order to compensate, while simultaneously increasing productive capacity, the management of the *chaebol,* controlled by families eager to maintain their control, decided to rely on domestic and foreign bank lending, instead of issuing stock. In 1997 it was estimated that fourteen of the thirty largest chaebol had a debt-equity ratio in excess of 300 percent and that eight of them surpassed 400 percent, a ratio two to three times higher than the normal situation in other economies. The average debt-equity ratio of 488 listed firms was 339.8 percent in 1997, up 87.7 percentage points from a year earlier (*Korea Economic Weekly* 1998). The four largest *chaebol* (Samsung, Hyundai, Daewoo, and LG), which together account for more than half of Korea's total exports, have interests in an average of no less than 140 different activities, that is, they compete aggressively among themselves.

Meanwhile, the domestic banking sector, which had financed the great bulk of this manufacturing expansion by relying on short-term external funds, faced increased difficulties. Nonperforming loans of Korean banks and other financial institutions amounted, already in 1996, to 70 percent of their net assets. In October 1997, it was estimated that at least a fifth of total lending was made of bad (or nonrecoverable) loans. The simultaneous deterioration of the financial position of manufacturing companies and the plunge in the stock market value of the financial institutions prompted a *banking crisis*.

4.2 *The Specificity of the Korean Crisis*

The Korean crisis of the second half of 1997 was in part similar and in part different from the crisis in Southeast Asia.

The main differences were related to macroeconomic management: Korea did not apply in 1995–97 a policy of anchoring the currency to a rising U.S. dollar in an environment of high current account deficits. Korea clearly did not display all the poor fundamentals that were common ground in Southeast Asia (for instance, real appreciation of the *won* or growing current account imbalances), although, as already mentioned, bad loans, overinvestment, and foreign debt accumulation were certainly important flaws (Corsetti, Pesenti, and Roubini 1998).

The evolution of the real effective exchange rate (REER) was much more negative in Southeast Asia than in Korea, especially in 1995–96. The REER (1990=100) was in 1996 roughly 105 in Malaysia and Indonesia, 110 in Thailand, and 125 in the Philippines, while it was only 98 in South Korea, according to IMF data (International Monetary Fund 1997a). Between December 1990 and March 1997, the real appreciation of the Korean *won* amounted to 11 percent, much less than the rise registered in Indonesia and Thailand (25 percent), Malaysia (28 percent), and the Philippines (47 percent), according to estimates from Radelet and Sachs (1998a: Table 10).

Moreover, as already mentioned, the current account deficit of Korea was lower than that of Thailand or Indonesia and in fact decreased in relative terms in 1997 with respect to 1996 (See Table 7.4).

Furthermore, the financial liberalization in Southeast Asia in the 1990s had been excessively rapid (see Stiglitz 1998). Although Korea eliminated many interest rate controls and restrictions on company debt financing and also allowed for more competition in financial services, its financial opening was more gradual and less intense than in Southeast Asia [Menzie and Maloney (1996); and for a comparison between Korea, on the one hand, and Indonesia and Thailand, on the other, see Johnston, Darbar, and Echevarría (1997)]. To be sure, in Korea financial

Table 7.4: *Current Account Balances in Several East Asian Economies (as Percentage of GDP), 1995–97*

	1995	1996	1997	Average 95–97
South Korea	−1.8	−4.8	−3.2	−3.2
Thailand	−8.3	−8.1	−3.9	−6.7
Malaysia	−9.0	−6.3	−4.0	−6.4
Indonesia	−3.6	−4.1	−3.2	−3.6
Philippines	−3.3	−4.1	−4.5	−3.9
Taiwan	+1.8	+3.7	+2.8	+2.7

Source: IMF (various issues); and author's calculations.

deregulation involved the removal or loosening of several controls: foreign banks were allowed to buy and sell large amounts of foreign and domestic currency; as banking supervision was weakened, domestic banks borrowed heavily from abroad and lent recklessly; manufacturing companies became free to take out loans from domestic and foreign financial institutions; and the government abandoned coordination of borrowings and investments. Despite the fact that financial liberalization has been more gradual than in Southeast Asia, it made the economy more vulnerable to external shocks (Amsden and Euh 1997). It seems paradoxical that some analysts have blamed Korea's recent troubles on excessive state interference in the economy and on the existence of so-called *crony capitalism.* In fact, in order to convert high private (household) savings into corporate debt, a cooperative, reciprocal, and long-term relation between firms, banks, and the government is needed, without necessarily implying corruption or favoritism (Wade and Veneroso 1998b). However, this was exactly what was lacking in Korea, due to what amounted later to have been an excessively rapid financial deregulation and, in more general terms, a too drastic domestic liberalization, both of which were vigorously pursued in the 1990s. In fact, the recent Korean crisis was not due to excessive state interference; on the contrary, it has been a *crisis of underregulation,* as the government abandoned in the 1990s — albeit gradually — its traditional role of properly monitoring foreign borrowing and of coordinating investments (Chang 1997).

The similar features of both kinds of crisis may be summarized as follows. First, the domestic financial institutions were ill-managed and lacked sufficiently prudential regulation by the monetary authorities. They financed, by increasing their short-term indebtedness in U. S. dollars, the spectacular increase of capacity of the manufacturing companies, infrastructure projects, and even real estate speculation. This was partly a result of political connivance and collusion, and even occasionally of corruption and nepotism. Second, the burst of the financial bubble, amplified by the export slowdown in 1996, and also the currency depreciation, which increased the domestic cost of foreign lending, acted as a powerful asset deflation (see Krugman 1997, 1998), and contributed to the liquidity crisis of many financial institutions. Third, the speculative attacks on the currency, which anticipated (and in fact prompted) the depreciation, exhausted the foreign exchange reserves (for an analysis of the factors behind speculative attacks on emerging economies' currencies, see International Monetary Fund 1997b: Chapter 4). Fourth, international private bank lending contracted abruptly after years of supplying large and cheap credit to the so-called emerging markets. According to data from the Institute for International Finance, net private capital inflows to five East Asian economies (Indonesia, Korea, Malaysia, Philippines, and Thailand) dropped from US$93 billion in 1996 to –US$12 billion in 1997, a swing of US$105 billion. The bulk of this decline came from a US$77 billion fall in commercial bank lending and from a US$24 billion decrease in portfolio investment, while direct investment remained virtually constant (Radelet and Sachs 1998a: 9). Therefore, foreign creditors not only stopped making new loans to East Asia but they also withdrew money from the region. In order to stop this self-fulfilling panic in the private sector from affecting national economies, the international financial community should have, already in mid-1997, reacted — as it failed to do. For instance, as Sachs (1998: 16) suggested, the U. S. government and the IMF should have insisted on bringing together the major private foreign creditors to discuss collective actions, and on the main Western central banks to extend credit lines to their counterparts in Asia.

5.   The IMF Rescue Package

In November 1997, the Korean government, swallowing its pride, asked the IMF for financial help. The IMF organized a rescue package of US$57 billion, the largest in the history of the Fund. The breakdown of this amount was as follows: US$22 billion from the main trade partners of Korea; US$21 billion directly from the IMF; US$10 billion from the World Bank; and US$4 billion from the Asian Development Bank (ADB).

The IMF's stand-by credit of SDR 15.5 billion (US$21 billion) involved an austerity program and several structural reforms, with four main areas:

5.1 *Macroeconomic Policies*

In order to eliminate the current account deficit and to contain inflation to single digits in 1998, the government has to pursue stringent fiscal and monetary policies. A package of tax increases and expenditure cuts is intended to render a small surplus in the budget balance in 1998 (from –0.5 percent of GDP in 1997). The IMF had initially demanded a fiscal surplus of as much as 1 percent of GDP but subsequently dropped this request. Interest rates will increase, in order to defend the currency, and the government will control the expansion of the monetary supply. The third Letter of Intent (International Monetary Fund 1998) of the government of Korea forecasts for 1998 a sizable current account surplus (2.5 percent of GDP), an inflation rate slightly below double digits in the whole year, and a real GDP growth of 1 percent, although "zero or negative growth remains a possibility."

5.2 Financial Sector Restructuring

The restructuring of the financial system involves strengthening prudential regulation by monetary authorities, the revocation of licenses of several merchant banks, and the rationalization of the commercial financial institutions.

5.3 Capital Account and Trade Liberalization

The financial opening will be accelerated, i.e., there will be full liberalization of money market instruments, allowance of foreign investment in domestic financial institutions, authorization for foreign banks and brokerage houses to establish subsidiaries, and elimination of ceilings on foreign investment in Korean equities; the trade opening involves abolishing trade-related subsidies and liberalizing merchandise imports and foreign financial services.

5.4 Labor Market Reform

The labor market will be made flexible, clarifying the circumstances and procedures for layoffs. Under the World Bank's US$10 billion Structural Adjustment Loan, the details of these measures will be discussed, in accordance with the Tripartite Accord reached between the government, the unions, and the business community on February 6, 1998.

6. Macroeconomic Perspectives

These restrictive macroeconomic policies will surely result in a drop in domestic demand, as consumer demand is expected to slow down or even decrease and as investment is estimated to contract sharply, as a result of higher interest rates. Together with the currency depreciation, this would allow for a substantial amelioration in the trade and current account balances. However, as Table 7.5 shows, if the IMF program is applied in all its aspects, a recession can be expected. It should be noted that the amelioration in the trade and current account balances — although generally positive — also has a negative side: more trade

Table 7.5: *Macroeconomic Perspectives, 1996–98*

	1996	1997	1998[a]
GDP growth (%)	7.1	6.0	<1.0[b]
Inflation rate (%)	4.9	6.6	9.0[c]
Exports (US$ billions)	129.7	136.6	144.0
Imports (US$ billions)	150.3	144.6	142.0
Trade bal. (US$ billions)	−20.6	−8.0	+2.0
Curr. acc. bal. (US$ billions)	−23.7	−13.8	+10.0
Curr. acc. (% of GDP)	−4.7	−3.2	+2.5

[a]   According to the IMF-sponsored program.
[b]   Private analysts forecast a −2.5% rate.
[c]   This figure might be too optimistic, as it does not take fully into account the effects of the currency depreciation.
Sources: International Monetary Fund (1998) and press reports (May 1998).

friction with the Western trading partners of Korea, many of which have sizable bilateral trade deficits.

However, the IMF-sponsored program has several important flaws. First, the restrictive character of the fiscal and monetary policies might induce a deep recession. Does it make sense to impose an immediate target of budget and current account surpluses and an inflation rate below double digits in an economy mired in recession and extremely affected by the currency depreciation? Several analysts, such as Levinson, Sachs, and Wolf, in articles published in late 1997 in the *Financial Times* and the *New York Times,* have criticized these excessively austere measures, as they will probably intensify the recession, increase the unemployment rate, and trigger social unrest.

On the fiscal side, as Radelet and Sachs have suggested:

> [I]t is not clear why government budgets were made so central to the [IMF's] programs, since fiscal policy had been fairly prudent across the region, and budget profligacy was clearly not the source of the crisis. Moreover, while the Fund argued that fiscal contraction was necessary to reduce the current account deficit, there was no clear rationale provided for why additional contraction was necessary on top of the massive contraction that was already automatically taking place in the region. The fiscal targets simply added to the contractionary force of the crisis. (1998a: 29)

The restrictive monetary policy relies on tightening the overall credit supply by the central bank and on rising interest rates in order to defend the exchange rate and to control inflation. The first measure has had an important pitfall, as it communicated to short-term creditors that the function of lender of last resort traditionally performed by the central bank has been switched off. The second measure calls into question whether its potential benefits with respect to the exchange and inflation rates compensate the immediate negative impact on overall production (see Feldstein 1998).

Second, the financial and trade opening will surely prompt important difficulties in the banking and manufacturing sectors, which had been traditionally protected against foreign services and goods. This is the case certainly of several financial institutions but especially of the Korean auto industry, which in 1996 exported 900,000 units and imported only 11,000 (less than 1 percent of domestic demand).

Third, despite the Tripartite Accord between labor, government, and business, it is clear that a radical reform of the labor market, in order to lower the cost of layoffs, may trigger social unrest. It should be recalled that in early 1997 labor militancy forced the government to cancel a similar initiative.

7.   Conclusions

The Korean economy is experiencing its worst situation since the early 1970s. The IMF-sponsored program is controversial, as its effects, if fully implemented, might be perfectly negative. Moreover, the current crisis certainly calls for a reassessment of past policies but should not be used as an argument for a complete overhaul of a developmental model that has certainly proved its success over the years.

7.1   A Controversial Bailout

The IMF-sponsored economic policies, if applied in their entirety, might aggravate the situation (Radelet and Sachs 1998b; Wade and Veneroso 1998a; Woo-Cumings 1997). First, the Fund is not familiar with the East Asian economies, as it has dealt before mostly with Latin American countries. Even its *World Economic Outlook* of October 1997 predicted a GDP growth for Korea of 6 percent in 1998, while it is now clear that the country will register a negative figure. The IMF's *Annual Report* of 1997 even praised the soundness of Korea's economic fundamentals.

Second, the IMF is treating different situations on an equal footing, such as Mexico in 1994 or Thailand and Indonesia in 1997, on the one hand, and Korea in 1997–98, on the other. The macroeconomic policies and the structural reforms suggested by the IMF are similar despite obvious different backgrounds:

- high current account deficits, exchange rate pegs, and very large external debts, like in Mexico in 1994 and in Thailand and Indonesia more recently;
- low and declining current account deficits, cautious exchange rate management, and relatively low debt-service ratios, like in Korea in 1997–98.

Moreover, the IMF's prescription seems to be totally independent of the state of economic fundamentals. Economies with budget surpluses (or small deficits), high savings rates, low inflation, and outward orientation, such as those in East Asia in the late 1990s, are equated with others affected by fiscal profligacy, low savings, high inflationary pressures, and inward-oriented growth, such as Latin America in the 1980s.

Third, the recessive impact of the excessively austere policies is especially important in economies with a long tradition of high and sustained growth. In 1990–97, the Korean GDP grew at an average annual rate in excess of 6 percent.

Fourth, the financial and trade opening will surely make Korea more and not less vulnerable (Akyüz 1998). The reaction of the international capital markets after the stand-by agreement with the IMF was signed in early December 1997 has been a clear sign of their mistrust. For instance, between December 4 and January 8, the exchange rate of the currency increased from 1,170 *won* to 1,788 *won* per dollar.

Fifth, the IMF programs have a clear bias in favor of private international financial institutions, as foreign creditors are not urged to take their share of responsibility in the crises, escaping instead unscathed. The latter are not even encouraged to roll over short-term debt into longer-term instruments, a process that was simply left to an eventual bilateral negotiation between Korea and its creditors.

Sixth, as a main agent for bailing out, not national economies, but in fact foreign private creditors, the IMF could perfectly well be accused of sowing the seeds of future crises. Private financial institutions, if assured that they will recover their loans, will continue to throw money recklessly at fragile economies.

Finally, the recent financial crises in East Asia have highlighted again the traditional lack of transparency and of political and social control of the Bretton Woods institutions (see Taylor 1997).

7.2 The Dangers of Globalization

In more general terms, the Korean crisis has demonstrated that even economies with a strategic (e.g., limited and controlled) integration into the world economy — rather than a close (or indiscriminate) one [see discussion in Singh (1995) and Lall (1996)] — are also vulnerable to rapid shifts in the international capital markets. It should be recalled that South Korea, similarly to Taiwan (see Bustelo 1997), has strictly controlled foreign direct investment and maintained several import protection measures throughout its industrialization process. Furthermore, as already discussed, the financial liberalization of the 1980s and 1990s had been more gradual and cautious in Korea than in Southeast Asia or Latin America. If even strategically integrated and gradually liberalizing economies are vulnerable, this certainly calls for global control of the international movements of short-term funds and for an even more careful approach in external liberalization in developing countries.

A second conclusion is that what is at stake in East Asia is the sustainability of an original developmental path, different in many aspects, such as state intervention and the degree of integration with the world economy, from the neoliberal orthodoxy. Korea might be compelled to abandon its previous strategy, a shift that will jeopardize its national economic prospects and put into question the appeal of its success story to other developing economies.

References

Typescript documents refer to texts available through the Internet, without hard copies released, to the author's knowledge, at the time of writing (May 1998).

Akyüz, Y. (1998). *The East Asian Financial Crisis: Back to the Future?* Typescript. Geneva: UNCTAD.
Amsden, A. H. (1989). *Asia's Next Giant. South Korea and Late Industrialization.* New York: Oxford University Press.
Amsden, A. H. and Y.-D. Euh (1997). "Behind Korea's Plunge." *New York Times,* 27 November.
Asian Development Bank (1997a). *Emerging Asia. Changes and Challenges.* Manila: ADB.
Asian Development Bank (1997b). *Asian Development Outlook 1996 and 1997.* Manila: ADB.
Bustelo, P. (1994). "La Banque Mondiale et le dévelopment économique des nouveaux pays industriels asiatiques: une analyse critique." *Asies Recherches* (Grenoble)13: 11–22.
Bustelo, P. (1997). "State Intervention and Strategic Integration in Taiwan's Economic Development." *Revista de Estudios Asiáticos* (Madrid) 4: 47–58.
Chang, H.-J. (1994). *The Political Economy of Industrial Policy.* London and New York: Macmillan and St. Martin's.
Chang, H.-J. (1997). "Perspective on Korea: A Crisis from Underregulation." *Los Angeles Times,* 31 December.
Cho, D. and Y. Koh (1996). "Liberalization of Capital Flows in Korea: Big Bang or Gradualism?" NBER Working Paper no. 5824.
Corsetti, G., P. Pesenti, and N. Roubini (1998). "What Caused the Asian Currency and Financial Crisis?" Unpublished, available at http: //www.stern.nyu.edu/~nroubini/ AsianCrises.pdf, March.
Feldstein, M. (1998). "Refocusing the IMF." *Foreign Affairs* 77(2, March–April): 20–50.
International Monetary Fund (1997a). *World Economic Outlook. Interim Assessment.* Advance Copy, December. Washington, DC: IMF.
International Monetary Fund (1997b). *International Capital Markets. Developments, Prospects and Key Policy Issues.* Washington, DC: IMF.
International Monetary Fund (1998). "South Korea's Third Letter of Intent." Unpublished, available at http: //www.imf.org/external/np/loi/020798.htm, February 7.
International Monetary Fund (various issues). *World Economic Outlook.* Washington, DC: IMF.
Johnston, R. B., S. M. Darbar, and C. Echevarría (1997). "Sequencing Capital Account Liberalization: Lessons from the Experience in Chile, Indonesia, Korea and Thailand." IMF Working Paper no. 97/157, Washington, DC.

Korea Economic Weekly (1998). "Debt-to-Equity Ratios of Listed Companies Shoot Up."
    April 6.
Krugman, P. (1997). "Currency Crises." Typescript, October. Cambridge, MA: MIT.
Krugman, P. (1998). "What Happened to Asia?" Typescript, January. Cambridge, MA: MIT.
Lall, S. (1996). "Paradigms of Development: The East Asian Debate on Industrial Policy."
    Oxford Development Papers 24(2) April. [Also in S. Lall *Learning from the Asian
    Tigers. Studies in Technology and Industrial Policy.* 1–26. London: Macmillan (1996).]
Menzie, D. C. and W. F. Maloney (1996). "Financial and Capital Account Liberalization
    in the Pacific Basin: Korea." NBER Working Paper no. 5814.
Radelet, S. and J. Sachs (1998a). "The Onset of the East Asian Financial Crisis." Draft
    and typescript. Cambridge, MA: Harvard Institute for International Development.
Radelet, S. and J. Sachs (1998b). "The East Asian Financial Crisis: Diagnosis, Remedies,
    Prospects." Draft and typescript. Cambridge, MA: Harvard Institute for International
    Development.
Sachs, J. (1998). "The IMF and the Asian Flu." *American Prospect* 37(March–April): 16–21.
Singh, A. (1995). "How Did East Asia Grow So Fast? Slow Progress Towards an
    Analytical Consensus." *UNCTAD Discussion Papers* (Geneva) 97(February).
Stiglitz, J. (1998). "The Role of International Financial Institutions in the Current Global
    Economy." Address (typescript) to the Chicago Council on Foreign Relations,
    February 27.
Taylor, L. (1997). "The Revival of the Liberal Creed — The IMF and the World Bank
    in a Globalized Economy." *World Development* 25(2): 145–52.
United Nations Development Program (1997). *Human Development Report 1997.* New
    York, UNDP.
Wade, R. and F. Veneroso (1998a). "The Asian Financial Crisis: The Unrecognized Risk of
    the IMF's Asia Package." Typescript, February. Russell Sage Foundation, New York.
Wade, R. and F. Veneroso (1998b). "The Asian Crisis: The High-debt Model vs. the Wall
    Street-Treasury-IMF Complex." Typescript, March. Russell Sage Foundation, New York.
Woo-Cumings, M. (1997). "Bailing Out or Sinking In? The IMF and the Korean Financial
    Crisis." Typescript, December 2. Economic Strategy Institute, Washington, D. C.
World Bank (1993). *The East Asian Miracle. Economic Growth and Public Policy.* New
    York: Oxford University Press.
World Bank (various issues). *World Development Report,* Washington, DC: World Bank.

CHAPTER 8

Tigers and Lambs

Asian Models of Development and the Island Pacific

Michael Goldsmith

1. Introduction

As the editors of this volume suggested in their original book proposal, for the so-called late industrializing countries, such as small and resource-restrained small island states — for example, in the Caribbean or in the Pacific region — the East Asian experience may either affect them directly (both positively and negatively) or, alternatively, furnish them with examples for viable development strategies in the context of (theoretically) unbridled global free trade.

Though there can be no doubt that the East Asian experience has exerted some influence on thinking about development in the Pacific region, this chapter will perforce concentrate on the first proposition, i.e., the ways in which developmental processes in (East) Asia affect Pacific Island states directly. It is clear, for Asia, that the Pacific functions mainly as a source of raw materials (timber and minerals, especially from Melanesia), food (especially migratory fish species), and tourist destinations. While it has performed these functions for many other parts of the world and continues to do so, what distinguishes the recent Asian involvement is its sheer size and potential for growth, its increasing intensity at a geopolitical and transnational corporate level, and its competition with alternative models of development. The situation is one where some of the largest and most rapidly developing economies in the world have come to exert influence on neighbors that happen to rank among the smallest and most underperforming. In the process, Pacific resources are exploited either by direct extraction or by loosely policed forms of investment and "joint" business enterprise between local and Asian partners.

In this chapter, I intend to explore some ramifications of Asian involvement in the Pacific Island Countries (PICs). First, I will briefly describe the constraints under which the economies of those countries operate. Then some intrinsic features and problems of "Asian models" will be discussed. That will be followed by an outline of the vexing issue of resource extraction. Toward the end, I will address the question of whether Asian and alternative models, influences, and institutions can (1) account for recent changes and (2) offer the possibility of economic solutions in the region. While Asian models as a whole may be inappropriate and destructive (as I argue), some aspects of their operation have been influential. Thus, the Asian Development Bank (ADB) and the New Zealand government jointly espouse "more market" models (including policies such as privatization and governmental "downsizing") in the former colonial possessions of the Cook Islands and Niue. These hybrid reforms show that Pacific societies are not immune to changing ideologies of governance and economic management. Nevertheless, their development is unlikely to follow the (East) Asian path. The specific quality of civil-military relationship exemplified in the Asian tigers may prove to be one of the greatest stumbling blocks, as Pacific Island economies are unable to sustain the high level of military spending that seems to be a crucial feature of the Asian model. The other stumbling block to greater diffusion of this particular ideology of economic growth and organization stems from the recent catastrophic problems of most East and Southeast Asian economies, the implications of which will be addressed in the conclusion.

2.   The Island Pacific

In general, the PICs are extremely small by world standards. The largest, Papua New Guinea (hereafter PNG), has some four million people; the next largest, Fiji, has only three-quarters of a million, and the Solomon Islands about 370,000. A few countries have populations of 100,000–200,000, such as French Polynesia, New Caledonia, Vanuatu, Western Samoa, and Tonga, and others have between 15,000 and 100,000, such as Kiribati, Marshall Islands, Palau, and the Cook Islands. At the low end of the demographic scale are some truly minuscule political entities: Tuvalu (about 10,000 people), Nauru (about the same but including a high proportion of immigrant workers), Niue and Tokelau (1,500 or so each). Since the internationally recognized threshold for microstate status is usually taken to be a population of under one million (Richards 1990: 40), the smallest Pacific states and territories represent a kind of political and economic category that is truly distinctive in the present world system. Even the middle-range PICs in terms of population and resource base are comparable only to some small states in the Caribbean and Indian Ocean.

For the purposes of economic growth and development, few PICs have enough raw materials to attract much outside investment. In particular, the high-island Melanesian states of Papua New Guinea, Vanuatu, the Solomon Islands,

New Caledonia, and Fiji (which occupies a transitional status between the Melanesia and Polynesia culture areas) all have either large mineral deposits or large tracts of tropical forest, or both. Most, if not all, PICs also have good-sized Exclusive Economic Zones — areas that, where other boundaries do not intervene, push formal sovereignty out to the 200-mile limit established by the Law of the Sea (Buchholz 1987). The zones of Kiribati, the Federated States of Micronesia, and French Polynesia are extremely large but any EEZ greatly enhances the size and resource base of the countries to which it belongs. Almost all large-scale fishing, however, is controlled from outside the region by the so-called Distant Water Fishing Nations (DWFNs), most of which are East Asian — Taiwan, South Korea, and Japan (Doulman 1989). While some progress has been made by the Forum Fishing Agency (FFA) in boosting returns to island nations from fish catches, employment, and licenses, the PICs still face considerable difficulties of policing the zones and of standing up to larger players in negotiations (Doulman 1992; Bergin 1995; Miller 1995; Sasako 1996; Sutherland 1984; Tsamenyi and Mfodwo 1995; Wolfers 1995). This issue will be addressed later in more detail.

Those countries with the largest populations and resource bases tend to face formidable problems of developing infrastructures and skilled labor forces, especially among younger cohorts for whom traditional subsistence activities are increasingly blocked by demographic pressures and land hunger.[1] PNG, Vanuatu, and the Solomons lack the safety valve of migration enjoyed by such Polynesian societies as Western Samoa and Tonga (which have entry quotas into Australia and New Zealand) and, in particular, those with guaranteed metropolitan access like French Polynesia, the Commonwealth of the Northern Mariana Islands, American Samoa, Niue, Cook Islands, and Tokelau. Yet these latter countries in turn lack the material advantages of the Melanesian ones and in many cases have equally dire infrastructural deficiencies in transport and communication. Not surprisingly, according to the ADB, about half the PICs are undergoing or have recently undergone some form of painful economic restructuring or crisis (Keith-Reid 1997a: 24).

3. Exploring the Asian Model

What, then, does the "Asian model" offer by way of inspiration to the PICs? As currently understood, this model embodies a number of well-known features. It connotes an industrial or rapidly industrializing economy, based not so much on the possession of raw materials as on a well-trained, cooperative, and industrious labor force. The latter is paid relatively low-wage rates (at least initially) and receives minimal welfare provision from the state (though employers may act as welfare providers in some cases). High rates of economic growth are achieved by cooperation between government and business and an environment in which the state offers little regulation but does direct some aspects of investment and training. In a world of "(theoretically) unbridled global free trade" (to quote the editors' prospectus), economies of this sort seem to offer a huge competitive advantage.

Ironically, however, to tout the shining examples of development afforded by the current generation of Asian tigers is not only to ignore their current difficulties but is also to run the danger of overlooking a very real and historically vexed relationship between Asian entrepreneurs and Pacific Islanders. The most politically contentious evolution of this relationship has occurred in Fiji, where the commercial aspirations of the substantial Indian segment of the population (largely the descendants of indentured plantation laborers) have encountered resistance from an indigenous Fijian politics of tradition (Ravuvu 1987, 1991). Chinese have also been present throughout the Pacific since the nineteenth century, both as a commercial segment that has intermarried with indigenous populations, particularly in the case of Western Samoa and French Polynesia, and as laborers who have played important roles in the extractive industries of Nauru and New Zealand.[2] Vietnamese and other migrants from the former French possessions in "Indo-China" settled many decades ago in the French Pacific territories, especially New Caledonia, though their numbers declined through repatriation in the 1960s and 1970s. The Japanese presence has also been intermittently powerful, first announcing itself by means of League of Nations mandates in former German territories in Micronesia between the First and Second World Wars (Peattie 1988), peaking with Pearl Harbor and the occupation of a number of Pacific territories, collapsing after defeat in 1945, but steadily reviving in the forms of trade, aid, and diplomacy in recent decades (Edo 1986; Numata 1990; Watanabe 1995). In the 1960s and 1970s, some observers expected Japan to become the dominant economic player in the region (see, e.g., Smales 1977; Mortimer 1979). In partial fulfillment of that prophecy, its relative prosperity and its diplomatic outreach have combined to make it currently the largest single aid donor in the Pacific. (A summit of Pacific Island leaders convened in Tokyo in October 1997 as recognition of that fact.) Nevertheless, while undoubtedly a hegemon, Japan's position has been challenged by transnational capital from South Korea, Malaysia, and Indonesia as well as by political overtures from Taiwan and China (Saffu and Roskies 1992; Pheysey 1996).

These connections reflect a historically entrenched and culturally policed arrangement of responsibilities that has reinforced the rhetorical distaste of many Pacific Islanders for business as an occupation. This suspicion results from stereotyping, admittedly, as there are no intrinsic barriers to engaging in either commerce or wage labor. All sources of cash attract Pacific Island recruits readily under the right circumstances. But there has long been a mutually convenient division of labor between Asian (and Western) entrepreneurs and Pacific landowners and laborers, a separation with implications for the recent reawakening of Asian interests.

In one sense, therefore, Asian influences and models are neither new nor unfamiliar in the Pacific. They have taken a new form, however, since the expansion of East and Southeast Asian economies over the last three or four decades. As the apparently most successful "developing" economies of the postwar era, the possibility that they may serve as a source of ideas for viable development strategies in the Pacific Islands cannot be lightly dismissed. David Lim (1993) has usefully formulated clear arguments in favor of this notion. I will outline his major points before suggesting some counterarguments. First, Lim (ibid.: 35–36) dismisses some hypotheses that purport to explain the growth of the East and Southeast Asian economies but that do not conform to the facts in his view. These hypotheses are (1) a paucity of abundant natural resources, which enables East and Southeast Asian economies to avoid the so-called "Dutch disease" of reliance on primary exports and consequent lack of international competitiveness; (2) historically massive aid flows from the United States and other Western countries to combat communist expansionism, allowing client states such as South Korea and Taiwan to establish the conditions for industrial "take-off"; (3) the Confucian heritage, which emphasizes hard work, thrift, and respect for authority (a cultural explanation that anyway works best for East rather than Southeast Asia).[3] Having dismissed these as significant explanations, the alternative hypothesis that, he contends, does explain Asian economic performance best is (4) the mix of macroeconomic policies that governments pursue in conjunction with markets. In Lim's exact words, "countries which pursue a market-friendly and internationally competitive approach to development will grow faster" (ibid.: 36). (For an opposing argument, which stresses chance factors and which questions the much-vaunted hegemony of Japan and the Asian tigers, see Palat 1996.)

What relevance does this hypothesis have for the Pacific island region? Lim concedes that the South Pacific economies have grown slowly or stagnated in part because of smallness, remoteness, and vulnerability to external pressures. But these factors are not the whole story, in his view. How else, he asks, can we explain the fact that the "small island economies of the Caribbean and the Indian Ocean, which are more or less similarly handicapped, have performed much better" (Lim 1993: 47–48)?

Lim's argument is undermined by large-scale issues of political economy as well as by flaws in the comparison.[4] To begin with, like many economists, he assumes that paths of development run on parallel tracks (and that where they do not there must be a distortion or obstacle that prevents them from following the otherwise "natural" course). The PICs, by contrast, have followed developmental paths that are often unique and certainly uneven. One does not have to advocate the sort of crude dependency theory that automatically attributes "underdevelopment" somewhere in the Third World to "(over)development" elsewhere to see that Pacific economies have tended to *complement* those of more industrialized nations, as opposed to *copying* them. They play a role in the international division of labor that simply is not, and never can be, the same as those of the Asian economies. Their interconnections are relational rather than mimetic.

Second, while the better-performing small Caribbean and Indian Ocean states face similar demographic and environmental constraints to those in the Pacific, the comparison is less convincing than it seems. In many PICs, "traditional" subsistence-based activities are more important than in the Caribbean. While these activities constitute less of the economic order than they used to, and have become thoroughly monetized in all sorts of ways, there is still a deep-seated reluctance among many Pacific Islanders to introduce market principles into certain aspects of their lives. True, there have been extractive industries based on commodities like sandalwood, kauri, and phosphate since the first decades of Western contact (Howe 1984). It is also true that labor has been bought and sold as a commodity since the whaling era, though this commoditization still runs up against limits imposed by cultural systems of reciprocity and exchange. Nevertheless, suspicion of commoditization has applied most strongly to one important factor of production: land (see Hooper 1993: 322). Withholding land from the commercial arena poses well-known obstacles to credit formation and investment. Though this retraction has always been applied selectively and there are signs of it being undermined in parts of the Pacific where it has hitherto been regarded as sacrosanct, rights over land continue to act as a powerful vehicle of resistance to commercialization.

To put it bluntly, then, the basis for Asian-style development does not exist in most Pacific states and territories. The few exceptions include some peripheral and possibly temporary "sweatshop" industries in Fiji and Micronesia, based on tax respite arrangements, migrant labor (often Asian in origin itself), and/or tariff advantages for entry into the American, Australian, and New Zealand markets. In general, however, Pacific Island economies suffer from diseconomies of scale and distance, and from a lack of technically trained work forces. Incentives also differ from those in Caribbean and Indian Ocean microstates, given (a) the continuing possibility of full-time subsistence activities and (b) relatively free or even open access to Western-style labor markets (New Zealand, Australia, the United States, and France). Both are more likely to attract effort than working in Asian-style production regimes.

Of course, it all rather depends on which version of the "Asian model" one chooses to highlight. As opposed to the high-growth, industrializing model implied by the "tiger" metaphor, a different ("earlier"?) kind of Asian parallel may reinforce low-growth sustainable development — one that entails efficient subsistence agriculture, low-intensity tourism, artisanal and petty commodity

production, and "appropriate technology." At the Third Southwest Pacific
Conference on Peace, Stability and Resilience, held in Ujung Pandang on Sulawesi
in early 1992, for example, a number of speakers from the "European" Pacific
Rim countries, such as the United States, Australia, and New Zealand, began to
acknowledge that some models of national development being pursued in countries
like Indonesia might be more suited to the resource-poor, tropical island states
of Melanesia, Polynesia, and Micronesia than strategies based on high capital
investment, high wage rates, and high-tech industries. Indeed, it is possible to see
historical precedents in development strategies pursued by Japanese colonial
administrators in Micronesia from the late nineteenth century until 1945 (Peattie
1984, 1988).[5] Nevertheless, this approach stands apart from the influence of Asian
models as conventionally depicted and it remains to be seen whether it can
compete in the ideological stakes against neoliberal economics.

4.   Resource Exploitation by Asian Tigers

Recent investigations have demonstrated the predatory nature of much of the
Asian interest, often in collaboration with local comprador entrepreneurs, in South
Pacific natural resources. This interest is especially notable in the forests of
Melanesian continental/high islands in Papua New Guinea (Garrett 1991; Barlow
1997), Solomons (Grynberg 1994; Frazer 1997: 64–66) and Vanuatu (Garrett 1993;
Decloitre 1994; Regenvanu et al. 1997). The move by Southeast Asian companies
into the Pacific reflects the increasing difficulty of domestic forestry in their own
countries as the most easily logged stands of tropical rainforest have been
exhausted. In addition, national legislation and international conservation cove-
nants against overexploitation of protected species and areas have taken effect.
By contrast, Melanesia has suffered from a strategy of open slather. The Barnett
Timber Industry Enquiry in PNG exposed stunning disregard of local environmental laws and corruption of local politicians by Indonesian and Malaysian corporations, such as Rimbunan Hijau, which has controlled about 85 percent of the
industry. Similar problems in Vanuatu and the Solomons have surfaced as
Southeast Asian entrepreneurs have turned their attention to these smaller but
equally tempting targets. By the early 1990s, Malaysian consortia came to control
50 percent of the Solomons timber business (Garrett 1993). Entrepreneurs who
take such an exploitative stance to the raw materials on offer have been aptly
named "robber barons," after a phrase from the Barnett Enquiry (Garrett 1991).
At least two forestry ministers in the PNG government have reportedly been
offered bribes to turn a blind eye to malfeasance in the logging industry. Where
monetary inducements have not worked, logging companies and/or their backers
have apparently issued death threats (Garret 1993; Keith-Reid 1995). In a move

that raises fears about freedom of the press to report such issues, one Asian forestry tycoon has even set up his own newspaper in Port Moresby (Robie 1993).

Roman Grynberg (1994) presents a compelling analysis of what he calls the "logging dilemma" in the Solomon Islands. The Solomons economy is actually quite diversified and soundly based by South Pacific standards. In theory, the country could produce enough commodities to ensure its own survival, as it has considerable fish stocks, forests, and cultivable land. Unfortunately, the exploitation of natural resources has in recent years been used to bolster a fragile financial base in a probably vain attempt to keep the country out of the clutches of the International Monetary Fund. There have been several alarms over potential bankruptcy since 1991 as foreign exchange reserves have come close to drying up. Commercial fishing, including a major Japanese-Solomons joint venture (Meltzoff and LiPuma 1985), used to supply much of the government's revenue but the catch declined after 1991 and the boom seemed to be over. With few mineral resources and a small tourism base, the Solomons turned to large-scale timber extraction as a way of keeping afloat. There are, however, serious doubts that the cutting rates are sustainable. Francis Hilly, Solomons prime minister (1993–94) predicted that stocks would run out in fifteen years if the exploitation were not checked.

Admittedly, local landowners in Melanesia have sometimes complied with treefelling and forestry projects. It is easy to accuse them of succumbing to commercial deals through a mixture of greed and naivete but the explanations are almost certainly more complex (Waiko 1981; Wood 1996). First, landowners may be lied to or not have the fine print of logging contracts made clear to them. Second, they simply may be unable to resist the industrial strength, legal expertise, and political power that large corporations can bring to the equation; they therefore attempt to get the best deal possible out of the situation, however bad that may be. Third, they may cooperate out of a genuine sense of frustration with the lack of initiative shown by central governments and their inability to provide even the basic infrastructure for development, in particular, roads that logging companies put into inaccessible areas for their own benefit. In the end, however, many of the expected returns from logging fail to live up to expectations because of underreporting of cutting rates, evasion of duties, and unfair pricing arrangements. An independent report to the 1994 South Pacific Forum estimated that "some Pacific countries were losing half their potential national income through unmonitored logging exports.... Papua New Guinea's losses were said to be equivalent to the A$327 million ($241 million) of aid it receives annually from Australia" (*Economist* 1994).

Reference was made earlier to the structural weaknesses of Pacific Island nations in negotiating favorable deals with the Distant Water Fishing Nations. Just as underreporting of timber cutting rates denies the Pacific states much-needed revenue, so does underreporting of fish catches. Grynberg (1993) reports that, according to the South Pacific Commission, the disparity in 1991 between the Asian DWFN purse seiner log books and the commission's own estimates were staggering: 94,000 vs. 170,000 metric tons (Japan), 11,000 vs. 242,000 tons (South Korea), and 26,000 vs. 176,000 tons (Taiwan). The figures show that Korea and Taiwan were the main offenders, with most of the Japanese discrepancy probably due to fishing in international waters as well as in Pacific EEZs. Nevertheless, Japan clearly uses access to the tuna fishing grounds as a bargaining chip in its aid allocations and has refused to conduct multilateral fisheries negotiations with PICs. Even where the metropolitan power concerned has decided to abide by Forum Fisheries Agency rules, as U. S. tuna fishing companies have done over the last decade, the maximum that PICs earn from the arrangement is 9 percent of the value of the catch. It has been calculated that, of the US$1,500 million worth of fish harvested from the Pacific each year, Forum nations receive a mere US$50 million (Keith-Reid 1997a: 25). Since 1994, however, the FFA, with the support of Australia and New Zealand, has achieved some success in bringing the island nations under a common umbrella for talks with the Asian DWFNs.

None of the allegations of Asian impropriety should be taken as suggesting that non-Asian corporations are squeaky clean when it comes to dealing with Pacific governments, elites, and landowners (Lafitte 1991, 1995). It is little wonder that accusations of hypocrisy flew when the Australian government threatened to withdraw aid from South Pacific countries breaching forestry regimes (Callick 1996). Most Western corporations, however, have concentrated on the exploitation of mineral resources in Melanesia, partly because they have their own timber reserves and partly because powerful mining interests based in Australia have simply extended their reach into neighboring regions (Connell and Howitt 1991). Sometimes, of course, Asian and Western firms cooperate to benefit from mining ventures. The most notorious current case is the huge copper and gold mine in the Grasberg mountains of Irian Jaya, which has been the subject of unsuccessful litigation by local tribespeople. Here the Indonesian government is directly involved alongside U. S.- and UK-based multinational corporations (Freeport McMoRan and Rio Tinto) that have aroused a great deal of opposition to their operations both abroad and domestically.

Almost none of the raw materials and natural resources extracted from the Pacific region by Asian business have value added to them in the Pacific islands themselves, other than in the forms of some Asian-financed fish canning in Fiji, Solomon Islands, and American Samoa, and Asian tourism in some island groups, especially in Micronesia (e.g., Japanese visitors to Guam and the Commonwealth of the Northern Marianas or Taiwanese visitors to Palau). Even tourism, however, which relies on pristine settings to sell itself, is threatened in the long term by accelerated processes of industrialization occurring in East and Southeast Asia, with their flow-on effects of pollution and global warming. There has been a steady growth of Asian investment in tourism, travel, hotel, and casino developments in such investment-friendly settings as the Commonwealth of the Northern Mariana Islands (McPhetres 1995, 1996, 1997) and Palau (Shuster 1997). Unlike the capital invested in sweatshop textile manufacture in the CNMI (Ray 1995) — which is highly mobile and directed to taking advantage of possibly temporary gaps in the U. S. tariff wall — these tourism ventures seem to promise relative stability. On the other hand, their social consequences are often negative and the economic returns to the host countries small in comparison to those gained by the Asian investors. Some local elites are wealthy or powerful enough to invest on their own behalf, of course, but for many families the gains from tourism are from one-off sales or long-term leases of land, a subject of much contention.

5.   The New Zealand Model

If, from the discussion so far, East and Southeast Asian economic activities look like the source of many of the Pacific's worst nightmares, it has to be conceded that the economic rationale implicit in many of those activities has gained a foothold in Pacific development circles. I have already mentioned the ADB's involvement in Pacific economic reform. The ideas that the ADB promulgates are not always modeled on the Asian economic boom as such but reflect a worldwide trend in economic ideology to purer notions of the market, state contraction, and free trade. This is not the place to discuss the reasons behind the ascendancy of new economic orthodoxy, but it has taken root in many parts of the world, not just Asia. No nation seems entirely immune from its influence but few governments have espoused the free market quite so fervently, at least among the capitalist democracies, as New Zealand since 1984, though Australia has also joined the chorus since the Liberal-National coalition took power there in 1995. The significance of this for the PICs is obvious: Australia and New Zealand have long been heavily involved in the region's political and economic circuits, are the only metropolitan countries in the South Pacific Forum, are members of what was formerly known as the South Pacific Commission (now the Secretariat of the Pacific Community), and have provided aid and economic advice for decades. Australia was the former colonial power in Papua New Guinea and has taken up a more active role in the Solomon Islands and Vanuatu since they gained independence from Britain and from a Franco-British condominium, respectively (Babbage 1995; Connell and Pritchard 1990; Firth 1994; Henningham 1996). Australia was also the dominant colonial administrator in the phosphate-rich island of Nauru and maintains a watching brief over much of Micronesia. New Zealand's colonial realm used to include Western Samoa and still includes the self-governing entities of Cook Islands, Niue, and Tokelau, whose residents have rights of New Zealand citizenship.

The recent history of the Cook Islands can stand as emblematic of the upsurge of economic reformism in New Zealand's relations with the Pacific. From the time that self-government was granted in 1965, successive administrations in the Cooks were generally able to count on Wellington's willingness to bail the country out of its financial woes — at least up until the economically rationalist Labour government of 1984–90 and the even more fiscally conservative National/ Coalition governments that have followed. Now government-to-government aid is being phased out and is due to expire completely in 2007. Failing to heed the signs, a popular but extravagant Cook Islands Party regime under the leadership of Sir Geoffrey Henry found itself in a fiscal crisis by late 1995. According to the ADB, external debt (excluding investment tied up in a stalled Sheraton hotel project) totaled about NZ$50 million, some 40 percent of which was owed to the ADB (Bell 1996: 10). The total debts amounted to US$107 million (NZ$158.49 million).

After surviving an abortive challenge to his leadership, Sir Geoffrey embraced a new strategy called *Upoko Tu* ("standing on one's own two feet") (ibid.). The nation, once known for policies reminiscent of a New Zealand-style welfare state and Crown ownership of assets, appeared to accept monetarist economics with evangelical zeal. Many of the country's major assets were put up for sale, including its international airport, the ports, the telecommunications company, the power authority, and government-owned hotels. Interestingly, in late 1996, a Malaysian businessman was rumored to be in the market for the purchase of state assets, though Sir Geoffrey denied there was any truth "to speculation that billionaire Malaysian businessman Tajudin Ramli had made a $100 million offer for the entire asset list" (Hill 1996: 5). Rather, Henry claimed, Australian and New Zealand investors were showing keen interest, a statement backed up by subsequent reports. On the other hand, some local landowners were also demonstrating keen opposition to the sale of assets, especially land, that they argued had only been made over to the government originally on condition that they remained under national control. Some traditional leaders, such as Pa Ariki, attempted to line up Cook Islands investors at home and abroad to keep ownership of the assets.

While the sale of public assets is still a matter of argument, there is no doubt that economic "reform," or its rhetoric, has taken root in the Cook Islands. The public service, which once made up about 60 percent of the entire work force, has been slashed. Reports have varied on how vigorous the pruning was intended to be. Some said the service was targeted for a cutback from 5,200 to 3,600 (still one of the largest public-private ratios in the Pacific, it has to be said), but other sources talked of a two-thirds reduction from 3,200 to just over 1,000 (*Dominion*

8 June, 1996, p. 2). These cuts were linked to a concomitant reduction in the number of government departments from 52 to 22 and in public service salaries by 15 percent (Kilroy 1996: 7). Indeed, the short-term salary cuts were in the order of 50 percent (*Dominion* 24 April, 1996, p. 1). Whatever the final figures, the cutbacks have been severe.

The neoliberal model is likely to have a twofold effect in the Island Pacific. First, there is the sheer momentum of the economic ideology, which is clearly gaining ground. One of the countries where the model has been most enthusiastically embraced is the resource-poor Micronesian atoll nation of Kiribati. A probusiness climate has recently emerged under President Teburoro Tito. His Christian Democratic party is attempting to foster a more investor-friendly environment, boost the private sector, and reform public management (IBP 1994; Fraser 1996; Johnson 1995; *Pacific Report* 1996; Skully 1997; Waqa 1997). The paradox in these developments is that they have required a substantial rise in public spending, which seems to go against the neoliberal orthodoxy. One aspect of the Asian model, however, has always been governmental willingness to back winners, even though this is a strategy now disclaimed by more purist state managers, such as in New Zealand. The Kiribati case shows Asian ideas and influences clearly at work. Further evidence of this influence has taken a rather direct form: like a number of other Pacific countries (e.g., Tonga and Western Samoa), Kiribati has discerned a market among Hong Kong and Taiwanese investors for passports and travel documents that offer the prospect of alternative nationality.

The second major effect of neoliberal reforms in the Pacific concerns the forced cutback measures impelled by declining aid and budgetary assistance budgets from both Australia and New Zealand. The resulting state contraction and fiscal stringency have led to discernible strains in state agencies. The effect on the Cook Islands public sector has already been mentioned. In particular, one area of reduction in scale or priority of public spending can quite literally lead to political instability of a spectacular sort. I am referring to the strains being felt by armed services in the Pacific. This problem surfaces selectively as, among the independent Pacific countries, only four have their own military forces: the PNG Defence Force (3,800 personnel) and the Fiji Military Force (about 6,000 at its maximum after the 1987 coups, but currently being trimmed back to about 3,500) are relatively large, while the Vanuatu Mobile and Tonga Defence Forces each musters only a few hundred staff (Keith-Reid 1997b). This is in clear contrast to the armed forces of the Asian tigers; whereas most of them have made defense spending a priority, it is difficult to see how Pacific nations could do so. Now that governmental cutbacks mean there is no longer assured state support for the armed forces, the result has been a blossoming of military discontent, especially in Papua New Guinea and Vanuatu.

The Fiji Military Force's gradual downsizing has not caused similar serious problems of adjustment. Despite occasional downturns, Fiji has a much more diversified and dynamic economy than any other Pacific nation, so the impact is less severe than it might otherwise have been. Moreover, the Fijian military continues to enjoy great prestige among ethnic Fijians as well as a reputation for professionalism outside the country, having been involved in the Allied war effort in World War II, the Malayan "emergency," and several UN peacekeeping operations (Lebanon, Sinai, and the Gulf). Such peacekeeping has proven to be an important source of funding and training. Not surprisingly also, it has served as one of the major symbolic links between the Fijian and Malaysian governments. Nevertheless, despite these signs of relative harmony between government and the military, the 1987 coups showed the army's readiness to intervene in politics, with immediate consequences for economic stability. There are almost certainly circumstances under which it would do so again.

More seriously, the PNG and Vanuatu forces have been involved in recent unsavory events reflecting serious declines in funding and morale, mismanagement, and political corruption. PNG's problems have been caused or at least exacerbated by the unpopular and bloody occupation of Bougainville. This large island in the east of the country is geographically and culturally part of the Solomon archipelago and has displayed secessionist tendencies for decades, tendencies highlighted by the development of the massive Panguna mine in the 1960s and early 1970s. The development brought in masses of expatriate and off-island workers who aroused local resentment. It also caused severe environmental damage, which has still not been resolved by the compensation arrangements set in place at the time. Growing animosity culminated in the formation of the Bougainville Revolutionary Army and guerrilla action against the mine in 1989. The Port Moresby government's desire to maintain its revenues and to deter any "domino effect" among other groups led to the deployment of troops. After seven or eight years of military operations costing an estimated $800 million kina (A$736 million), the conflict may only now be coming to an end with the signing of a New Zealand-brokered peace agreement in April 1998. In the process, however, a series of ugly incidents has blighted the reputation of the PNG Defence Force.

By November 1996, soldiers were reportedly refusing to serve on Bougainville in frustration over a lack of logistics and administrative support from the headquarters and the government (Wambi 1996a). Infantrymen cited serious deficiencies in combat rations, uniforms and footwear, weapons, helicopter and transport backup, and failure by the headquarters in processing pay and combat allowances. The situation was bad enough to warrant public comment by the Defence Force Commander, Brigadier-General Jerry Singirok, to the effect that servicemen refusing to follow orders or carry out official duties were free to leave the force. But the action was preempted in July by the sacking of nineteen soldiers who had earlier refused to go to Bougainville and by other retrenchments among the officer corps. News of the dismissals was accompanied by admissions of "an alarming breakdown in morale and discipline" (Palmer 1996), none of which was helped by the spectacular failure of Operation High Speed II, supposedly designed to bring the war to a quick conclusion in the middle of the year. Brigadier-General Singirok even "admitted he was alarmed at the hundreds of illegal army-issue weapons already in the community" (ibid.), mostly the result of apparent theft by members of the Defence Force (Wambi 1996b).

Instead of replenishing the men, matériel and morale of the PNGDF, the Chan government took the audacious step of trying to recruit mercenaries through Sandline, a British company, to carry out new operations in Bougainville. When news of this plan, which would have contracted the services of a South African-based group called Executive Outcomes, erupted in early 1997, the reaction among Opposition politicians and the public encouraged a near-mutiny among soldiers in Port Moresby. Sir Julius was forced to step aside as prime minister and though he was later cleared by a commission of inquiry, his popularity had sunk to such an extent that he lost his parliamentary seat in the general election of June 1997.[6]

The recent Vanuatu problems have been smaller in scale but similar in nature (see Ambrose 1997: 503–4). As in PNG, personnel had not received promised allowances, and tensions rose. On 12 October 1996, troops in the capital broke into the VMF armory, neutralized fifteen commissioned officers, and seized President Leye from his bed at gunpoint. Others surrounded Police Headquarters and held the police commissioner under house arrest. The extraordinary actions that followed included flying the president to the neighboring island of Malekula, picking up the acting prime minister, and returning them both to Vila for an emergency meeting of the Council of Ministers. In the meantime, armed troops had kept the airport closed until the return of the plane, had cut international telephone lines, and had forbidden Radio Vanuatu to broadcast any news. An agreement was reached under which the outstanding allowances were to be paid in two tranches, one immediately and the other after parliament passed an appropriation bill. The agreement included a provision that no member of the VMF could be disciplined for their actions. Within days, however, the mutineers had been arrested in a predawn raid by the police force. The operation seemed to go off peacefully and all the arrested VMF members except for the ringleaders were released, subject to their swearing an oath of allegiance. As "coups" go, this one was remarkably restrained but it still revealed the same problems of military governance as the much more serious situation in PNG. There have even been claims that the VMF had a plan in reserve to take over government, suspend the constitution, and impose military rule (apparently the police raid uncovered documents along these lines).

Most military power in the Pacific remains in the hands of metropolitan powers like France, the United States and, to a lesser extent, Australia and New Zealand. Where a local military is present, however, it depends excessively on external funding and on the competence of its political/bureaucratic masters. The disturbing developments in PNG and Vanuatu show the vulnerability of such military/political relationships to changes in state constitution — changes that are increasingly dictated by metropolitan powers' tougher aid regimes. The mix of economic and military strength that seems to be an essential feature of the "Asian model" does not appear viable in the Pacific context. Furthermore, as previous sections of this chapter have indicated, given the lack of resources and labor power in many of the Pacific microstates, their diseconomies of scale and distance, and burgeoning political instability in the region, the prospects for industrial development on Asian lines are extremely remote. More than economics is at issue. Despite the beliefs of fervent free-marketeers, economic models cannot be divorced from political conditions. Nor can they be understood in isolation from cultural ideals in the conduct of business or from forms of state-military relations that have evolved in an environment more suited to them.

In the end, the impact both of "Asian models" and of the region's predation of PIC resources may have been stymied for the time being by the Asian economic crisis that began in mid-1997. That economies that had been touted as the most powerful sources of innovation and success in the contemporary world could stumble so spectacularly will have damaged the credibility of their proponents for a long time to come. Concomitantly, rates of timber extraction in Melanesian PICs have declined greatly due to falling Asian demand, causing some short-term problems for economic development but allowing a breathing space for the resources on which prosperity depends to recover. In April 1998 came a signal rejection of free-market philosophy and openness to Asian involvement: the Solomon Islands government declared that it would nationalize the logging industry, including the Malaysian interests that had dominated for the previous decade (Atkins 1998).

Notes

1. Under some projections, these tendencies are seen to foreshadow a "doomsday scenario" that condemns many independent countries in the Pacific to urban congestion, rising unemployment and crime rates, social polarization and political instability, and other signs of Third World immiseration against which they have historically been insulated (Cole 1993).

2. Though Indians in Fiji have endured the most intensive local-level anti-Asian prejudice by Pacific Islanders, the Chinese have not been immune and have been exposed on an everyday basis by virtue of owning local stores in many parts of the region. Their commercial success has sometimes provoked resentment. In parts of Papua New Guinea, for example, rioters were reported to have targeted Chinese-owned stores in urban centers in the aftermath of the Sandline affair in March 1997. The then PNG prime minister, Sir Julius Chan, has Chinese ancestry

and is reported to be very wealthy from business dealings. The unpopularity he suffered, and which was projected on to other (part-)Chinese residents, followed accusations that he flouted the constitution by signing a contract for mercenary assistance to end the conflict on Bougainville (see the final section of this chapter).

3. Susan Strange provides a slightly different mix of explanations, though they all count as variants and elaborations of Lim's second and third hypotheses: the Asian states' strategic geopolitical situations led to "generous military and economic aid from the Americans, aid which was combined with their exceptionally high domestic savings and low patterns of consumption"; it also led to their exemption from foreign competition while being "given relatively open access...to the large, rich US market." Lastly, according to Strange, the technology necessary for industrialization "was available to be bought on the market" (1996: 6).

4. Henke (1997) mounts a similar critique with respect to the application of the "Asian model" to the Caribbean.

5. Echoes of that earlier policy recur in the Indonesian government's policy of *transmigrasi* in Irian Jaya/West Papua since the 1960s. The negative aspects of this development strategy for the indigenous Melanesian population, however, have been reinforced by political oppression, leaving locals almost powerless to resist large-scale resettlement of Javanese migrants.

6. Most of the information in this paragraph is distilled from a constant stream of e-mail postings by Vikki John in Sydney — an information service known as "Bougainville Update." The sources are too numerous and too varied to cite here but see Dinnen (1997), Hunter (1997), Sasako (1997), and Vulum (1997).

References

Ambrose, D. (1997). "Vanuatu (Melanesia in Review: Issues and Events, 1996)." *Contemporary Pacific* 9(2): 497–505.

Atkins, G. (1998). "Solomons Moves on Logging Industry." Agence France-Presse (via Clarinet).

Babbage, R. (1995). "Australia." Pp. 177–213 in *Strategic Cooperation and Competition in the Pacific Islands,* edited by F. A. Mediansky. Sydney: Centre for South Pacific Studies, University of New South Wales.

Barlow, K. (1997). "Regulating the Forest Industry in Papua New Guinea: An Interview with Brian Brunton" *Contemporary Pacific* 9(1): 150–56.

Bell, C. (1996). "Cooks Forced to Sink or Swim." *Dominion* (September 4): 10.

Bergin, A. (1995). "The High Seas Regime — Pacific Trends and Developments." Pp. 183–98 in *The Law of the Sea in the Asian Pacific Region: Developments and Prospects,* edited by J. Crawford and D. R. Rothwell. Dordrecht: Martinus Nijhoff.

Buchholz, H. J. (1987). *Law of the Sea Zones in the Pacific Ocean.* Hamburg: Institute of Asian Affairs/Singapore: Institute of Southeast Asian Studies.

Callick, R. (1996). "Logging Causes Axe to Fall on $2 Million Aid." *Islands Business Pacific* 22(2, February): 49–50.

Cole, R., ed. (1993). *Pacific 2010: Challenging the Future.* Canberra: National Centre for Development Studies, Research School of Pacific Studies, Australian National University.

Connell, J. and R. Howitt, eds. (1991). *Mining and Indigenous Peoples in Australasia.* South Melbourne: Sydney University Press and Oxford University Press.

Connell, J. and B. Pritchard (1990). "Tax Havens and Global Capitalism: Vanuatu and the Australian Connection." *Australian Geographical Studies* 28(1): 38–50.

Decloitre, P. (1994). "Logging Dilemma." *Pacific Islands Monthly* 64(8, August): 17–18.

Dinnen, S. (1997). "The Money and the Gun — Mercenary Times in Papua New Guinea." *Journal of Pacific History* 32(3): 52–65.

Doulman, D. J. (1989). "Japanese Distant-Water Fishing in the South Pacific." *Pacific Economic Bulletin* 4(2): 22–28.

Doulman, D. J. (1992). "Aspects of Fisheries Cooperation Between Indonesia and South Pacific Countries." *Papers in Indonesia-South Pacific Relations. Yagl-Ambu* (Special Issue, edited by Y. Saffu and D. Roskies) 16(2): 85–107.

Economist (1994). "The New Colonisers." 6 August, p. 24.

Edo, J. (1986). *Japanese Aid to the Pacific Islands Region.* Honolulu: Pacific Islands Development Program, East-West Center.

Firth, S. (1994). "Australia and the Pacific Islands." Pp. 75-90 in *The ANZUS States and Their Region: Regional Policies of Australia, New Zealand, and the United States,* edited by R. W. Baker. Westport, CT: Praeger.

Fraser, H. (1996). "How Do You Make a New Singapore? Watch, Says Tito." *Islands Business* 22(11, November): 50.

Frazer, I. (1997). "The Struggle for Control of Solomon Island Forests." *Contemporary Pacific* 9(1): 39–72.

Garrett, J. (1991). "Robber Barrons [*sic*] of the Logging World." *Pacific Islands Monthly* 61(6, June): 5.

Garrett, J. (1993). "Facing the Robber Barons." *Pacific Islands Monthly* 63(9, September): 19.

Grynberg, R. (1993). "The Tuna Dilemma." *Pacific Islands Monthly* 63(5, May): 9-11.

Grynberg, R. (1994). "The Solomon Islands Logging Dilemma." *Pacific Islands Monthly* 64(3, March): 11–13.

Henke, H. (1997). "The Rise of Industrial Asia and Its Implications for Small Developing Countries: A Perspective from the Caribbean." *Australian Journal of International Affairs* 51 (1, April): 52–72.

Henningham, S. (1996). "Australia and the Pacific Islands: The Limits of Influence." Pp. 148-159 in *Asia-Pacific Security: Less Uncertainty, New Opportunities?* edited by G. Klintworth. Melbourne: Addison Wesley Longman.

Hill, D. (1996). "Cooks PM Keen to Replace 'Pits of the Pacific' Tag With New Look." *National Business Review* (November 1): 5.

Hooper, A. (1993). "Socio-Cultural Aspects of Development in the South Pacific." Pp. 314-342 in *The Future of Asia-Pacific Economies: Pacific Islands at the Crossroads?* edited by R. V. Cole and S. Tambunlertchai. Canberra: National Centre for Development Studies.

Howe, K. R. (1984). *Where the Waves Fall: A New South Sea Islands History from First Settlement to Colonial Rule.* Sydney: George Allen and Unwin.

Hunter, R. (1997). "Arms and the Man." *Pacific Islands Monthly* 67(8, August): 30–31.

Islands Business Pacific (IBP) (1994). "Teburoro Takes Charge." 20(12, December): 28.

Johnson, G. (1995). "Tito Talks of a Pro-Business Climate." *Islands Business Pacific* 21(4, April): 35.

Keith-Reid, R. (1995). "Threats of Death Come With Jean Kekedo's Job." *Islands Business Pacific* 21(9, September): 59–60.

Keith-Reid, R. (1997a). "It's The Economy, Stupid; How the Islands Are Shaping Up." *Islands Business* 23(1, January): 24–30.

Keith-Reid, R. (1997b). "Armed and Ready." *Islands Business* 23(8, August): 18–20.

Kilroy, S. (1996). "Hidden Cost in Aid Cut." *Dominion* 7 June, p. 7.

Lafitte, G. (1991). "Top Down Bottom Up: The Colonel Takes the Rap." *Arena* 96: 25–30.

Lafitte, G. (1995). "Big Ugly Australian: Ok Tedi, BHP and the PNG Elite." *Arena Magazine* 19: 18–19.

Lim, D. (1993). "Relevance of East Asian Development Experiences to the South Pacific." Pp. 33-55 in *The Future of Asia-Pacific Economies: Pacific Islands at the Crossroads?* edited by R. V. Cole and S. Tambunlertchai. Canberra: National Centre for Development Studies.

McPhetres, S. F. (1995). "Twenty Years After: The Commonwealth of the Northern Mariana Islands in Political Union with the United States of America." *Umanidàt* 3(1): 1–6.

McPhetres, S. F. (1996). "Micronesia in Review: Commonwealth of the Northern Mariana Islands." *Contemporary Pacific* 8(1): 170–73.

McPhetres, S. F. (1997). "Micronesia in Review: Commonwealth of the Northern Mariana Islands." *Contemporary Pacific* 9(1): 198–202.

Meltzoff, S. and E. LiPuma (1985). "Social Organization of a Solomons-Japanese Joint Venture." *Oceania* 56(2): 85–105.

Miller, B. (1995). "Combating Drift-Net Fishing in the Pacific." Pp. 155-170 in *The Law of the Sea in the Asian Pacific Region: Developments and Prospects,* edited by J. Crawford and D. R. Rothwell. Dordrecht: Martinus Nijhoff.

Mortimer, R. (1979). "The Japanese Connection." Pp. 78-93 in *Development and Dependency: The Political Economy of Papua New Guinea,* edited by A. Amarshi, K. Good, and R. Mortimer. Melbourne: Oxford University Press.

Numata, S. (1990). "Japan's Cooperation with the South Pacific Region." *Pacific Economic Bulletin* 5(2): 8–14.

Pacific Report (1996). "Kiribati Aims for Major Development in New Business Centre." 9(19, 4 October): 1–2, 4.

Palat, R. A. (1996). "Pacific Century: Myth or Reality?" *Theory and Society* 25(3): 303–47.

Palmer, L. (1996). "Troops Sacked For Refusing to Serve." *Sydney Morning Herald,* 22 November. ("Bougainville Update" on ANU Pacific Islands List 26 November.)

Peattie, M. R. (1984). "Nanyo: Japan in the South Pacific, 1885–1945." Pp. 172–213. In *The Japanese Colonial Empire,* edited by Ramon H. Myers and Mark R. Peattie. Princeton, NJ: Princeton University Press.

Peattie, M. R. (1988). *Nanyo: The Rise and Fall of the Japanese in Micronesia.* Honolulu: Center for Pacific Islands Studies, School of Hawaiian, Asian, and Pacific Studies, University of Hawaii/University of Hawaii Press.

Pheysey, C. (1996). "Oceania Searches for New Friends." *New Zealand International Review* 21(3, May/June): 24–27.

Ravuvu, A. (1987). "Fiji: Contradictory Ideologies and Development." Pp. 230-241 in *Class and Culture in the South Pacific,* edited by A. Hooper, S. Britton, R. Crocombe, J. Huntsman, and C. Macpherson. Suva: Institute of Pacific Studies, University of the South Pacific/Auckland: Centre for Pacific Studies, University of Auckland.

Ravuvu, A. (1991). *The Facade of Democracy: Fijian Struggles for Political Control 1830–1987*. Suva: Reader.

Ray, B. (1995). "Exploitation in the Marianas." *Pacific Islands Monthly* 65(1, January): 28–29.

Regenvanu, R., S. P. Wyatt, and L. Taconi (1997). "Changing Forestry Regimes in Vanuatu: Is Sustainable Management Possible?" *Contemporary Pacific* 9(1): 73–96.

Richards, J. (1990). "Micro-States: A Specific Form of Polity?" *Politics* 10(1): 40–46.

Robie, D. (1993). "Timber Tycoon's Media Wars." *NZ Monthly Review* 341(Nov./Dec.): 17–19.

Saffu, Y. and D. Roskies, eds. (1992). *Papers in Indonesia-South Pacific Relations. Yagl-Ambu* (Special Issue) 16(2).

Sasako, A. (1996). "Fishy Deals — Is the Pacific Losing Out?" *Pacific Islands Monthly* 66(7, July): 8.

Sasako, A. (1997). "Mercenaries and Mayhem." *Pacific Islands Monthly* 67(5, May): 13–14.

Shuster, D. R. (1997). "Micronesia in Review: Belau." *Contemporary Pacific* 9(1): 196–98.

Skully, M. (1997). "Micronesia in Review: Kiribati." *Contemporary Pacific* 9(1): 208–10.

Smales, G. (1977). "Japan — PNG: Ah, What a Change Was There!" *Pacific Islands Monthly* 48(11, November): 17–18.

Strange, S. (1996). *The Retreat of the State: The Diffusion of Power in the World Economy.* Cambridge: Cambridge University Press.

Sutherland, W. (1984). "Exclusive Economic Zones and Ocean Policy in the South Pacific." *Review* (USP) 4(11): 56–61.

Tsamenyi, B. M. and K. Mfodwo (1995). "South Pacific Island States and the New Regime of Fisheries: Issues of Law, Economy and Diplomacy." Pp. 121-153 in *The Law of the Sea in the Asian Pacific Region: Developments and Prospects,* edited by J. Crawford and D. R. Rothwell. Dordrecht: Martinus Nijhoff.

Vulum, S. (1997). "Sir Julius — Just Where Did He Go Wrong? Singirok — I'm No Hero; Enuma — Of Few Words and Quick Action; The Sandline Saga; A Saga of Corruption and Dirty Deals; Business — But Not Quite as Usual." *Pacific Islands Monthly* 67(5, May): 15–21.

Waiko, J. D. (1981). "Land, Forest and People: Villagers Struggle Against Multinational Corporations in Papua New Guinea." *Kabar Seberang: Sulating Maphilindo* 8/9: 33–41.

Wambi, D. (1996a). "Soldiers Refuse Duty on B'ville." *National* (PNG) (21 November).

Wambi, D. (1996b). "PNGDF Alarmed Over High Weapons Theft." *National* (PNG) (22 November).

Waqa, V. (1997). "The Kiribati Experience." *Islands Business* 23(2, February): 50–51.

Watanabe, A. (1995). "Japan." Pp. 237-265 in *Strategic Cooperation and Competition in the Pacific Islands,* edited by F. A. Mediansky. Sydney: Centre for South Pacific Studies, University of New South Wales.

Wolfers, E. P. (1995). "The Law of the Sea in the South Pacific." Pp. 41-49 in *The Law of the Sea in the Asian Pacific Region: Developments and Prospects,* edited by Crawford, J. and D. R. Rothwell. Dordrecht: Martinus Nijhoff.

Wood, M. (1996). "Logs, Long Socks and the 'Tree Leaf' People: An Analysis of a Timber Project in the Western Province of Papua New Guinea." *Social Analysis* 39: 83–117.

CHAPTER 9

Conclusion

The Asian Model in Crisis and the Transferability of Development Experiences[*]

Holger Henke   Ian Boxill

1. Rallying around the neoliberal "cake": Asia and the developing world

There can be little doubt that the current financial crisis in East Asia has brought into question the validity of the so-called Asian "model." Neoliberal critics have used the crisis to discredit any and all government involvement in the process of economic development, thereby staying closely in line with the current orthodoxy, which calls for the total, uninhibited reign of the market. It is no secret that respected economists, including Jeffrey Sachs, felt that the East Asians were on the right path to economic development. In a lecture at the University of the West Indies in February 1997, Sachs pointed to East Asia's economic strategy as the way forward. Here was a region with high rates of economic growth as a result of the openness of their economies. There was no hint that a crisis or even difficulties were looming. Far from it, as he used East Asia as an example of what was possible for "closed" backward economies in this part of the world, only if they opened up. Perhaps more than any other, the debate over the nature of the "Asian miracle" exposes much of the opportunism, intellectual dishonesty, and weaknesses of social scientific thought. In the halcyon days of the East Asian miracle, neoliberal social scientists would point to the speed of deregulation and privatization as indicators that the East Asian model was in line with orthodox Western economic thought. (Incidentally, since the crisis many now, amazingly, argue that these economies were not deregulated enough.)

In contrast to this view (and although in his chapter Jayasuriya reminds us

---

*   This chapter draws significantly on two of Ian Boxill's previously published papers: "Science in the Social Sciences: A View from the Caribbean," *Journal of Human Justice* 6(1), 1994; and "Globalization, Sustainable Development and Postmodernism: The New Ideology of Imperialism," *Humanity and Society* 18(4), 1994.

that our perspective might also be too static), to both editors and the majority, if not all, of the contributing authors it is obvious that — notwithstanding the value of comparative empirical analysis — industrialization and economic development are the results of very complex social, political, and economic processes both at the domestic and the international level, rather than the result of abstract economic formulas. While most accounts attempt to tiptoe delicately between rival camps, this complexity is not always acknowledged among the makers and breakers in — what Robert W. Cox would term — the oligopolist system of international finance. Here and at the various levels of policy implementation in development programs suggested, monitored, and/or supervised by international financial agencies or donors, public servants in small countries are often lectured about the virtues of export orientation, prudent fiscal management, and a favorable "investment climate" without being also enlightened about the role of East Asia's visible hand "governing the market" (to use the title of Robert Wade's book). This one-sided account is frequently given with an explicit reference to the rapid industrialization in East Asia during the 1960s, 1970s, and 1980s. Indeed, in numerous cases an abstract Asian "model" of development was utilized in order to legitimize neoliberal structural adjustment policy prescriptions in indebted developing states. Despite, or rather because, of this emphasis on essentially wrong assumptions and premises, the number of "least developed countries" (LLDCs) increased from twenty-four in 1972 to forty-one in 1990 (cf. Broad and Cavanagh 1995).

It appears, therefore, that neoliberal critics of the current financial crisis may have thrown out the baby with the bathwater. As World Bank economist Joseph Stiglitz (1998) recently argued:

> The accusations of "crony capitalism," overbearing state direction of investments, and lack of transparency have, in some minds, discredited government involvement in development. I would argue that the critics have been too harsh — after all, the past achievements in accumulating savings, promoting investment, and developing human capital cannot simply be erased. In historical perspective, financial crises and economic downturns are not new phenomena in capitalist economies. Furthermore, several countries in the region, most notably China and Taiwan (China) seem to have weathered the storm quite well. Nevertheless, the depth of the crisis in countries such as Korea, Thailand, and Indonesia does provoke questions.

Clearly, this conclusion is fully congruent with the findings of several of the preceding chapters (see, e.g., Chapter 7). In reading some of the other chapters (see, e.g., Chapters 4, 5, and 8) the question has to be asked if the lessons that neoliberal economists often chose to focus all their attention on — that is, export orientation, openness of the economy, no barriers to trade and investments, to name the most often cited — might not be the right recipe for a developmental headstart. Indeed, there are a number of influential economists and development theorists (including Bustelo) who argue that even in the South Korean case some of the current IMF prescriptions are bound to further aggravate the crisis. Indeed, as a recent cross-country study found, besides macroeconomic factors (low GDP growth and high inflation), high real interest rates, vulnerability to capital outflows, and ineffective law enforcement, domestic financial liberalization ranks among the most important predictors of banking crises (see Stiglitz 1998). Similar conclusions can be drawn for other regions (see, e.g., Henke 1997).

One of the axiomatic assumptions of neoliberal development theory is that by opening and liberalizing their economies, developing countries — independent of their stage of development — will inevitably attract increasing amounts of foreign investment capital. However, according to the World Bank, in 1995 twelve mostly middle-income countries accounted for over 80 percent of total private capital flows to developing countries. East Asia's share of such flows increased from 41 percent in 1993 to 59 percent in 1995 — largely at the expense of Latin America. Although foreign investment may remain subject to temporary fluctuations (such as the investment slump that hit several South Asian countries in mid-1997), the fact remains that East Asian borrowers enjoyed maturities almost three times longer than did Latin American issuers in 1995 — and average spreads were about one-half those of Latin America. Thus, while private capital flows in this year to the East Asia/Pacific region totaled $84,137 million, they only amounted a quarter of this amount ($22,096 million) for the Latin American/Caribbean region (excluding Mexico and Brazil), $9,128 million for Sub-Saharan Africa, $5,191 million for South Asia, and a relatively meager $1,141 million for the countries of the Middle East/North Africa region. Within Asia itself foreign direct investment is largely concentrated in the special production zones and large cities (see Chapters 2 and 3), whereas the rural hinterland remains relatively detached from the increasing capital flows (see Chapters 1, 4, and 8). These data clearly indicate that for the foreseeable future the lives of large segments of the population in most developing regions will probably remain unaffected by whatever amounts of foreign direct investment may pour into their countries and that for many regions urbanization will remain or become an even bigger problem than it is already. It is therefore quite evident from the preceding chapters that the development process within developing countries, and indeed in Asia itself, is quite uneven. There is sufficient evidence that even in the context of newly liberalized and transparent economies catering to the world markets, international direct investment — by all means a very important variable and precondition for development in most small, developing economies — remains highly skewed.

As the preceding chapters intended to show, the Asian model is by no means a homogenous experience and indeed the lessons abstracted from the so-called Tiger nations did not even work well in several other Asian countries (see, e.g., Chapters 4 and 8). The current financial crisis in the region has further sharpened the awareness that the neoliberal interpretation of the "model" is far from impeccable. Pablo Bustelo's chapter calls our attention to South Korea's difficulties and the costs of remaining financially afloat in the face of the crisis, and World Bank economist Stiglitz (1998) recently argued that "deep, efficient, and robust financial systems are essential for growth and stability":

> But left to themselves, financial markets will not become deep, efficient, or robust. The government plays an essential role, both in directly overseeing and regulating the financial system and also in establishing the correct incentives to encourage prudential and productive behavior.

Nevertheless, neoliberal orthodox pundits are continuing their work of imposing their vision of a free market Eldorado on small countries in East Asia and other regions of the world. Thus, current plans for a Multilateral Agreement on Investment (MAI), secretly (before they were leaked on the Internet in January 1997) drafted by the OECD in Paris, by aiming to make capital mobility a legally enforceable property right, are likely to undermine development. This global property right will override internationally recognized human rights because it will be legally enforceable at the international level, while human rights are not. It will probably make it considerably harder to assert high standards for workplace safety and protection of adjacent communities from industrial waste and catastrophic accidents like the industrial disaster in Bhopal, India. Finally, it will make illegal efforts by states and municipalities to promote locally owned and controlled enterprises and almost certainly lead to even greater concentration of wealth and power of multinational conglomerates. As we shall further argue in the next two sections, the lessons from the Asian industrialization experience have therefore been drawn only in part and improperly used as a prescriptive blueprint for international development and assistance programs.

2.   Global Dedifferentiation and Peripheralization

Few development specialists would gainsay the view that development is a complex multifaceted process. Even when we speak of economic development we are talking about more than simply economic factors. Economic development encompasses a constellation of factors, among them social, political, economic, psychological, and ecological. Yet in discussing economic development, development analysts, partly because of their training and perhaps because of the nature of the process that they seek to unravel, tend to isolate and deal primarily with a matrix of "economic" factors. In addition, some analysts are of the view that the process of globalization makes it legitimate to assume that economic opportunities and choices are relatively open for virtually all countries that are part of this "global village." What these countries need to do is to recognize where the possibilities are, and with the help of international capital, take advantage of them (Reich 1991). However, globalization is an extremely uneven process; thus "the supposition that domestic economies are now submerged in a seamless, unified world market is belied by the evidence" (Rodrik 1997: 21). Clearly, globalization has led to different results for different countries.

In light of the above two observations, problems of abstraction and application are likely to arise when we try to analyze and transfer the East Asian experience. We begin by looking at the implications for abstraction and application posed by the problematic of globalization.

Globalization may be referred to as "a process through which cross-border interactions intensify, spaces of social action extend beyond the nation state and detach themselves from territories respectively, and social awareness for a globalized world increases" (Beisheim and Walter 1997: 157). Globalization has been largely facilitated by the spread of international capitalism, which has resulted in the creation of a global economy through the activities of multinational corporations and international financial agencies such as the International Monetary Fund and the World Bank. Therefore, the single most defining characteristic of globalization is the capitalist forms of production, distribution, and consumption at the local and international levels.

It is important for us to understand that globalization is not a recent phenomenon. The process of globalization as it is discussed today has its roots in the European conquest of the "New World" and African slavery. According to Hall:

> [w]hen we are talking in the present context, we are talking about some of the new forms, some of the new impetuses in the globalizing process.... I do want to suggest that it is located within a much longer history.... The United Kingdom rose with, and is declining with, one of the eras, or epochs, of globalization: that era when the formation of the world market was dominated by the economies and cultures of powerful nation states. It is that relationship between the formation and transformation of the world market and its economies of powerful nation-states which constituted the era within which the formation of English culture took its existing shape. Imperialism was the system by which the world was engulfed in and by this framework. (1991: 20)

However, it has been argued that there is an important difference between the old form of globalization and the new. For one, the new globalization is characterized by the near omnipresence of capitalist forms of production (Hall 1991; Wallerstein 1991). Second, and importantly, the new globalization is not English: it is American. In cultural terms the new kind of globalization has to do with a new form of global mass culture, very different from that associated with English identity, and the cultural identities associated with the nation-state in an earlier phase (Hall 1991: 27).

One of the features of globalization is simultaneous convergence and divergence in the living styles and standards of large segments of the world. The process of globalization has ensured that large sections of humanity use similar capital markets and consume similar goods. Mobility of capital, goods, and services has indeed played a large role in the growth of East Asian economies. However, it is also true that globalization is characterized by a situation where many countries have been excluded from such cross-border money flows and groups of people live in enclaves of abject poverty and alienation.

Rodrik (1997) contends that contrary to popular belief the mobility of capital across the world is highly selective and highly skewed. The evidence, he states, is not consistent with current notions of capital mobility. He argues:

> Popular discussions take for granted that capital is now entirely free to cross national borders in search for the highest returns. As economists Martin Feldstein and Charles Horioka have pointed out, if this were true, the level of investment that is undertaken in France would depend only on the profitability of investment in France, and it would have no relationship to the availability of savings in France. Actually, however, this turns out to be false. Increased savings in one country translate into increased investments in that country almost one for one. (ibid.: 22)

Rodrik's view is supported by the evidence advanced in the first section of this conclusion, where it is shown that capital flows to developing countries have been quite uneven for a number of years, economic conditions notwithstanding.

This raises another dimension of the globalization process and, by extension, of what has been taking place in East Asia and other developing countries seeking to emulate the East Asian miracle. Notwithstanding the huge gains made from industrialization, researchers are coming to the realization that there has also been much fallout from this process. Ash Amin (1994), in commenting on industrialization and its post-Fordist characteristics in matured and maturing industrial economies, points to an emerging pattern of urbanization characterized by significant enclaves of poverty and informal activity. The growth of cities and its consequent increased urbanization, along with an increased role for the market and the emergence of the "flexibly organised economy" has led to a situation where there is "a vast underclass of low-income or no-income communities increasingly abandoned by welfare programmes, and isolated from the areas of the city 'embellished' for the well-off" (Amin 1994: 32). This "vast underclass" is present in East Asia and other emerging nations, and in some cases has become even more peripheralized even as the industrialization process proceeds. The extent of this peripheralization varies enormously among the Asian Tigers.

To be sure, this peripheralization also has a gender component to it. Numerous case studies cited in Ward (1990) illustrate that globalization has intensified the exploitation of women, especially in the informal sector (see, e.g., Truelove

1990: 48–63). Many developing countries now have a dual labor market sector — informal and formal — in which an informal sector that is dominated by women suffers high levels of exploitation, poor working conditions, and low levels of remuneration.

At this point we would like to make it clear that we are not opposed to the idea of industrialization along the lines of the Tigers; our concern is with assessing the experiences of these countries and the attempt to transplant such experiences to other sociopolitical and economic spaces. Indeed, our research points to the fact that some countries have not fared well in their effort to attract foreign direct investment (FDI) and attempt to emulate features of the East Asia economies (see, e.g., Henke 1997). Many developing countries that have been seduced into the global economic web find themselves trapped when foreign companies take advantage of their lucrative investment climate and cheap labor and then leave unceremoniously. Governments are then faced with a sudden upsurge in unemployment and social chaos. Green (1993: 28–33) has attributed the rapid debt burdens and the growth of dualistic sectors in Caribbean economies to a globalization process that forces many countries to the periphery. She states:

> The adoption of an export led strategy by Caribbean governments, based on assembly manufacture and U. S. investment in areas serving U. S. interests, is leading to renewed colonization of these countries. It is drawing them into an endless series of boom and bust cycles, one island temporarily exchanging places with another along a trajectory of the spiral of dependency. (ibid.: 32)

However, in the eyes of some analysts, Green offers a pessimistic representation of a largely positive process. Robert Reich, former secretary of labor in the Clinton administration and author of *The Work of Nations,* argues that the growth of global webs means that when nations trade, we no longer have the exchange of commodities entirely produced in one country. He states:

> When an American buys a Pontiac Le Mans from General Motors, for example, he or she engages unwittingly in an international transaction. Of the $20,000 paid to GM, about $6,000 goes to South Korea for routine labor and assembly operations, $3,500 to Japan for advanced components (engines, transaxles, and electronics), $1,500 to West Germany for styling and design engineering, $8,000 to Taiwan, Singapore and Japan for small components, $500 to Britain for advertising and marketing services, and about $100 to Ireland and Barbados for data processing. (Reich 1991: 113)

This transnational form of production, Reich argues, has created a global web of workers, many of whom share more in common with each other than with people in their countries. These people he calls "symbolic analysts." That is, "people engaged in problem solving, problem-identifying, and strategic brokering activities" (ibid.: 177). These workers are normally well educated and include the likes of lawyers, design engineers, real estate developers, and management consultants.

We have no quarrel with Reich's argument except that he seems to assume, incorrectly, that all countries involved in the manufacturing of "global" commodities receive fair compensation for the product they manufactured. Also, Reich does not explore the relative bargaining powers of those countries engaged in the production. Reich — like so many who see economic relations more in global terms — also seems to make the unrealistic assumption of a "level playing field." Furthermore, implicit in Reich's conception of the global web is the presence of laws of demand and supply that are universal. This universalism is rationalized on the basis of capitalism, which produces economic and social institutions and conditions that are similar across cultures (ibid.: Chapter 14). Of course, the reality of the economic situation in most developing countries contradicts this assumption of universalism of capitalism across cultures. Thus, for example, one has to be very cautious when comparing the impact of macroeconomic policy in, say, the economies of the industrialized North with Latin America and Caribbean economies, where in many places there is a huge informal economy; more than 60 percent of the families live in poverty in some places; and disguised unemployment is as high as 55 percent. The historical evolution of these countries — where powerful ruling elites control monopolies in the business sector and where large-scale corruption in the private and public sectors exists — makes a mockery of the notion of a free market. In other words, to talk of a global economy in which the market defines economic relations is to ignore the vast differences between countries of the industrialized and nonindustrialized world.

The other questionable aspect of Reich's view is that the presence of symbolic analysts have the same consequences for developed and developing countries. Whereas in countries of the North levels of education are fairly even, in many countries of the South more than 40 percent of the population is illiterate. The growth of another cadre of people who are highly educated and whose lifestyles are closer to people in the North than in the South has only exacerbated the already serious inequalities in the South.

Now it is precisely this idea of the universalism of economic systems and values that has basically informed the policies of international lending agencies such as the World Bank and the IMF. The policies of these lending agencies quite often threaten the sovereignty of many developing nations (Payer 1974; Dell 1984; Girvan 1984; Levitt 1991; George and Sabelli 1994). Levitt argues that "the modalities of the IMF/World Bank designed adjustment programs breed a psychology of failure and impotence" (1991: 63). In outlining the rationale for her book on the dangers posed by the IMF and World Bank to developing nations, Cheryl Payer states "my intent is to extend the critical analysis of the IMF as an obstacle to autonomous national development" (1974:x). Levitt, in discussing Jamaica's relationship with the IMF, which has since the mid-1970s been characterized by the IMF exercising enormous leverage in the running of the

Jamaican economy, refers to a situation in which the Jamaican government "in 1986 asserted its independence in refusing to undertake further devaluations" (1991: 26). The IMF had been recommending devaluation of the Jamaican currency as one of its policy prescriptions — one of many prescriptions that have been opposed by social scientists and policymakers from developing countries. The main criticism of such policies is that they are not sensitive to the political, social, and economic realities of developing countries. Furthermore, they result in large-scale foreign ownership of important sectors of the economy, high prices, and massive social dislocation (Payer 1974: Chapter 2; Girvan 1984: 172). In other words, these programs, which assume cultural and institutional universalism in terms of the operation of market, are blind to the particularities of the developing countries, many of which operate on the periphery of the global economy (Girvan 1984: 172).

Another important policy prescription of the IMF and World Bank that is potentially detrimental to developing countries is rapid privatization. Privatization is premised on the belief that the private sector is more efficient than the public sector — a view based primarily on the experience of industrialized countries. After privatization, developing countries are encouraged to remove barriers to international trade because of the notion that privatization leads to greater efficiency. While it is true that privatization has led to greater efficiencies in some sectors of these countries, given the fragility of the economies of many developing countries, rapid privatization has also resulted in the destruction of local industries either before they have had time to develop their competitive edge or without viable replacements in the export sector (Levitt 1991).

At present a number of developing nations are caught in a catch-22 situation: If they fully liberalize, most of the local industries are likely to be destroyed, and there is no guarantee that alternative industries will fill the employment and revenue void created by liberalization. On the other hand, if they do not liberalize, they risk being unprepared to compete in the liberalized global economy. Consequently, there seems to be a divergence between the theoretical and practical benefits to be derived from liberalization/globalization at the present moment.

This leads us to another problem that we as social scientists face when we extrapolate from the experiences of others, when we construct models, and when we apply these models to real-world situations. We are talking about the inherent dangers associated with abstraction.

3.   The Problem of Abstraction

Historically, development specialists, particularly economists, have been construct-ing various models of economic development. For those countries that are yet to achieve industrial development these models are supposed to be a road map to progress. There was a time when the British industrial revolution represented the development model of the future, while for others not persuaded by the benefits of capitalism there was the Soviet model and, later, the Chinese model. The emergence of the East Asian economies, along with the demise of the USSR, stimulated greater interest in the "Asian model" of development. Among scholars in the developing world, and particularly in the Latin American region, there is talk of the Latin American models, such as Mexico, Costa Rica, and Chile. Within CARICOM there are some who now speak of the Barbados and Trinidad models of development. It would appear that as a developing country begins to "take off," this process leads to the creation of a new model of development.

The plethora of so many models of economic development, at different points in time, begs two questions: First, if it is true that these models are universal, why is it that almost every new success story emerges with its own unique model? Second, if there is something universal about these models, why is it that we have so many models in the first place? Given the current trend it is quite possible that in the next twenty years we may be talking about a St. Lucian model, a Nigerian model, or a Fijian model. By having a plethora of models are we not, implicitly, accepting that in reality economic behavior is culturally relative, and also not transhistorical? And if human behavior is culturally relative and period dependent, how is it possible to have a science of human development?

Some may argue, as a number of commentators on Caribbean development do, that the problem is not with the universality of these models or features that can be extrapolated to the Caribbean context, but that the political systems in the Caribbean prevent the implementation of very rational policies that may lead to economic development. There appears to be a problem with this type of reasoning. To separate political and cultural practices from economic practices is to suggest that economic behavior is something very different and can be seriously isolated from other forms of social behavior. The question therefore is: When is an act purely economic, political, or cultural? In our view there is no uncontestable empirical or theoretical answer to this question. The truth is that when we talk about economic or political behavior we are doing so clinically, that is, outside the "real world." Therefore, it would seem that part of the problem we social scientists face in analyzing development experiences is that the models of economic development that we construct inadequately capture the complexity of human ideas, choices, and actions — all of which are at the core of the development process itself.

But there is also another problem: While these models abstract from particular situations, they are not abstract enough to be applied universally. Methodologists refer to this as a problem of reliability. However, the conundrum is that as one's analysis becomes more reliable through abstraction the less valid it is due to a lack of specificity. It is this tension between external validity and reliability that currently haunts our attempt to assess what is and also prescribe what is to be done.

Notwithstanding these problems of abstraction and application, most social scientists, like those in this book, believe that the lessons of development are transhistorical and transcultural, in other words, that social, political, and economic regularity can be measured and manipulated. In this regard the experiences of East Asian economies are not specific to that region's space but have a global dimension. We have no problem with this position, as long as it is recognized that there are limitations inherent in this type of project.

References

Amin, A. (1994). "Post-Fordism: Models, Fantasies and Phantoms of Transition." Pp. 1–41 in *Post Fordism: A Reader,* edited by A. Amin. Oxford: Blackwell.

Beisheim, M. and G. Walter (1997). " 'Globalisierung' — Kinderkrankheiten eines Konzeptes." *Zeitschrift für Internationale Beziehungen* 4(1): 153–80.

Broad, R. and J. Cavanagh (1995). "Don't Neglect the Impoverished South." *Foreign Policy* 101(Winter 1995–96): 18–35.

Dell, S. (1984). "Stabilization: The Political Economy of Overkill." Pp. 222–247 in *The Political Economy of Development and Underdevelopment,* edited by C. K. Wilber. New York: Random House.

George, S. and F. Sabelli (1994). Faith and Credit: The World Bank's Secular Empire. Boulder: Westview Press.

Girvan, N. (1984). "Swallowing the IMF Medicine in the Seventies." Pp. 169–81 in *The Political Economy of Development and Underdevelopment,* edited by C. K. Wilber. New York: Random House.

Green, C. (1993). "Export Processing Industry and the New Peripheralization of the Commonwealth Caribbean." Unpublished paper. Eastern Michigan University, Department of Africana Studies.

Hall, S. (1991). "The Local and the Global: Globalization and Ethnicity." Pp. 19–40 in Culture. *Globalization and the World System,* edited by A. King. London: Macmillan.

Henke, H. (1997). "The Rise of Industrial Asia and its Implications for the Developing World: A Perspective from the Caribbean." *Australian Journal of International Affairs* 51(1): 53–72.

Levitt, K. (1991). "The Origins and Consequences of Jamaica's Debt Crisis, 1970–1990," Consortium Graduate School of Social Sciences, University of the West Indies, Mona.

Payer, C. (1974). *The Debt Trap: The International Monetary Fund and the Third World.* New York: Monthly Review.

Reich, R. (1991).*The Work of Nations.* New York: Alfred A. Knopf.

Rodrik, D. (1997). "Sense and Nonsense in the Globalization Debate." *Foreign Policy* (Summer): 19–36.

Stiglitz, J. (1998). "Sound Finance and Sustainable Development in Asia." Keynote address to the Asia Development Forum. Manila, March 12.

Truelove, C. (1990). "Disguised Industrial Proletarians in Rural Latin America: Women's Informal-Sector Factory Work and the Social Reproduction of Coffee Farm Labor in Colombia." Pp. 26–63 in *Women Workers and Global Restructuring,* edited by K. Ward. New York: ILR Press, Cornell University.

Wallerstein, E. (1991). "The National and the Universal: Can There Be Such a Thing as a World Culture?" Pp. 91-105 in *Culture, Globalization and the World-System*, edited by A. D. King. London: Macmillan Education Ltd. (in association with the Department of Art and Art History, State University of New York at Binghamton).

Ward, K., ed. (1990). *Women Workers and Global Restructuring.* New York: ILR Press, Cornell University.

About the Editors and Contributors

IAN BOXILL is Lecturer in the Department of Sociology and Social Work at the University of the West Indies (Mona, Jamaica). He received a Ph. D. in sociology from Colorado State University, and his research interests include Caribbean and Pacific societies, race and ethnic questions, culture, development issues, and research methods. Dr. Boxill recently concluded a research and teaching assignment at the University of Waikato in New Zealand. He has published numerous books and articles about Caribbean regional integration, research methods, human resource management, race relations, culture, and ethnicity.

PABLO BUSTELO is Director of Asian Studies at the Complutense Institute of International Studies and Associate Professor of Applied Economics at Complutense University of Madrid. In his research he concentrates on development economics, the Asian newly industrializing economies, comparative paths of industrialization in East Asia and Latin America, and the economic reform in China. Professor Bustelo, a fellow of the Salzburg Seminar, is author of eight books on the Asian NICs, China's economy, development theory, and the world economy and is a contributor to journals such as *The European Journal of Development Research* (London), *Comercio Exterior* (Mexico DF), *Issues & Studies* (Taipei), *Ciclos* (Buenos Aires), *Asies Recherches* (Grenoble), *Información Comercial Española* (Madrid), *Economistas* (Madrid), and *Economía Exterior* (Madrid). He was external advisor to the ADB study *Emerging Asia* (1997). Professor Bustelo is also the founder of the European Association for Co-operation with Asia (Brussels).

MICHAEL GOLDSMITH is the Director of the Anthropology Programme at the University of Waikato (New Zealand). He received his M. A. and Ph. D. from the University of Illinois at Urbana-Champaign, and has a background in anthropology and history. Dr. Goldsmith's current research interests include political sociology and anthropology, Pacific politics, and sociocultural theory.

HOLGER HENKE is a Research Fellow at the Caribbean Research Center (Medgar Evers College, CUNY) and has taught sociology and history at Hunter College and Iona College. He earned an M. A. degree in Political Science from the University of Munich and a Ph. D. in International Relations from the University of the West Indies (Mona), where he previously taught in the Department of Government. In addition, he is the Assistant Editor of *Wadabagei. A Journal of the Caribbean and its Diaspora*. Dr. Henke's research interests include various aspects of Caribbean studies and foreign relations, international political economy, migration, race relations, and (political) culture. His book about Jamaica's international relations will be published toward the end of 1999 (The University of the West Indies Press) and he is currently preparing a manuscript about English-speaking Caribbean immigrants in the United States, which will be published in 2000 (Greenwood Press). In addition, Dr. Henke — a Fellow of the Salzburg Seminar (Harvard University) — has published several articles in academic journals and magazines.

HENK W. HOUWELING is Associate Professor of International Relations in the Department of Political Science at the University of Amsterdam, Instructor at the Amsterdam School of International Relations, Adjunct Professor of International Relations at Webster University (Leyden), and Outside Instructor at the NATO Defense College (Rome) and at the Netherlands Defense College (Rijswijk). He received a Ph. D. from the University of Amsterdam and a Ph. D. from the University of Leyden. Dr. Houweling's research interests include development in East Asia, East and Central Europe, and Africa.

W. G. HUFF is Senior Lecturer in the Department of Economics and Centre for Development Studies at the University of Glasgow. Dr. Huff has taught economics in Canada, the United States, and England, at the universities of Lancaster and Durham, and his research interests include the development experience in Asia. He has published a number of journal articles on Singapore's economy and is the author of *The Economic Growth of Singapore: Trade and Development in the Twentieth Century* (Cambridge University Press, 1994).

KANISHKA JAYASURIYA is a Research Fellow at the Asia Research Centre of the Department of Politics and International Studies at Murdoch University, where he leads a research project on the political economy of institutional change in East Asia. He has held teaching and research positions at the National University of Singapore and several Australian universities. Dr. Jayasuriya is a coauthor of *Towards Illiberal Democracy in Pacific-Asia* (Macmillan 1995) and coeditor of *Dynamics of Economic Policy Reform in South West Pacific* (OUP 1992). He recently edited a volume entitled *Law, Capitalism and Power in Asia: The Rule of Law and Legal Institutions* (Routledge 1998).

PATRICK MENDIS is currently a Graduate Faculty Member at the University of Maryland in the European Division. In Europe, he is teaching the U. S. and NATO forces enrolled in the graduate programs in business and public administration in England, Germany, and Spain. He received a Ph. D. from the University of Minnesota and is a recipient of Harvard, Humphrey, McMillan, Coolidge, UN, and several other awards. At the time of writing this chapter he was serving as a Visiting Scholar in Applied Economics and Lecturer in International Relations at the University of Minnesota. Dr. Mendis has also taught at the University of St. Thomas, Augsburg College, Concordia University, and Yale University. Dr. Mendis also participated in the Salzburg Seminar as a Sasakawa Peace Fellow. His research interests include human development and culture, world agriculture and food security, poverty alleviation, sustainable development, and globalization. His published work includes several books, staff papers, and journal articles about development programs in Sri Lanka.

PHILIPPE RÉGNIER has been Director of the Modern Asia Research Centre (MARC) at the University of Geneva since 1992, Associate Professor in East Asian Development Economics at the National Institute of Oriental Studies (Paris) and at the Graduate Institutes of Development and International Studies (Geneva). His research interests include development in East Asia and the economics and geopolitics of ASEAN. Dr. Régnier has published a widely acclaimed book about Singapore and regional geoeconomics and several articles about Singapore and other NICs.

JOE REMENYI is Associate Professor of International Development at the School of Australian and International Studies at Deakin University. His various research projects and consultancies for international foundations and organizations (e.g., World Bank, UNDP, Ford Foundation) have led him to conduct field research throughout the Asia-Pacific region and Africa. His research interests focus on poverty alleviation, microenterprise development, food aid, and community development. Dr. Remenyi earned a Ph. D. from Duke University and has published numerous articles and books about his research.

Index

John Benjamins Publishing Company publishes Advances in Organization Studies as a reformulated continuation of the De Gruyter Studies in Organization.

1. ZEYTINOĞLU, Işik Urla (ed.): *Developments in Changing Work Relationships in Industrialized Economies.* 1999.
2. HENKE, Holger and Ian BOXILL (eds.): *The End of the 'Asian Model'?* 2000.
3. QUACK, Sigrid, Glenn MORGAN and Richard WHITLEY (eds.): *National Capitalisms, Global Competition, and Economic Performance.* 2000.
4. MAURICE, Marc and Arndt SORGE (eds.): *Embedding Organizations. Societal analysis of actors, organizations and socio-economic context.* 2000.